1979

Aids to Psycholinguistic Teaching

Second Edition

Aids to Psycholinguistic Teaching
Second Edition

Wilma Jo Bush
West Texas State University

Marian T. Giles
Giles Institute for Research
Fort Collins, Colorado

Charles E. Merrill Publishing Co.
A Bell & Howell Company
Columbus   London   Toronto   Sydney

THE SLOW LEARNER SERIES
Founding Editor, Newell C. Kephart

Published by Charles E. Merrill Publishing Co.
A Bell & Howell Co.
Columbus, Ohio 43216

This book was set in Century Expanded.
The production editor was Jan Hall.
The cover was prepared by Will Chenoweth.

Cover photo by Tom Hutchinson.
Photo on p. 3 by E. F. Bernstein.

International Standard Book Number: 0–675–08525–X

Library of Congress Catalog Card Number: 76–58077

1   2   3   4   5   6   7   8   9—82   81   80   79   78   77

PRINTED IN THE UNITED STATES OF AMERICA

Foreword

Drs. Bush and Giles have compiled a plethora of activities and games for kindergarten to eighth-grade children for the purpose of fostering linguistic and psychological processes necessary for normal development. The games and activities are generated from the hypothetical constructs of Osgood, Piaget, and Guilford, and are based on the model of the *Illinois Test of Psycholinguistic Abilities*.

There has been some question about the value of training psycholinguistic processes. These questions tend to arise from sophistic reasoning and from a one-sided point of view concerning processes and process training. Actually there are two kinds of process training, namely: (1) training a process to develop a skill or product at a later stage, such as training body image at an early age to develop reading at a later age, and (2) training a linguistic or psychological function for its own sake. Opponents of process training tend to refer to the first process.

The second type of process training, namely training a process for its own sake, is not controversial. If the child does not understand language, does not decode language (defined by Osgood as a process) we try to teach the child to understand language using the games and activities described by Bush and Giles under "Auditory Reception." If the child cannot relate what he hears to his past experience, we play games with him to help the child associate auditory materials. These games and activities are described under "Auditory Association." Likewise, if a child does not talk or does not clearly express himself at his expected age level, we provide him with games and activities described by Bush and Giles under "Verbal Expression." These activities attempt to develop in the child processes for their own sake.

Teachers will find in *Psycholinguistic Teaching* many appropriate games and activities which will aid them in developing instructional tasks for children who exhibit disabilities in linguistic and psychological functions.

Samuel A. Kirk

Preface

This book has been written with both the preservice and the inservice teacher in mind. It concerns the pressing issue of language development in children and youth. The child with inadequate experiences and the child with learning disabilities may be inadequate in one or a number of psycholinguistic skills. Through familiarity with the activities found in this book, the preservice teacher will become knowledgeable about psycholinguistic components of the learning process and will be better equipped to aid children who have deficits in these skills.

Teachers will find this book useful due to its organization. Since activities in the book are divided into both skill groups and interest levels, the book readily can be incorporated into the studies of the student teacher in these areas. Furthermore, at the end of the book there is a materials list which contains the addresses of the manufacturers who make the major equipment mentioned in the book. The teacher in training may start a supply of teaching aids through this list, and the regular teacher may add new materials to an already established supply.

A new feature in this revision is the index of the activities into arithmetic, phonics, and spelling categories. For example, if a teacher chooses to use psycholinguistic activities that aid spelling, this index will expedite the selection of these specific activities at a specific grade level interest.

The schema of this book is planned after the remediation techniques recommended by Dr. Douglas E. Wiseman. The activities are organized around the format of the *Illinois Test of Psycholinguistic Abilities* which was developed by Dr. Samuel A. Kirk, Dr. J. J. McCarthy, and Mrs. Winifred Kirk.

The study of this book by preservice and inservice teachers can further their abilities to attack the programs for the development of language skills and can lead to an enriched educational program required for remediation of specific language deficits.

Wilma Jo Bush
Marian T. Giles

Acknowledgments

Very special thanks are extended to:

Colleagues and friends who supported our efforts by offering suggestions, needed information or encouragement—Dr. Kenneth W. Waugh, Claud "R" Zevely, Avaril Wedemeyer, Dr. Jean Scott, Dr. Ruth Lowes, Dr. Kenneth M. Laycock, Dr. Max Manley, Jack Shelton, Dr. Emmett D. Smith, Dr. Dorothy Bell, Dr. Dan White, Dr. Lloyd Watkins, Dr. O. P. Kolstoe, and Jan Lambert.

Authorities who were the pioneers in psycholinguistic training—Dr. Samuel A. and Winifred Kirk, Dr. Jeanne M. McCarthy, Dr. James J. McCarthy, and Dr. D. E. Wiseman.

West Texas State University graduate students of 1967 who made the major activity contributions in the first edition—Harold G. Andrews, Attie M. Berry, Catherine C. Bray, Charlyn Carder, Tommie L. Daws, Cassandra S. Deaver, Dorothy C. Dodgen, Martha L. Drake, Roland T. Drake, Charles E. Gaither, Elizabeth Garlitz, Nannie L. Gibbs, Marian Taylor Giles, Iona M. Haag, Jimmy C. Howell, Elma B. Hughes, Elwyn C. Hulett, Mable A. Johnson, Baynard B. Kendrick, Raymond C. Killingsworth, Jack E. Lancaster, Dorothy M. McClure, Margaret C. Mills, Patti L. Nivens, Peggy J. Pemberton, Jimmy W. Pope, Zelma P. Poston, Mabel W. Reese, Doris E. Reid, Bob G. Schneider, Mallie Sheets, Martha L. Sheets, Creda A. Smith, Rolly D. Spradling, Bonnie K. Staten, Leona P. Stone, Martha A. Tooms, Billie A. Vestal, Dorothy M. Whitfield, Pauline E. Abney, Bobbie C. Austin, Johnnie Blackwell, David C. Cole, Alice J. Cox, Jauquin E. Crawford, Ethel Florence, Evie M. Froehner, Mary D. Goff, Mary V. Griffith, Cordia M. Hargesheimer, Sarah E. Hillhouse, Della B. Jones, Loman D. Jones, Eva B. Kelly, Martha J. Lacewell, Peggy L. Lindley, Zacharita B. Lowrie, Edwin A. McCreary, Lula V. Needham, Minnie L. Parkan, Francis L. Plumlee, Fay J. Potts, Adelia B. Sanders, Hubert C. Schmidt, Jr., Tommie L. Sharp, Helen C. Smith, Tyne L. Sturdevant, Shirley K. Testerman, Vesta G. Tubbs, Lorene H. Waller, Mary E. Ward, Lola M. Whitaker.

Graduate students who contributed kindergarten activities and aided in the completion of the index for the revised edition—Marie Shamburger and Frances Duke.

Our typist—Mary Whitten.

Those who posed for the pictures—Jo Betsy and Jason Huber, Inell Zeverly, Jean Waugh, Linda Brotherton, Ronald Tidmore, Myrtle Fitzpatrick, Richard Browder, Martha Phillips, Marzee and Susan Lee, Michael Salinas, Tom McKay, Kory Ford, Carlton Grant, Jay Lamb, Richard Anderson, Larry Stegal, Noland Clayton, Tesha Lodholm, Kay Scholl, Cathie Moreland, Julian Martinez, Bettie Davis, Julie and Susie Norman, Michael Seely; and to the Brim Youth and adults who also posed for pictures in the first edition, Burl, Jr., Shelly, Shannon, Heather, Trina, and Barry.

Those who helped in the editing of the book in such a helpful and diplomatic way—Tom Hutchinson, administrative editor, and Jan Hall, production editor, both at Charles E. Merrill Publishing, College Division.

The photographers—Wilma Jo Bush, Gort Rushmer, and Randy Miller.

Our families—Guy E. Bush, Mil Wallis, Jo Betsy, Jason and Dwight Huber, and Sheila and Steve Giles.

Contents

Part I

PSYCHOLINGUISTIC TEACHING   1

Chapter 1
     Psycholinguistic Teaching   *Wilma Jo Bush*   **3**

Part II

AUDITORY MODALITY   27

Introduction   *Wilma Jo Bush*   **27**

Chapter 2
     Auditory Reception   **31**

Chapter 3
     Auditory Association   **67**

Chapter 4
     Grammatic and Auditory Closure   **91**

Chapter 5
     Auditory Memory   **117**

Part III

VISUAL MODALITY   145

Introduction   *Marian T. Giles*   **145**

Chapter 6
     Visual Reception   **149**

Chapter 7
     Visual Association   **177**

Chapter 8
     Visual Closure   *Marian T. Giles*   **203**

Chapter 9
     Visual Memory   **217**

Part IV

EXPRESSION   249

Introduction   *Wilma Jo Bush and Claud "R" Zevely*   249

    Activities: Poems and Jingles   252

Chapter 10

    Verbal Expression   265

Chapter 11

    Manual Expression Activities   295

Part V

PERCEPTUAL-MOTOR ACTIVITIES   321

Introduction   *Wilma Jo Bush*   321

Chapter 12

    Multisensory Activities   323

Chapter 13

    Recreation and Motor Activities   337

Part VI

EDUCATIONAL PLANNING   363

Chapter 14

    Guidelines for Teachers   *Marian T. Giles*   365

Bibliography   *Wilma Jo Bush*   374

INDEXES   377

Phonics Activities   379

Math Activities   380

Spelling Activities   382

Subject Index   382

Author Index   384

Materials List   386

Part I

Psycholinguistic Teaching

Wilma Jo Bush

1

Psycholinguistic Teaching

INTRODUCTION

In the past three decades, there has been an intensive search for the critical factors which influence growth and development in children. These efforts have evolved from the pressures to understand individual differences—differences which have been considered by educators for centuries. Since the time of Locke, who devised a *tabula rasa* theory suggesting that environment was responsible for individual differences, experimenters and writers have sought ways and means of identifying these differences. The work of Galton, the Cattell, Thorndyke, and Thurstone provided milestones of data. These data became the basis which supported much of the work of later experimental enthusiasts.

The ensuing research has resulted in many beneficial systems of measurement and educational planning. From the discipline of training for the basic skills we have many approaches to the teaching of reading, spelling, and arithmetic. Systems which have been satisfactorily used in the teaching of reading are abc's, language-linguistic experience, phonics, flash card, and programmed readers. Systems which have been satisfactorily used in the teaching of arithmetic are the traditional techniques of presenting multiplication, division, addition, and subtraction, modern math, the use of Cuisenaire Rods and/or the Catherine Stern Blocks, and such systems as Key Math. In the teaching of spelling, the traditional or rote memory procedure, the phonics method, and much later the kinesthetic methods (such as Fernald [1943] described) have proved to be of value.

Other disciplines dealing with measurement, growth and development, and linguistic and intellectual analysis have also made great strides towards progress, each making valuable contributions to the education process. From the discipline of measurement, we have the *Stanford-Binet Intelligence Test,* the *Wechsler Intelligence Tests,* and many other achievement and aptitude tests. In addition, there are communication-type tests, such as the *Illinois Test of Psycholinguistic Abilities,** and perceptual assessment instruments, such as the *Frostig Visual Perceptual Test* and *Wepman's Auditory Discrimination Tests,* to name only a few. From the discipline of growth and development studies, we have the significant work of Gesell and Piaget. From the discipline of linguistic and intellectual analysis, we have the work of Osgood and Guilford along with the theoretical positions of Chomsky, Lennenberg, and Vygotsky.

All of these earlier works influence today's concept of educational planning, whether developmental or remedial, and all have had their share of positive beneficial results. Because learning is such a complex matter, there will never be an all-or-none system, methodology, or technique as a means in educational planning. To make such an assertion would be proclaiming an educational Tower of Babel which, like in Biblical history, will itself become confounded by different viewpoints and interpretations. Such a "single lens" theory would be like looking through a prism from one specific point and declaring that what one sees is the total picture.

This book, which deals with products of some of the earlier investigators, is concerned with activities relating to individual differences and involves the field of psycholinguistics. The activi-

---

* The *Illinois Test of Psycholinguistic Abilities* has been adapted for use in Greece, Persia, Germany, Japan, Denmark and Finland.

ties included are presented for the purpose of aiding the language development of children and youth. Carroll (1960) states that the quality of a child's early linguistic environment is the most important external factor affecting the rate of language development and that the lack of a stimulating linguistic environment seems to inhibit the development of cognitive (intellectual) skills. Whereas our philosophy embraces more than one system or construct for education planning, we feel that language, being one of the key influences on intellectual development, should be a major emphasis. A construct such as the psycholinguistic model (Kirk, McCarthy and Kirk, 1968) provides an organization which emphasizes language experiences under expression, comprehension, association and discrimination, closure, and memory.

Neisworth and Greer (1975) cite principles taken from Stevens, Quay, Iscoe, and Payne which highlight important aspects of a language system and also suggest a framework for instructional organization. The third point supports the concept of meaningful categories as necessary for planning objectives for educational grouping and intervention.

1. Language systems are based on a common foundation (education), as opposed to terminology coming from various non- or para-educational perspectives.

2. Labels for children based on cause or condition are avoided.

3. Categories are based on educational variables that facilitate pinpointing of educational objectives and that suggest guidelines for feasible educational grouping and intervention.

We suggest that a psycholinguistic construct, or a language science construct, provides categories based on educational variables as comprehending, expressing, associating, and memory. It is further suggested that educational planning based on such a construct will not necessitate examination of cause and that it will lend itself to behavior modification techniques, as well as cognitive-field techniques. It is not portended that a psycholinguistic construct is the ultimate or the only desirable means for educational planning. The suggestion is that such a construct is a viable, workable means of presenting information to students and provides opportunity for performance in comprehending, associating, expressing, and remembering, which are all a part of the communication process.

The necessity of providing a variety of different language experiences for young children cannot be overemphasized. Pribram

(1971) has pointed out that documentation is well established to show the versatility of the adaptational functions of the brain.* Consequently, if children have deficits caused by brain pathology, we must double our efforts to provide the variety of psycholinguistic procedures which will *facilitate this adaptation process while the child is young.*

HISTORICAL ASPECTS OF PSYCHOLINGUISTIC TERMINOLOGY

The psycholinguistic model is a verbal language construct, and can be vocal, nonvocal, and/or manual. The term *psycholinguistic* denotes processes which underlie the acquisition and use of language. It is specifically identified with the ways and means that language is acquired, stored, integrated, and retrieved. Although the term is relatively new when considered as an organization depicting essential aspects of language processing, the terms identified with this construct can be traced back in part to writings of experimentalists who were concerned with the disturbance or loss of the faculty of communication. Reports show that these studies were made on cases where the problems were caused by injuries to particular brain structure, from trauma, infection, or due to disturbance of blood supply (Goodglass & Blumstein, 1973). In the early 1800s, Bouillaud, a teacher of medicine in France, recognized that the cerebral structures controlling the

---

* The most graphic example of this known to the author is the account by J. Victor Ellis, M.D., F.R.C.S., who was the neurological surgeon and who describes the case of a five-year-old girl as follows:

[She] had been shot accidently from side to side through the occipito-parietal area of the head. She was becoming moribund from intracranial bleeding. The problem was complicated by the fact that this girl had lost both forearms in an earlier farm accident and had become most adept in the use of artificial limbs which, of course, demanded that she have vision. It was reasonably certain that loss of the damaged part of the brain would leave her blind. However, it was elected to proceed. After opening the skull, it was evident that there was extensive maceration to both occipital poles of the brain, which had to be amputated. On both sides the stripe of Gennari (identifying the visual cortex) was observed in the parts of the brain removed.

The child survived the surgery but was blind as anticipated. Surprisingly, within a period of nine months, she recovered full vision without color perception. A visual acuity of 20/20 in each eye with normal visual fields was confirmed by a prominent opthalmologist.

In a follow-up conversation about 18 years later, the neurosurgeon learned that the patient had satisfactory vision with good color perception, but that she did not remember when the color perception had developed. Ellis (1976) ends his account by stating, "This remarkable case would suggest that in a young person certain special functions of the brain can be transferred to a new area."

use of language were partially independent of those controlling the nonspeech movements of the articulatory organs (Head, 1963). Bouillaud stated that the loss of speech did not necessitate want of movement. Medical authorities such as John Hughlings Jackson (1878) reported information regarding the loss of speech and/or the meaning of speech; the loss of ability to understand and/or recognize printed symbols; and the loss of ability to interpret sound and/or words. Pick (1924) spoke of impressive and expressive speech, explaining that impressive or sensory aphasia was the inability to understand the verbal aspects of language. Other early reports of communication problems vary from the mystical writings of the saints, who spoke of how words and letters would lose their meaning when they were experiencing states of ecstasy, to the case of John Schmidt, a physician, 1624–1690, who described the loss of the ability to read.

Such expressions as *word-blindness, word-deafness, aphasia,* and *dyslexia* evolved to professional use among physicians after reported accounts of problems such as those cited previously. These terms, identified and accepted by the medical profession, were not quickly accepted by educators or psychologists unless it was understood that the underlying source of the problem was emotional blocking. Eventually the terms *dyslexia* and *aphasia* did become associated with the education process.

Goodglass and Blumstein (1973) cite other terms identifying learning problems and state that certain deficiencies can only be defined in linguistic terms. Some of the less common ones are introduced in the following paragraph:

> One of these was "agrammatism," the dissolution of syntactic relationship, which some writers considered an independent form of aphasia and others a common accompaniment of motor aphasia. In agrammatism, speech is laborious, reduced to isolated substantives and short phrases. In order even to describe this disorder it was necessary to recognize the distinction between content words and function words, the latter most often being omitted and confused with each other. It was also noted that inflectional endings disappeared. The term *telegraphic speech* was applied to indicate the resemblance between the resulting form of expression and the abridged style of a telegram. (p. 5)

Other terms, such as *paragrammatism,* the garbled syntax and omitted or confused particles of inflections, and *paraphasia,* the unintended or meaningless utterances during the efforts to speak, also are representative of the attempts to understand and describe the facets of the communication process encompassed in the meaning of the term *psycholinguistics.*

Though much of the earlier references to psycholinguistic problems were couched under the heading of speech and communication problems, the term *psycholinguistics,* denoting a particular branch of science, has unquestionably become a meaningful term and no doubt has become prominent because of the early work of Osgood (1957a; 1957b). His model of human language usage lists essential linguistic abilities and is specifically concerned with meaningful communication as opposed to mechanistic concepts, which considered only the overt stimulus-response aspects of communication. Figure 1 shows the model*as including three processes at three different levels. The processes are decoding (understanding), association (relationships), and encoding (expression). The levels include representation, integration, and projection.

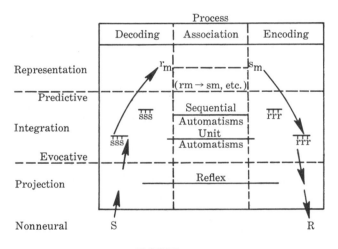

FIGURE 1-1

A multistage model of behavior proposed by Osgood (1963).

Note. From *Approaches to the Study of Aphasia* by C. E. Osgood and M. S. Miron, p. 100. Urbana, Ill.: University of Illinois, 1963. Reprinted by permission.

Osgood sought to show intervening activities in the brain occurring between a stimulus and a response. In the diagram in Figure 1, the S is the initial and observable stimulus and the R is the observable and measureable response; s and r denote the

---

* This model is considered now by Osgood to be simplistic. His later model still includes the main aspects of psycholinguistics—two levels, semantics and integrational, and three processes, encoding, decoding, and association (Osgood, 1976). These aspects are the basic framework for the Kirk et al. model.

fractional stimulus and response activity evoked from the original *S* and *R*. It is the *s–r* which characterizes the representational level of activity and signifies the meaning of the *S* (stimulus). The integrative part of the activity level is concerned with the processing of nonmeaningful information (see Figure 11–30 from Hilgard, 1967, p. 306). The projection level deals with reflexive behavior, which is physiological in nature and is not a known significant variable in the acquisition of language.

Kirk, McCarthy, and Kirk (1965) modified the Osgood model into a more complex model for the *Illinois Test of Psycholinguistic Abilities* and changed some of the terms used in their revised edition. They added the term *memory* to both editions of their test. Their changes, as shown in the 1965 edition, included visual and auditory reception (decoding), visual and auditory association, visual and auditory closure, grammatic closure, visual and auditory sequential memory, and verbal and manual expression (encoding). Myklebust (1967) and Johnson and Myklebust (1967), among others, are also noted for having used psycholinguistic terms in their writings: *receptive language, inner language,* and *expressive language.*

Both the earlier and the later terminology have made visible the attempts to classify the many processing functions in communication. The advantage of such categories seems to lie in their relationship to the performance of children in the classroom. In order to be "schooled," children must understand instructions and relate these instructions to assigned tasks. They must be able to express themselves effectively in both oral and written fashion and they must be able to remember what they have learned in order to build a hierarchy of skills.

ASPECTS OF THE PSYCHOLINGUISTIC CONSTRUCT

There are three processes, two channels, and two levels in the Kirk model (Figure 2). The three processes are receptive process, organizing process, and expressive process. The two channels are the auditory-vocal channel and the visual-motor channel. The two levels are representational and automatic (Paraskevopoulos & Kirk, 1969; Kirk & Kirk, 1971).

The subtitles of the psycholinguistic construct used in this text taken from this Kirk modification of the Osgood model previously described include one change. The authors choose to use the term *memory,* i.e., *auditory memory* and *visual memory,* as subtitles, rather than *auditory sequential memory* and *visual sequential memory,* as does the Kirk modification. Individuals who need

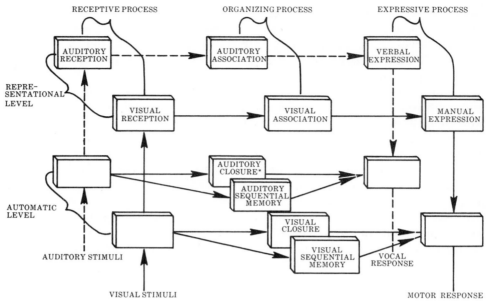

RECEPTIVE PROCESS   ORGANIZING PROCESS   EXPRESSIVE PROCESS

*Auditory Closure, Grammatic Closure, and Sound Blending subtests

FIGURE 1–2

Three-dimensional model of the *ITPA*.

Note. From *Illinois Test of Psycholinguistic Abilities* by S. Kirk, J. McCarthy, and W. Kirk, p. 8. Urbana, Illinois, 1968. Reprinted by permission.

specific help with memory processing do not have needs confined to sequential memory skills. The storing and retrieval of information deals with many problems other than arrangement or order, thus the activities in this text involve other memory tasks in addition to sequential ones.

Levels

The construct includes representational and automatic levels of learning. These two levels are emphasized by Hilgard and Atkinson (1967). They state "that a provisionally satisfactory position regarding learning is that any given illustration of learning can be graded on a crude scale, with the most automatic kind of learning (explained best as conditioning) at the one end and the most rational (explained best as involving cognitive structures) at the other." To highlight this view they graph a rectangular model with insightful learning cutting across in diagonal fashion. The other half represents habit or automatic learning. These learnings are cited as moving from conditioned gastric secretion (habit) to learning higher mathematics (most insightful). While automatic learning occurs without awareness and with a minimum of understanding, rational learning involves cognitive structures.

According to Kirk et al., the representational level deals with some aspect of symbols that have meaning, and the automatic level deals with nonmeaningful uses of symbols. We see the latter as requiring the kind of attentive skills described by Rapaport (1945). He discriminates between attention and concentration, saying that attention requires a passive state which *takes in* without effort, whereas concentration is an active state which requires effort. It is not meant that "automatic" activities are *purely* automatic, requiring only attentive skills as opposed to concentration skills. It is not meant that "automatic" activities are free of meaning. The receptive, associative, and expressive activities at the representational level do deal with meaningful materials, as described by both Kirk et al. and Hilgard and Atkinson; however, the closure and memory activities at the automatic level are not confined to such nonmeaningful skills as the *Illinois Test* measures. As Hilgard and Atkinson (1967) explain, most learning falls somewhere between the two levels as a kind of mixture. Thus automatic learning overlaps with representational learning by degree and according to the requirements of the task.

Memory

Guilford (1967) has found after 15 years of research that where learning is concerned, *content* makes a difference. Semantics is found to be involved in the process of memory, understanding (cognition), evaluation, and other operations. Through factor analysis Guilford has identified 16 kinds of memory. Whether these memories require automatic versus representational skills was not the pertinent problem of his research. The problem as it relates to the design of this book involves whether or not the activities on memory should be confined to sequential tasks, as they are in the automatic learning memory tasks in the Kirk model (in the *Illinois Test of Psycholinguistic Abilities*).

The importance of memory and its many components should not be deemphasized in the learning process. Thurstone (1938) found *memory* to be one of the seven primary mental abilities in his early research. Biochemists, psychologists, neurologists, and psychiatrists include memory as one of the major considerations when they theorize or experiment in the field of learning. It is considered to be of significant importance in the training of children with learning disabilities. It has great practical value in learning, and for this reason it seems to warrant a position wherein activities are planned to cover both representational and automatic learning.

REMEDIATION AND PSYCHOLINGUISTICS

The implementation of psycholinguistic training in school programs has unquestionably had its impact following the first edition of the *Illinois Test of Psycholinguistic Abilities*. There has been no *specific* system other than the *ITPA* model as a guide. In most instances, the use of a psycholinguistic model (or part) has been added as a supplementary part of a day's program, usually covering a period lasting between 15–30 minutes. Some research has reported only one or two short periods a week to comprise the time element for training. More often the construct has been used in remedial programs which have been individualized for specific problems, the assumtion being that if there are deficits shown in certain processes as, for example, comprehending what one sees or hears, then specialized training dealing with these processes would be beneficial.

Research to date has shown both positive and nonsignificant results. Some of these studies have dealt with only the attempt to show the validity of the *ITPA*, since it is the most commonly used psycholinguistic measuring instrument. Other studies have dealt with the results of training for specific psycholinguistic processes or for determining the effects of psycholinguistic training on academic skills.

Opposing views to psycholinguistic teaching are reported by Hammill and Larsen (1974), Newcomer and Hammill (1976), and by Sowell, Larsen, and Parker (1975). Proponents of psycholinguistic training are Kirk (1966), McCarthy, James (1964), McCarthy, Jeanne M. (1967), Minskoff, Wiseman, and Minskoff (1972), Minskoff (1976), Karnes (1968, 1972), Dunn and Smith (1966), McLeod (1976), Bush and Giles (1969) and Bush (1976). These latter educators see the construct as a workable organization which provides motivational impetus for creative efforts, as well as provides a means for planning materials after a diagnosis has been made showing deficit processes or skills necessary for reading, writing, or spelling.

There have been good results, negative results, and nonsignificant results in (1) flash card/insight methods of teaching reading, (2) in phonics approaches to teaching reading, (3) in the use of Cuisenaire Rods, (4) in aspects of psycholinguistic teaching, and (5) in any traditional method of teaching any subject; however, it might be done. Life has a way of protecting its survival elements and all of the previously mentioned approaches will continue to show satisfactory results for the majority of children if other variables in each teaching situation are held within equal limits. Also, any of these systems may be helpful in remediation if used appropriately.

Perhaps one of the major aspects arising regarding differences in research on remediation of learning problems (regardless of the plan or system used) is that the term *learning disabilities* is not and can never be a term encompassing one single specific problem. No two visual problems are ever the same. No two auditory problems are ever the same. No two processing problems are ever the same. For example, an auditory reception problem may be due to lack of experience with words, to brain pathology which defies the understanding of words, or to poor auditory discrimination, to name only a few reasons. Successful remediation of the problem would depend upon how a teacher *modified her own approach to the treatment of auditory reception.*

Space does not permit the views that have been presented by both protagonists and antagonists of psycholinguistic teaching; I encourage the reader to study the issue for greater clarification. The wise teacher or diagnostician will use the materials in this book (and/or any teaching materials) judiciously, i.e., according to personal skills of presentation, to appropriateness of material, and to the needs of the child.

RELATIONSHIP TO TASK ANALYSIS

Among the most significant approaches to analyzing and evaluating is that of analyzing the demands that a task makes upon a child. One asks what skill is needed in order for the child to respond to that task: does he have to pay attention, does he have to have a certain amount of information, does he have to remember relationships, and does he have to be able to speak. There are many more and the questions one might ask are dependent on the task at hand.

Chalfant and Scheffelin (1969), Junkala (1973), and Johnson (1968), among others, suggest excellent means of examining a task for the purpose of trying to determine just where along a continuum that a breakdown in skills occurs. The reader is referred to these authors for further information. Bush and Waugh (1976) analyze a subtest from the *ITPA* based on the Chalfant and Scheffelin guidelines. Figure 3 shows the process to follow in the analysis of this subtest.

FIGURE 1–3

Auditory association process: Task analysis of a subtest from the ITPA.

1. *Attention.* Attention to vocally produced auditory sound units (i.e., noises, speech sounds, words, phrases, sentences)

2. *Discrimination.* Discriminate between auditory-vocal sound units found in two sets of sentences or phrases

3. *Establishing correspondences.* Establish reciprocal associations between the auditory-vocal sound units and objects or events.
   (a) Retrieve and identify auditory-vocal sound units as meaningful auditory-language signals. Substitute auditory language signals of the two sets
   (b) Establish word order sequences and sentence patterns of the two sets

4. *Automatic auditory-vocal decoding.*
   (a) Shift attention from the auditory-language signals to the total meaning that is carried by the signal sequences
   (b) Retrieve a common denominator term (aud-vocal symbol) that makes association between the two sets
   (c) Retrieve the auditory-vocal symbol that stands for the common denominator to fit set two

5. *Terminal behavior.* Respond with appropriate auditory-vocal symbol to complete set two

FIGURE 1–4

Application of task analysis to auditory association task.

"Grass is green—sugar is _____"

1. *Attention* to vocally produced words and phrases "Grass is green, sugar is _____"

2. *Discriminate* sound units of *grass, is, green, sugar*

3. *Establish correspondence.*
   Associate object (*grass*) with color (*green*) and object (*sugar*)
   (a) Retrieve and identify *grass* and *green* and *sugar* as meaningful auditory language signals. Substitute

Psycholinguistic Teaching

auditory language signals for actual objects and
events
   (b)   Establish word sequences and sentence patterns of
"Grass is green, sugar is _____"

4.   *Automatic auditory-vocal decoding.*
   (a)   Shift attention from auditory language signals to
the total meaning that is carried by the sequence
"Grass is green, sugar is _____"
   (b)   Retrieve a common denominator term (auditory-
vocal signal) which makes association between the
two sets of signal sequences—"*color*"
   (c)   Retrieve the auditory-vocal symbol that stands for
the common denominator to fit the second set—
"*white*"

5.   *Terminal behavior.* Respond with appropriate auditory-
vocal symbol to complete second set, "*white*"

Figures 3 and 4 provide examples of how to make task analyses
of subtests. The next step to follow would be to find the position
of development of the individual who needs training. Perhaps
this person needs to be able to pay attention. Perhaps this person
cannot retrieve (remember) a common denominator term as in
Figure 4. Whichever the case, the procedure to follow is described
in Figure 5.*

You may take any subtest, any reading system, or any behavioral response of an individual and examine the necessary
information or skills needed to perform that function. Chalfant
and Scheffelin (1969) describe in detail how a task analysis can
be made of auditory receptive language, auditory expressive
language, vocal-motor production, encoding graphic language
symbols, developmental hierarchy of writing tasks, a whole-word
system of reading, and a sound-symbol system of reading. After
the task analysis is made, you can determine where in the developmental process the individual is having trouble. If, for
example, in the auditory expressive language analysis, the individual is not able to retrieve and sequence the appropriate
vocal-language signals, your responsibility at that point is to
begin remediation in memory and sequencing of words in a sequence. In the memory section of this book are found many
activities provided to help individuals retrieve and sequence
words. These and other psycholinguistic activities in this book
can be used to aid in training and remediation after a task anal-

*Figures 4–6 from *Diagnosing Learning Disabilities* (2nd ed.) by W. J.
Bush and K. W. Waugh, pp. 83–85. Columbus, Ohio: Charles E. Merrill, 1976.
Reprinted by permission.

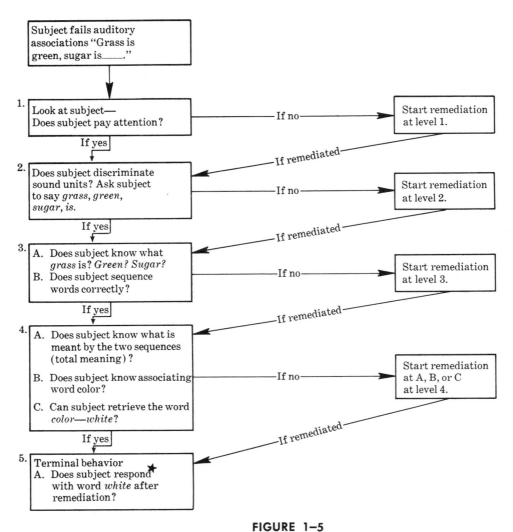

FIGURE 1–5

Flow chart for remediation.

ysis has been made and it has been determined where the breakdown in learning has occurred. For developmental training where no remediation is needed, the psycholinguistic activities also may be used to aid in the development of skills.

RELATIONSHIP TO PIAGETIAN DEVELOPMENTAL STAGES OF INTELLIGENCE

Among the most prominent theories concerning development of intellectual skills is that of Piaget. His emphasis on the steps involved in a child's ability to see relationships has prompted many teachers to include classification activities in their training programs. Since this theory is often used as a basis for educational planning, the writer suggests that the developmental training planned after Piaget's theory might be enhanced if the planner examined the possibility of using ideas from a psycholinguistic construct in conjunction with their programs.

The rationale for use of the psycholinguistic construct lies in its organization in terms of what children "do" in a classroom, i.e., understand, remember, express and engage in closure procedures to facilitate the learning process. The rationale for use of the Piagetian tasks lies in the possibility that some *learning skills* are dependent on maturity that must develop prior to the skills waiting to be developed.

Before relating the two in terms of educational planning, their differences should be examined.

"Piaget views development as an inherent, unalterable, evolutionary process; yet within this developmental process he locates a series of distinct developmental phases and sub-phases" (Maier, 1965, p. 91). A psycholinguistic construct, such as the Kirk model, suggests that language can be seen as having certain operational differences. The saltatory pattern of the Piagetian theory is that the phases and subphases of development occur in a chronological sequence, one stage necessitating the occurrence of the next stage. Thus we see a vertical order of development. The psycholinguistic (language-science operation) pattern could be considered horizontal; that is, a pattern, or parts of a pattern, are observable and measurable at any stage.

"Piaget's theory is not consistent with a diagnostic-prescriptive approach to education where the weaknesses of the child are systematically explored, nor does it encourage a premature emphasis on achievement; rather it allows the teacher to accept and nourish at appropriate times what is positive and best in every child, namely his capacity for further intellectual development" (Furth and Wachs, 1975). Within this statement is seen another inference of a difference between application of the Piagetian theory and the psycholinguistic construct taken from the *ITPA*. The specific difference lies in the original intent for use of the two systems. The *Illinois Test of Psycholinguistic Abilities* was designed to measure psycholinguistic functions and to highlight strengths and weaknesses, whereas the Piagetian theory deals with the nature and development of thinking. Stated in another way, the *ITPA* deals with what goes on in *communication,* and Piagetian theory involves what goes on in *thinking* or intellectual development. Though this difference in intent lies between the

ITPA construct and Piagetian tasks, let us examine how one may use the theory of Piaget in conjunction with a psycholinguistic construct. If one considers separately the processes of reception (comprehending or understanding), association, expression, closure, and memory as skills which can be developed without consideration of measurement for ascertaining normative data, one can envison these communication processes being operative at each "thinking" stage according to Piaget. The sensorimotor stage (0–2 years) encompasses a progress from autism to egocentricity. During this period, the child learns to deal with his muscles, senses, and the specific objects and events in his environment; language has its beginning here. It is composed of six substages:

1.   Reflexive action (0–1 years) is characterized by simple reflexive activity; the child is stimulated and his reflexes respond. He does not recognize objects as distinct from himself. No *psycholinguistic* functions are differentiated at this stage except communications of pain and contentment.

2.   Primary circular reactions (1–4,5 months). The reflexive behavior becomes more sophisticated and coordinated (eye-hand and eye-ear coordination). Developmental aspects are observed here as the child follows hand movement with his eyes and tries to focus attention to sounds. Beginning signs of *expression* are identified as cooing.

3.   Secondary circular reactions (4,5–8 months). Attempts are made to repeat or reproduce events so as to cause an interesting change or effect. Signs of early stages of *reception*, both *visual* and *auditory*, are observed when the child repeats acts with musical toys or swinging mobiles.

4.   Coordination of secondary schemata (8–12 months). Means to attain an end are observed. Within this stage can be seen the first clear acts of intelligence. Beginning signs of *association* are evidenced as the baby demonstrates that he sees the relationship between his hand movements and an object.

5.   Tertiary circular reactions (12–18 months). Through active experimentation, the child discovers new means to gain desired ends. Both *reception* and *association* are observed as the child demonstrates that he can reach around a transparent plastic screen to secure a toy.

6.   Invention of new means by mental combinations rather than actions (18–24 months). The child mentally solves simple problems; there is the appearance of elementary memory and planning. *Reception* and *expression* are clearly distinguishable

as the child recognizes an object by name, for example, *ba* for *ball.*

The pre-operational period (2–7 years) exhibits the child's progress from sensorimotor organization to the beginnings of internalization of actions to form operations. The single most important development of the pre-operational period is the *development of language.* Between the ages of 2 and approximately 6 is the greatest period of language growth experiences by the individual. This period is divided into two stages:

1. Preconceptual stage (2–4 years). Most language acquisition occurs between 2 and 4; speech is repetitious here. Behavior is egocentric and nonsocial. *Expression* is through imitation. *Auditory closure* is observed as child begins to discriminate sounds and make sentences (*grammatic closure*).

2. Intuitive stage (4–7 years). The child's conversations become largely communicative and social. His reasoning is still very egocentric. All heretofore described psycholinguistic functions can be observed as children show signs of *comprehending* (reception), *association, expressing, "closing"* and *remembering.* Also the functions can be measured through the remaining stages of the Pigeatian tasks.

During the third period, concrete operations (7–11½ years), the child attains the use of logical operations for the first time. Capable of decentering his perceptions and attending to transformations, the child can now solve conservation problems (conservation of length, number, mass, quantity, weight, and volume). Two other operations developed during this period are classifications and seriation (association is emphasized). The period is characterized by reversibility (an essential quality in all operations); but the two forms of reversibility (inversion and reciprocity) are not yet integrated into a whole. The child can assume the viewpoints of others (not as egocentric as he once was). His language is social and communicative. The last period, formal operations (11½ years and up), is the accumulation and culmination of the development of the cognitive structures. This period carries the greatest mobility and flexibility of all the developmental periods. The beginning of the formal operations period coincides approximately with the onset of adolescence. The adolescent is capable of thinking logically in relation to all classes of problems; he can think abstractly. He is able to solve hypothetical problems, verbal problems, and he can use scientific or deductive reasoning. Whereas the child can only consider the real, the adolescent is capable of considering the

these factors relate to listening skills, which are recognized universally as necessary for reading. Using a systematic plan for listening should give you a plan which would utilize key aspects of training without presenting unneeded stimulus materials.

Since there are activities found in this text to aid in the training of listening skills, you are advised to consult the phonics index in the appendix in order to quickly find aids specifically related to such activities.

A creative means of aiding in the development of intellectual functions as defined by the *SOI* is to use as many of the psycholinguistic processes as is possible to develop any factor in the *SOI*. For example, if you chose to train for development of cognition of visual figural units (CFU–V), which is one of the factors found to be necessary for reading readiness and a psycholinguistic function (though not measured by the *ITPA**), one could follow the example following.

You should begin with a specific idea (content) to teach a child. In this instance the shape of and understanding of the meaning of *square* is chosen. The objective is to help the child recognize a square (CFU–V).

If the psycholinguistic process were used to aid in this skill, the following procedure would be recommended:

1. Show the child a square within a template, but one that could be removed. Let the child trace around the square and then make the square in the air. (visual reception)

2. Have the child hear the word *square* as he traces. (aud. rec.)

3. Have the child repeat the word *square* and make a sentence with the word *square*. (expression)

4. Have the child associate the square with anything else in the room that is square or has similar properties. (association)

5. Give child opportunity to pick a square out of a series of geometric designs. (closure)

6. Give the child a chance to show how well he remembers the shape of a square. (memory)

A student who understands the *SOI* would readily recognize that more than one *SOI* factor would be developed through such a procedure; but it would appear that such an approach would provide many opportunities for the individual to really recognize and perceive a square. In order to insure that the child remembers, he should be allowed to see the square among other designs and be able to pick it out over a period of time to reinforce his recognition and memory.

---

*Not all psycholinguistic tasks are measured by the *ITPA*.

SUMMARY

The present approaches to teaching can be traced back in history to earlier research designed to identify individual differences. Through the years this research has resulted in many beneficial systems of teaching. One of these, emphasized in the teaching of reading, is the language experience approach. This approach can be seen in the psycholinguistic construct. Since 1957, the Osgood model of psycholinguistics has been modified by Kirk et al. (1968) and Osgood (1976).

The major points covered in this chapter are:

1. Earlier psycholinguistic terms are introduced with the later terms identified in the *Illinois Test of Psycholinguistic Abilities.*

2. The psycholinguistic construct is related in a meaningful way to the Piagetian developmental tasks and the Structure of Intellect model by Guilford (1967).

3. A procedure to run a task analysis on the psycholinguistic subtests is described. This procedure can aid the teacher in determining where to begin remediation within a process deficit.

4. Psycholinguistics and teaching is briefly reviewed with reference to those who hold protagonistic and antagonistic views.

REFERENCES

Bush, W. J. Psycholinguistic remediation in the schools. In P. L. Newcomer & D. D. Hammill, *Psycholinguistics in the schools.* Columbus, Ohio: Charles E. Merrill, 1976.

Bush, W. J., & Giles, M. T. *Aids to psycholinguistic teaching* (1st ed.). Columbus, Ohio: Charles E. Merrill, 1969.

Bush, W. J., & Waugh, K. W. *Diagnosing learning disabilities* (2nd ed.). Columbus, Ohio: Charles E. Merrill, 1976.

Carroll, J. B. Language development. In C. W. Harris (Ed.), *Encyclopedia of educational research.* New York: Macmillan, 1960.

Chalfant, J., & Scheffelin, M. A. *Central processing dysfunctions in children.* NINDS Monograph No. 9, U.S. Department of Health Education and Welfare, Washington D.C.: U.S. Government Printing Office, 1969.

Dunn, L. M., & Smith, J. O. *The Peabody language development kits.* Circle Pines, Minn.: American Guidance Service, 1966.

Ellis, J. V. Written communication. December 1976.

Feldman, Bernard. Seven specific factors of intelligence. Unpublished document, June 29, 1972. (Available from the SOI Institute, El Segundo, Cal.)

Fernald, G. *Remedial techniques in basic school subjects.* Manchester, Miss.: McGraw-Hill, 1943.

Furth, H., & Wachs, H. *Thinking goes to school.* New York: Oxford University, 1975.

Goodglass, H., & Blumstein, S. *Psycholinguistics and aphasia.* Baltimore: Johns Hopkins, 1973.

Guilford, J. P. *The nature of intelligence.* New York: McGraw-Hill, 1967.

Hammill, D., Larsen, S. The effectiveness of psycholinguistic training. *Exceptional Children,* 1974, *41* (5), 5–16.

Head, H. *Aphasia and kindred disorders of speech.* New York: Hafner, 1963.

Hilgard, E. R., & Atkinson, R. C. *Introduction to psychology* (4th ed.). New York: Harcourt, Brace and Jovanovich, 1967.

Jackson, J. On affections of speech from disease of the brain. In H. Goodglass & S. Blumstein, *Psycholinguistics and aphasia.* Baltimore: Johns Hopkins, 1973.

Johnson, D. Educational principles for children with learning disabilities. In *Minimal brain dysfunction.* Chicago: National Easter Seal Society for Crippled Children and Adults, 1968.

Johnson, D., & Myklebust, H. *Learning disabilities: Educational principles and practices.* New York: Grune and Stratton, 1967.

Junkala, J. Task analysis: The processing dimension. *Academic Therapy,* 1973, *VIII* (4), 401–409.

Karnes, M. B. *Activities for developing psycholinguistic skills with preschool culturally disadvantaged children.* Washington, D.C.: Council for Exceptional Children, 1968.

Karnes, M. B. *Goal program: Language development.* Springfield, Mass.: Milton Bradley, 1972.

Kass, C. *Inservice program for Canyon public school teachers.* Canyon, Texas, Sept. 1973.

Kirk, S. *Diagnosis and remediation of psycholinguistic abilities.* Urbana, Ill.: University of Illinois, 1966.

Kirk, S., McCarthy, J. & Kirk, W. *Illinois Test of Psycholinguistic Abilities.* Urbana, Ill.: University of Illinois, 1968.

Kirk, S. A., & Kirk, W. *Psycholinguistic learning disabilities: Diagnosis and remediation.* Urbana, Ill.: University of Illinois Press, 1971.

Maier, H. W. *Three theories of child development.* New York: Harper and Row, 1965.

McLeod, J. A reaction to *Psycholinguistics in the schools.* In P. Newcomer & D. Hammill (Eds.), *Psycholinguistics in the schools.* Columbus, Ohio: Charles E. Merrill, 1976.

Minskoff, E. H. Research on the efficacy of remediating psycholinguistic disabilities: Critique and recommendations. In P. Newcomer & D. Hammill (Eds.), *Psycholinguistics in the schools.* Columbus, Ohio: Charles E. Merrill, 1976.

Minskoff, E. H., Wiseman, D. E., & Minskoff, J. G. *The MWM program for developing language abilities.* Ridgefield, N.J.: Educational Performance Associates, 1972.

McCarthy, J. M. How to teach the hard to reach. *Grade Teacher,* 1967, May-June, pp. 97–101.

McCarthy, J. J. The importance of linguistic ability in the mentally retarded. *Mental Retardation,* 1964, *2,* 90.

Meeker, M. N. *Structure of intellect.* Columbus, Ohio: Charles E. Merrill, 1969.

Myklebust, H. R. *Progress in learning disabilities* (Vol. 1). New York: Grune and Stratton, 1967.

Neisworth, J. T., & Greer, J. G. Functional similarities of learning disability and mild retardation. *Exceptional Children,* 1975, *42,* 17–21.

Newcomer, P., & Hammill, D. *Psycholinguistics in the schools.* Columbus, Ohio: Charles E. Merrill, 1976.

Osgood, C. E. A behavioristic analysis. In *Contemporary approaches to cognition.* Cambridge, Mass.: Harvard, 1957 (b).

Osgood, C. E. Motivational dynamics of language behavior. In *Nebraska Symposium on Motivation*. Lincoln: University of Nebraska, 1957 (b).

Osgood, C. E. Personal communication. Nov. 1976.

Paraskevopoulos, J., & Kirk, S. A. *The development and psychometric characteristics of the revised* Illinois Test of Psycholinguistic Abilities. Urbana, Ill.: University of Illinois Press, 1969.

Pick, A. In O. Spreen, Psycholinguistics and aphasia: The contribution of Arnold Pick. In H. Goodglass & S. Blumstein, *Psycholinguistics and aphasia*. Baltimore: Johns Hopkins, 1973.

Pribram, K. H. *Languages of the brain: Experimental paradoxes and principles of neuropsychology*. Englewood Cliffs, N.J.: Prentice-Hall, 1971.

Rapaport, D. *Diagnostic psychological testing* (Vol. 1). Chicago: The Yearbook Publishers, 1945.

Sowell, V., Larsen, S., & Parker, R. The efficacy or psycholinguistic training through the MWM Program. Unpublished Manuscript, University of Texas, 1975.

Thurstone, L. L. Primary mental abilities. *Psychometric Monograph*. No. 1, Chicago: University of Chicago, 1938, pp. 427.

Part II

Auditory Modality

Wilma Jo Bush

It appears axiomatic that the auditory channel is one of the most important avenues through which children and adults receive information about their environment. The qualitative aspects of speaking and the understanding of meaning of sounds are dependent upon this sensory channel. Experiments involving the auditory system have shown that speech can be impaired when the subject hears her own words delayed a few seconds (McGaugh, Weinberger, & Whalen, 1967). Also, deficiencies in hearing acuity which block incoming stimuli will affect the perceptual process (Myklebust, 1967). Discrimination of sounds, localization of sounds, and the selection of pertinent sounds for appropriate integration and association are all important aspects influencing learning. The educational planning for children, whether developmental or remedial, must view the auditory channel as a major consideration if proper communication is to develop.

Since the research is controversial regarding teaching to the intact channels or to the deficit channels, either auditory or visual, the organization of activities in this text under the auditory modality is not designed to suggest that language training be confined to this modality as opposed to others. Our organization is meant to meet the needs of speech and hearing therapists and remedial or regular teachers. Sometimes specific modality training will be most useful. However, you may have doubts about the similarity of the problems of a particular group, in which case single modality training would not be efficacious. Individualized instruction would seem to demand that some activities be planned on the basis of modality emphasis; therefore this text's organization fits such a need. For those who do not have this need, they will not find it inconvenient to choose from both the visual and the auditory activities as well as from the motor activities.

This is not a book designed for the discussion of research, but we do feel that some mention be made regarding the controversy of academic training with emphasis on modes of learning.

There is ample research to show that problems in learning can occur from specific modality deficiencies (Luria, 1973). Strauss and Lehtinen (1947), while pointing out the paucity of evidence regarding reading and auditory perception, offer clinical observations to show that weaknesses or disturbances of differentiation of speech sounds may be compensated for by visual or context clues so that the confusions are not as conspicuous as speech defects. They also observe that boys who have struggled with indifferent success to acquire a phonic approach toward apprehending new words suddenly "catch on" at the approximate onset of puberty and tend to progress with more ease following that period. They further emphasize the need for specific perceptual training, whether visual or auditory, in specific cases and their successes in the past attest to the efficiency of such training.

In a review of the research, Wallace and McLoughlin (1975) report several researchers who tend to refute significant gains through preferred modality training (auditory modality instead of visual, and vice versa): Bateman (1968), Ringler and Smith (1973), and Waugh (1973). To provide possible reasons for this lack of significant gains when teaching by a preferred modality, they cite Tarver (1973), who suggests that modality training could have been unsuccessful because of the lack of emphasis on (*a*) task analysis at different stages of learning to read, (*b*) the roles of reinforcement and repetition in increasing learning rates, and (*c*) the cognitive aspects of learning to read.

Bateman (1969), in a later report, suggests the importance of the role of auditory perception. Zigmond (1969) reports the need for other channels than the visual channel alone to be necessary for developing reading skills. McLeod (1966) has shown that dyslexics are inferior to the normal readers in a control group in discriminating spoken English. He found that if the verbal English words were more uncertain (as in nonsense vs. meaningful words), the dyslexics had more difficulty than normal readers. This finding suggests the need for more opportunity for hearing and discrimination in language activities among dyslexics.

There are numerous systems and teaching strategies which involve both modalities and many principles of learning (Gearhart, 1973; Lerner, 1976). Before you choose a specific strategy, you should: (*a*) read the documented evidence and the evidence refuting the strategy, (*b*) consider the specific child and her nonhomogeniety traits in comparison with children with similar problems, (*c*) consider the reputation and skill of the diagnostic referral sources, (*d*) consider your own skills in teaching the particular strategy, (*e*) consider your own knowledge about the alternatives available, and (*f*) evaluate the daily progress of a child when using a specific strategy, e.g., graphs, charts or criterion tests. The feedback should then regulate changes in a strategy. Further, we recommend that you read Myklebust (Johnson & Myklebust, 1967, pp. 58–63), who suggest excellent principles to follow if you are involved in remediation procedures. If you have a need or goal for guiding children through auditory training, the following group of activities are offered as additional aids to the systems and/or strategies being used. In addition, we recommend that (for remediation purposes) the pitch, amplification, and rhythm of the spoken words/sounds be varied until the best mode of presentation is determined.

The following activities are organized under auditory reception, auditory association, auditory memory, and grammatic and auditory closure. You will be able to refer to subtitles of discrimination, figure-ground, and/or sound blending as you read through the various tasks. Please see the Appendix for quick reference to activities that help in the teaching of *phonics, math,* and *spelling.*

REFERENCES

Bateman, B. The efficacy of an auditory and a visual method of first grade reading instruction with auditory and visual learners. In H. Smith (Ed.), *Perception and reading*. Newark, Del.: International Reading Association, 1968.

Bateman, B. Reading: A controversial view—Research and rationale. In L. Tarnopal (Ed.), *Learning disabilities*. Springfield, Ill.: Charles C. Thomas, 1969.

Gearhart, B. R. *Learning disabilities: Educational strategies*. St. Louis: C. V. Mosby, 1973.

Johnson D., & Myklebust, H. *Learning disabilities: Educational principle and practice*. New York: Grune & Stratton, 1967.

Lerner, J. W. *Children with learning disabilities.* Boston: Houghton Mifflin, 1976.

Luria, A. R. *The working brain.* New York: Basic Books, 1973.

McGaugh, J. L., Weinberger, N. M., & Whalen, R. E. *Psychobiology.* San Francisco: W. H. Freeman, 1967.

McLeod, John. Psychological and psycholinguistic aspects of severe reading disability in children: Some experimental studies. In S. Kirk & J. McCarthy (Eds.), *Learning disabilities.* Boston: Houghton–Mifflin, 1975.

Ringler, L. H., & Smith, I. Learning modality and word recognition of first grade children. *Journal of Learning Disabilities,* 1973, *6,* 307–12.

Strauss, A. A., & Lehtinen, L. *Brain injured child.* New York: Grune and Stratton, 1947.

Tarver, S. Deficit vs. strength teaching: Is this a crucial issue? Unpublished Manuscript, University of Virginia, 1973.

Wallace G., & McLoughlin, J. A. *Learning disabilities.* Columbus, O.: Charles E. Merrill, 1975.

Waugh, R. P. Relationship between modality preference and performance. *Exceptional Children,* 1973, *6,* 465–69.

Zigmond, N. K. Auditory processes in children with learning disabilities. In L. Tarnopal (Ed.), *Learning disabilities.* Springfield, Ill.: Charles C. Thomas, 1969.

Auditory Reception

In the acquisition and use of language, auditory reception is the process of recognizing and/or understanding what is heard. It is one of the auditory functions which involves decoding information that is symbolic or representational. Does a word have meaning for an individual when heard? Does a sentence have meaning for an individual when heard? These questions may be asked when we are planning materials for children and youth. Games and a variety of activities may be beneficial in this training for the development of the skill in auditory reception processing.

For remediation you may frame a question, e.g., "What do we do with our eyes?" or "What do we see with?" or "The eyes do what?" If the child does not understand, begin a series of statements to explain: "I see with my eyes. I look at you with my eyes. My eyes look. My eyes see the book. My eyes see the table. I close my eyes, and I cannot see. *Now,* what do you do with *your* eyes?"

If the child cannot concentrate, in order to hold his attention you may touch the child on the arm as you explain. You may also play games with sentences, e.g., asking the child to stand when a correct statement is heard or having the child lift his right arm when a correct statement is made.

If the child does not discriminate sounds, you may make a sound with a bell and say, "A bell makes this sound." After slamming a door you may follow with the question "What is the sound of a door slamming?" The discrimination may progress to more discrete and different sounds. Each time the sounds may be identified. Training should then continue to different sources for the sounds and then different backgrounds for the sounds. Questions may be asked and followed by the teacher's identification of the sounds and finally by the child's identification.

SELF INTRODUCTION

Introduce the children individually to themselves in a full-length mirror. Say, "That is (*child's name*)." Hold out your hand to him in the mirror. "What is he doing? Put your hand on your head; your shoulder; touch your nose. Does he do everything you do?"

FOLLOWING DIRECTIONS

Say, "This morning, boys and girls, I will see how well you can follow directions. Listen carefully and do just what my sentence tells you. Sometimes I'll ask you all to do something together, and sometimes I'll just ask one of you to do something by yourself."

All of you stand in back of your chair; now in front of your chair.

(_____), bring me a book, a pencil, and a crayola.

Everyone, jump two times and stomp one foot.

(_____), say "My name is (_____)."

Everyone, stretch up high, touch your toes, and then turn around two times.

WHISPER GAME

Choose a child to be the messenger and whisper a "message" to him. He chooses a child to receive the message and whispers the message to this child. Sample messages: "Take off one shoe. Turn around three times. Stand on one foot." The child who receives the message acts out the request. The other children then guess out loud what they thought the message was. When the children master the game, they can make up their own messages and you will not need to initiate the messages.

SIMON SAYS

Begin as Simon and give commands: "Simon says, 'Thumbs up.' Simon says, 'Thumbs down.'" The children follow the directions. If the command is given without saying *Simon says,* the children are not to follow the command. When the children have mastered the game, they may take turns giving the commands.

COLOR GAME

"Look very carefully at the clothing you are wearing. If you are wearing something red, will you please come up and stand by me? What are you wearing that is red, (*child 1*)? What are you wearing that is red, (*child 2*)?" Continue in this way until all children have shown their red items of clothing. "You may return to your places now."

"Is anyone wearing something brown? Please come and stand by me." Continue in this way until as many colors as desired have been named.

WHO KNOWS?

"This morning I am going to read some sentences to you. Listen carefully to each sentence and answer *yes, no,* or *maybe.*" Suggested content follows:

1. *Body image.*

    Our feet are on the ends of our arms.
    You have one head.
    Your arm does not bend.
    We are sitting down.

2. *Immediate environment.*

The light is on.
The floor is moving.
We can pick up chairs.

3. *Familiar classes or concepts previously taught (fruits, animals, colors, seasons, number, weather, properties of objects).*

Bananas are found.
A triangle has four sides.
Horses, cows, and ducks are four-legged animals.
A fish can walk.
An ice cream cone is hot.
John is the name of a boy.
Mud is good to eat.
Acorns grow on maple trees.
Leaves turn red and yellow in the fall.
All apples are red.
People turn off their furnaces in the fall.

ANIMAL NAMES

Select or invent a story that includes the names of familiar animals and one that entails repetition of these names. ("The Little Red Hen" is an example.) After the children are seated and ready to listen, assign each child the name of an animal that is in the story and show him how to "talk" like that animal. Whenever a child's animal name is mentioned in the story, the child must make the sound of that animal.

DELAYED RECALL

"This morning I shall read some very short stories. Be good listeners. When I finish a story, I shall ask you some questions. If you can answer the questions, then you are good listeners. Ready?"

1. "We have fun in the spring. We jump rope. We play marbles and fly kites. *What time of the year is it? Name three games we play in the spring.*"

2. "Today it is raining. We wear our raincoats and hats. Our boots splash in the puddles. We like the spring rain. *What kind of weather did I mention in the story?* What kind of clothes do we wear when it rains?"

3. I am a baby bird. I live in a nest. I am learning to fly. When I am big, I can sing. *Where did the baby bird live? What was it learning to do? What will it do when it is a grown-up bird?"*

4. Tell a story in which children have to remember a specific category, such as color. "There was once a boy named Pedro. Pedro lived in a white house with his mother and father. One day Pedro's father brought a dog home for Pedro. The dog was brown. One day Pedro forgot to shut the big green door and the dog ran away. *What was the color of Pedro's house? What color was the dog? What color was the big door?"*

RECTANGLE FOLDING

A large piece of construction paper or newsprint can be divided into work areas for pasting and other activities by careful folding. "Pick up the left edge of the paper and bring it over to the right edge. Hold it there while you press the paper flat with your other hand. Good. Now bring the bottom edges up to the top and then press the paper flat. Has everyone done that? Now, unfold the paper. You can see four rectangles. Let's count them together. We will make a design in each rectangle." Precut geometric shapes are given each child and he is directed to select an ice cream cone, a clown and balloons. The materials pasted, colored, or printed in each rectangle will vary according to the content currently being taught.

LISTEN AND CORRECT

Changing sentences. "Today I am going to say some sentences with wrong or silly words in them. Listen to the sentence. If you can change it into a sentence that makes sense, raise your hand." Examples: Water is dry. A nail has a tail. An ax is an animal. Cows have four wings. Jane is the name of a boy. An apple is square. Ice is warm. A pig can fly.

RHYMING

No knowledge of letters is required for this game.

"I will name a word such as *star*. Raise your hand if you can think of any word that rhymes with *star*." (Children might name such words as *far, jar, car*, etc. If a child names a word that does not rhyme, help him understand why the two words don't rhyme. If he says *step*, you might say, *"star* and *step* begin alike, but rhyming words must end alike. Listen: *Star. Jar.* Can you hear them rhyme?" (Other good key words to use for this activity are: *sand, fit, book, cat, day, sing, mail, pin, man, cold, light.*)

COMMON SOUNDS

Make a tape recording of various ordinary sounds: the piano, drum, door shutting, children clapping, someone walking, water running, a teacher talking. Leave a space after each sound for the children to identify it: "Listen closely to the sounds. If you know what any of them are, raise your hand. Close your eyes and tell me what this sound is." Draw a chair on the floor. "All right, open your eyes."

RHYTHM CLAPS

"Listen while I clap. When I finish clapping, I will call on someone to tell me how many times I clapped. Sometimes I will clap, stop, and clap again. Don't let that fool you, just count how many times I clap in all."

Clap such patterns as:
Clap . . . (pause) . . . clap, clap . . . (pause . . . clap.
Clap, clap, clap . . . (pause) . . . clap, clap.
Clap . . . (pause) . . . clap, clap, clap . . . (pause) . . . clap.

CAREER GAME

"Who brings our mail to the house?"
"Who owns the cow that gives us milk?"
"Who puts medicine in bottles for us?"
"Who puts out fires?"
"Who preaches at church?"
"Who helps children learn at school?"
"Who sells us groceries?"
"Who helps us get well when we are sick?"
"Who travels to the moon?"
"Who washes and sets our hair?"

Sing number games slowly and distinctly to allow time for all children to process the sounds. Gradually pick up normal speed until children can demonstrate that they are understanding the sounds that they hear. The object is to discriminate number sounds.

G
R
A
D
E
1

General Techniques

A. Understanding Stories Read Orally

B. Following Verbal Directions

C. Identifying Nonsense

D. Verbal Description

E. Identifying Familiar Sounds

Specific Ideas

UNDERSTANDING FAMILIAR STORIES READ ORALLY

Read aloud the following verse:

> Three little kittens
> lost their mittens
> and they began to cry,
> "Meow, meow, meow."

Ask the children to listen carefully as you read the poem again and tell them that they will be asked questions after the story is read. Reread the poem and ask the following questions: "What animal did I read about? How many animals were mentioned? What did they lose? What did they do?"

FOLLOWING VERBAL DIRECTIONS

1. Play hopscotch with numbers in the squares. Tell children to hop to #1, hop to #6, hop to #7, etc.

2.   Use the same game, except use beginning *letters* in the squares and have each child tell a word that begins with the letter to which he has hopped.

3.   The preposition game is good. Ask children to follow instructions such as: *put the book on the table, crawl under the chair, go up the slide,* and *come here to me.*

4.   Use the story of Melinda the Cow in "Talking Time." *See, the cow likes to moo! What letter sound does Melinda like to make?* The response to this is good if proper preplanning has been done by the teacher. An air of mystery and secret creates interest and enthusiasm.

5.   The magic wand game is good. Touch each child with a pointer and give a direction or ask for a sound or blend.

6.   Use the finger plays as auditory training material for establishing better listening habits. (Learning to follow directions, learning to hear specific sounds, words and phrases, or learning to hear rhyming words will result from this game.) This helps to teach the voiceless *th* and the difficult letters, including *l, s, r,* and *f.* **See Saw** is excellent for *s* sounds:

See Saw

(hold out arms)
Up and down we go—
(move arms up and down)
See Saw
High and then down low—
(move arms up and down)
See Saw
Fun as you can see—
(move arms up and down)
See Saw
Play the game with me.
See Saw, See Saw
See — Saw — See.

Through these finger plays, children come to learn the concepts of size (short, tall, large, small) and shape (round, square, triangular) and place (over, under, behind, before, up, down).

IDENTIFYING NONSENSE

You can readily devise examples of nonsense, such as the following, to suit your own group of children. Encourage them to answer in full sentences.

1. John has green hair.
2. Mary is a boy.
3. The cat barks.
4. Fish walk.
5. Bears talk.

VERBAL DESCRIPTION

Riddles are wonderful! There seems to be a magic quality about them.

1. What do cats like to chase?
2. What hides its face with its hands?
3. What has four legs but cannot walk (it has a back, too)?
4. Mary and Joe went to visit Grandmother and Grandfather in the country. They rode over bumpy roads and had a flat tire. Did Mary and Joe ride in a boat, on a plane, or on horseback?
5. Categorizing can also be used: What three words belong together?
   duck, chicken, turkey, baby
   bread, meat, eggs, house
Perhaps you might need to begin with only three things.

IDENTIFYING FAMILIAR SOUNDS

Make tape sounds which your children would like—sounds they hear around them: home sounds, town sounds, country sounds, sounds of different animals and of babies.

GRADE 2

UNDERSTANDING STORIES

READ ORALLY

Read a story to the child and then ask questions about it.

The Puppy that Wanted to Fly

Once upon a time, there was a funny little puppy that wanted to fly. He jumped up on his house with a towel tied to his hands and feet and jumped off. After awhile a big dog came along and saw the little puppy jumping up and down from his house. The big dog asked the little dog what he was doing. The little puppy said, "I am trying to fly." The big dog said, "Trying to fly?" "Dogs can't fly," said the big dog. The little puppy was sad for awhile, but he soon learned he could have just as much fun walking and running on his four little paws. Anyway, he was a little tired of jumping off his house!

FOLLOWING AND UNDERSTANDING VERBAL DIRECTIONS

For numbers three and four of the following, use either pictures or tops of a car, train, bus, or airplane. Do not go on to the more complex directions until the child has continued success with the less complex instructions.

1. Stand up.
2. Sit down.
3. Show me the car.
4. Give me the train.
5. Put your paper on my desk.
6. Put your pencil in your desk.
7. Open your book to page seven and show me the first word on that page.
8. Go to the sink and wash your hands with soap and water. Then dry them with a paper towel.

IDENTIFYING NONSENSE

Ask the child to tell what word is silly or what word should be changed in the following sentences. Explain.

1. I drink water out of a *table*.
2. I walk on the *ceiling*.
3. I turned *off* the TV so we could watch cartoons.
4. I like to *jump* my bicycle to school.

5. *Close* your book to page 23.
6. Put your shoes on your *hands*.
7. Go to the closet and get your *toat*.
8. Do you *wemembuh* your phone number?
9. She is in the *sslecond* grade.

UNDERSTANDING VERBAL DESCRIPTIONS

Have a picture of each object. After each sentence, ask what the answer might be.

1. I have something that is round. It is silver. It is warm on my arm. It is a (bracelet).

2. I am thinking of something. It is cold. It melts in the sun. It is not ice. It is (snow).

3. I am listening to something. It has rhythm. There are words. There are also sounds from some instruments. It is a (song).

4. I am listening to a noise. It's louder than a tiptoe. It comes nearer and gets louder as it comes to the door. It is someone (walking).

5. I heard something last night. It made a whistle and I heard a roar as it went by. It was a (train).

6. I have something in my hand. It is small. It is round and flat. I buy something with it. It is (money).

7. I do something in the fall. I use a rake. I put something in a barrel. Sometimes I sweep. I (rake the leaves).

8. I do something everyday. I do this in school. I look at printed words. I say these out loud. Sometimes I do not say them out loud. I am (reading).

IDENTIFYING FAMILIAR SOUNDS

Let the child select a picture of the object when attempting to identify the sound. Use a tape recorder.

1. Tape animal sounds. (bird, dog, cat, pig, cow)
2. Tape human voices. (child, man, woman, baby)
3. Tape bells or horns. (door bell, school bell, siren, telephone, car horn, truck horn)
4. Tape home noises. (running water, laughter, door slamming, mixer, vacuum cleaner)

BUILDING RECEPTIVE VOCABULARY

Ask the children to answer *yes* or *no* to the following questions.

1. Do dogs fly?
2. Do cats meow?
3. Do balls bounce?
4. Does grass grow?
5. Do doors open and close?
6. Do you have three feet?
7. Are fires cold?
8. Is water wet?
9. Can an airplane walk?
10. Is the sky red?

GAMES

While directing games, be certain that at no time the child feels he has failed completely. Here are instructions for a simple game:

Tell the children to clap their hands once for *yes* answers and twice for *no* answers. Make a train with two box cars. For each correct response place a colored button in the first car. For each incorrect response, place a colored toothpick in the second car. Drop play money in a bank when the child is ready to answer or after each response. Let the child hold the correct picture or object after he has responded, whether or not he gave the correct response.

UNDERSTANDING
VERBAL CONCEPTS   G R A D E **3**

This task should help determine whether the child understands information necessary for problem solving in math and in following directions for any task. If the child does not understand, you should explain with concrete examples and not force continued failure. Once the child does understand, presenting these questions or statements speedily should help develop confidence and result in responses given with more assurance. (These exercises are good for atypical language-speaking children.)

After each statement the child is asked *to show or explain* whether he *really* comprehends.

1. Three balloons are more than two balloons.
2. Six bats are less than ten bats.
3. An ocean is larger than a sea.
4. A wagon is larger than a cart.
5. Here are three items, a desk, a waste basket and a chair. The biggest one is the desk.
6. The tallest thing in this room is the door.
7. *Add* means to put more together.
8. *Minus* means we take away.
9. *Greater than* means more than.
10. Three plus four are seven.

This game may be varied by making negative aspects of the statement and allowing the child to (*a*) nod yes or no, or (*b*) make correct statements to indicate that the statement was not true. Example, you say, "*Greater than* means that something is not as large or not as many." The child should affirm, "*Greater than* means it is bigger or larger" or "It has more."

UNDERSTANDING AND FOLLOWING VERBAL DIRECTIOI

Games:

1. Simon Says This is a game in which the leader gives commands which must be obeyed when preceded by "Simon says ..."

2. Birds Fly This is a game similar to **Simon Says**. The leader names animals with the word "fly," at the same time always moving his arms to show flying motion. If it is an animal that can fly, players are to imitate flying, but if the animal named does not fly, the children are to remain still.

3. I Say Stoop This is a game in which the leader gives commands that are to be followed regardless of the leader's actions.

Verbal directions are given and the child complies:

1. Go to the chalkboard. Pick up the chalk. Make a mark on the chalkboard.
2. Touch the door with your right hand. Touch the floor with your left hand.

3. Stand up. Turn around. Look down at the floor. Sit down.
4. Take five hops. Turn around. Take three hops.
5. Touch your head with both hands. Turn around. Sit down.
6. Take two hops on left foot. Take three hops on right foot. Walk back to your seat.
7. Clap your hands. Close your eyes. Touch your nose.
8. Walk to the window. Turn around. Skip back.
9. Stretch as high as you can. Stand on tiptoe. Turn around.
10. Raise your right foot. Raise your left foot. Open and close your mouth.

Directions for drawing activities:

1. Draw a tree. Color it green. Put a bird in the tree. Color the bird blue.
2. Draw a circle. Put two eyes, a mouth, and a nose in the circle. Draw a yellow hat on the circle.
3. Draw a house without any windows. Put a tree with six branches on the left side of the house. Draw a porch with three steps in front of the house. Draw a boy on the top step. Draw a girl on the bottom step. Draw a wagon under the tree. Draw a bird's nest in the tree. Draw a mother bird flying over the tree. Draw two windows and one door in the house. Put a chimney on the house. Draw some smoke coming out of the chimney. Draw some flowers under one window. Draw a dark cloud in the sky.

Directions for writing activities—dictate sentences with familiar words:

1. It is time for father to come home from work.
2. Mother will cook supper before six o'clock tonight.
3. The man wears a brown hat on his head.
4. We all went to the birthday party last Wednesday.
5. I did all my work at school today.

Children like to write about first things:

1. Write your first name.
2. Write the first letter in your first name.
3. Write the first letter in your last name.
4. Write the name of the first day of the week.
5. Write the first letter in the alphabet.

6. Write the name of the first month of the year.
7. Write the title of the first story in your reader.
8. Write the name of our first President.

IDENTIFYING NONSENSE

Choose the word that sounds silly or does not make sense.

1. Susan was playing with her little grey *kitchen.* (*kitten*)
2. Jimmy could *smile* the cake baking in the oven. (*smell*)
3. Timmy fed the *cars* at the zoo. (*animals*)
4. Mary rode to school in a *tree.* (*car*)
5. I like to eat bread and *napkins.* (*butter*)
6. We eat bacon and *books* for breakfast. (*eggs*)
7. You eat with a knife and *glove.* (*fork*)
8. Mother sews with a needle and *book.* (*thread*)
9. When it is cold, I wear a cap and a *glass.* (*coat*)
10. It was raining very hard as Dick walked home. He saw a stream of water running *up* the rain spout. (*down*)
11. Mary had pancakes for breakfast. She put butter on them first. Then she put syrup on them to make them *sour.* (*sweet*)
12. Jimmy was hungry. His mother gave him a sandwich to eat. He *saved* it. (*ate*)

UNDERSTANDING VERBAL DESCRIPTIONS

Ask the child to identify what is being described.

1. It hops and has long ears. It is an animal. (It is a *rabbit.*)
2. It is an animal. It gives milk. It says *moo.* (It is a *cow*).
3. It is an animal. It has puppies. It says *bow-wow.* (It is a *dog.*)
4. It has hands and numbers. It tells you the time. (It is a *clock.*)
5. It is in the sky. It is white and fluffy. (It is a *cloud.*)
6. It is a game. It is played in summer with a ball and bat. (It is *baseball.*)
7. It grows in a garden. It is used at Halloween. It is big and fat. (It is a *pumpkin.*)
8. It is red and round. It grows on a tree. It is good to eat. (It is an *apple.*)

IDENTIFYING FAMILIAR SOUNDS

Sounds can be produced by the teacher or by a tape recorder for the child to identify.

1. The *meow* of a cat.
2. The *oink* of a pig.
3. The *moo* of a cow.
4. The *quack* of a duck.
5. The *cheep* of a chick.
6. The *bow-wow* of a dog.
7. The *neigh* of a horse.
8. The *buzz* of a bee.
9. The *ring* of a telephone.
10. The *siren* of a fire truck.

Hold short listening periods for familiar sounds.

1. The child closes his eyes for a short time to see how many different sounds can be heard.
2. The child closes his eyes, and the teacher makes different sounds for him to identify. Examples: tapping pencil on desk, writing on chalk board, tapping on chalk board, tapping on the window, tearing paper, running water in the sink, clapping hands, snapping fingers.

BUILDING RECEPTIVE VOCABULARY

Ask the child to answer *yes, no,* or *maybe* questions.

1. Do you have any sisters?
2. Is your house white?
3. Do you like candy?
4. Is a bird as big as a horse?
5. Are your eyes blue?
6. Are boys bigger than girls?
7. Can a turtle run as fast as a horse?
8. Is an ant small?
9. Can you pick up a tree?
10. Does the mailman bring letters?
11. Is a dog an animal?

12. Is a brick heavy?
13. Is a knife sharp?
14. Is a ball round?
15. Is a banana round?
16. Do all girls have long hair?
17. Are some clothes made of cotton?
18. Does the milkman bring milk?
19. Does Sunday come after Wednesday?
20. Is Easter a holiday?
21. Does the fire feel warm?
22. Is bubble gum sweet?
23. Does the washing machine need water?
24. Can a squirrel run up a tree?
25. Do birds fly south in winter?
26. Do you go to school on Saturday?
27. Is grass always green?
28. Does a letter need a stamp?
29. Do cars run on electricity?
30. Are you older today than you were yesterday?
31. Is the desert hot and dry?
32. Do you wear shoes on your head?
33. Do you wear gloves on your feet?

GRADE 4 — UNDERSTANDING STORIES, PARAGRAPHS, AND SENTENCES

Let the children listen to a short story or paragraph. Tell them things to listen for in the story and, when it has been read, ask questions about it. The following short story might be used:

Joe Smith was a little boy nine years old. He lived with his father, mother, and three brothers.

Joe had to walk to school, and it had rained all day while he was in school. He walked home in the rain, and his shoes were very wet when he arrived at home. He had a new pair of shoes, and he was very sad that he had gotten them so wet and muddy.

When Joe arrived home his mother told him to clean his shoes and set them up to dry. Joe washed his shoes in the sink, and put them on top of the stove to dry. Can you imagine what happened to Joe's shoes? The toes began to curl up, and they became very dry and cracked. Joe had ruined his shoes and had to buy another new pair.

These questions might be asked the child:

1. What is this story about?
2. What kind of weather was it?
3. What did Joe do?
4. What happened to his shoes?
5. Do you think Joe's mother was happy? Why?

Another experience with this story would be to let the child retell it to the teacher.

UNDERSTANDING AND FOLLOWING VERBAL DIRECTIONS

The child is given verbal directions, which he follows without repeating them, if possible. This can be used as a game or in giving instructions for an assignment in class.

Good games to play are **Simon Says** and **What Will I Take on My Trip?** In **Simon Says**, give such directions as *Simon says put your hands on your head*. If you do not say *Simon says*, the child knows he isn't to do what is said.

In **What Will I Take on My Trip?** the first child will say, *I am going on a trip, and I will take a pair of shoes*. Each child will repeat what the other has said and add another item to it.

The children could do exercises by following directions such as *touch your toes, jump up and down, run in place*, and so on. Things like *go to the blackboard, put the chalk on the board*, and so on, can be used right in the classroom.

As you continue, make each task a little harder, and continue these until someone fails to follow directions.

When using verbal directions in lessons, form a "One Time Club" in giving assignments and directions. You might ask some member of the club to repeat what you have said. Verbal directions can be used in almost any subject area. If a child realizes that one time is all the assignment will be given, he will learn to listen more carefully.

IDENTIFYING NONSENSE

The child will enjoy this type of exercise, and it will help him to understand what he hears. This can be done by reading a story, a paragraph, or just sentences. Ask the child if he hears anything wrong in the following paragraph:

There was a man on a four-engined jet airplane on his way to New York City. About halfway there, the plane flew through an ice storm and lost two of its propellers. The plane kept flying and a few miles further the other two propellers fell off. The plane crashed, and the man had to finish his journey on foot.

This story might also be used:

When Mr. and Mrs. Jones started to bed, Mr. Jones set his wind-up alarm clock for six o'clock. During the night the electricity went off because of a storm. Mr. Jones was late for work the next morning because his clock had stopped as a result of the storm.

UNDERSTANDING VERBAL DESCRIPTIONS

Auditory reception is practiced together with imagery. The teacher gives the child a description by giving only one clue at a time. The child will try to guess after each clue. When enough clues have been given, the child will name the object being described. This takes logical thinking and understanding of causal relationships. For example: The children could be given clues for an object in the schoolroom, such as a picture, or a classmate could be described. As the clues are developed, the child will begin to see what, or who, is being described.

ANSWERING "YES, NO, MAYBE" QUESTIONS

Ask the children questions that can be answered *yes, no,* or *maybe.* These statements should help children concentrate in order not to miss responses, thus, attention should be improved. You will be able to determine what concepts the children know and you also will be able to direct logical thinking by asking the children to explain why the statements are true or not true.

1. Apples are just little red homes for worms.
2. The banana was red.
3. The ice was hot.
4. The ball is square.
5. The wind is blowing.
6. You are a fourth grade boy/girl.
7. The fire was cold.

8. An apple is pointed.
9. A load of logs is light.
10. An electric stove is soft.
11. Dry sand is sticky.
12. A metal button is shiny.
13. A shoestring is heavy.
14. A feather pillow is hard.
15. A pancake is flat.
16. The end of the pin is pointed.
17. The wings of a bee are light.
18. Butter on a warm day is soft.
19. A piece of paper is flat.
20. Candy on a warm day is sticky.
21. A brick wall is hard.
22. A mirror in the sun is shiny.
23. A box of bricks is light.
24. The end of an arrow is pointed.
25. A balloon is light.
26. Crayons that have been in the sun are soft.
27. A hill is flat.
28. Wet paint is sticky.
29. A wooden doll is hard.
30. The bark on a log shines.
31. A school bus is heavy.
32. A washing machine is light.
33. The blade of a pocketknife is pointed.
34. Bread and jam are sticky.
35. A handkerchief is soft.
36. A round ball is flat.
37. Bananas can telephone.
38. You can hear a telephone roar.
39. You can hear a bee meow.
40. You can hear a lion ring.
41. You can hear a kitten buzz.
42. The seat of a chair is flat.
43. The children went to the ice cream shop and bought a truck.

44. Bacon smells good when it is cooking.
45. Bubble gum is not sticky.
46. The trees are purple and blue.
47. It was raining cat and dogs.
48. A monkey has nine hands.
49. The water at the lake was hot.
50. The blanket felt warm.
51. The mud felt squishy between the boy's toes.
52. Rocks can hurt your feet when you are barefoot.
53. A duck goes "bow-wow-wow."
54. A kitten goes meow.
55. Kittens like to eat worms.
56. Saturday comes after Tuesday.
57. Boys and girls need to drink milk.
58. Dogs like to eat hay.
59. Christmas is a holiday.
60. The car had a tiger in its tank.
61. The mailman brought the milk.
62. The wooly lamb said, "Oink, oink."
63. When a person cries, he is sad.
64. An air conditioner makes you feel hot.
65. Some dresses are made of wool.
66. When a person laughs, she is sad.
67. A heater feels good in the summer.
68. Boys wear sashes on their coats.
69. You can rattle a napkin.
70. Bread, butter, and jam make a good sandwich.
71. A raccoon can scamper up a tree.
72. A gallon of water is more than a handful.
73. A hammer is the same as a hatchet.
74. To make a dress you need a pattern.
75. A boy is never bashful.
76. Boys with good manners do not snatch.
77. You can wrap a package with a shadow.
78. The captain takes a nap when there is a battle.
79. A balloon travels on a stick.
80. Travelers are people who travel.

81. Frank felt fine after he drank a gallon of gasoline.

82. Children look for colored eggs on Ground Hog Day.

83. A lobster likes to ride on a donkey's back.

84. Goggles are something good to eat.

85. A cottage is a place where cots are made.

86. Black is the opposite of white.

87. Does a girl have three arms?

88. Is cheese made to eat?

89. Do you hear with your nose?

90. Can a bee read?

91. Are geese green in color?

92. "Jack and the Beanstalk" is a true story.

93. The ocean is filled with wheat.

94. The sailor lived in the desert.

95. A red light means *go*.

SHORT-ANSWER QUESTIONS   GRADE 5

Have the children answer questions on student evaluation sheets:

In Square No. 1, draw your picture. If you have a small picture of yourself, you may bring it to school and paste it in Square No. 2.

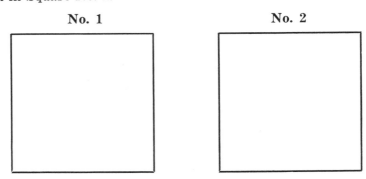

No. 1   **No. 2**

You are an important person. Let's find out more about you. If you fill in the next page or pages correctly, you will know more about yourself, and I will know more about you!

Facts

Write in the right answers:

1. My name is _____ _____.
    (first)   (last)
2. My age is _____.
3. The street I live on is _____.
4. The name of my town is _____.
5. The name of my state is _____.
6. The name of my school is _____.
7. I like school because _____

    _____.

8. I do *not* like school because _____

    _____.

Family

9. My father's name is _____ _____.
10. My mother's name is _____ _____.
11. I have _____ sisters.
12. I have _____ brothers.

Self-Description

13. I am a boy. _____

14. I am a girl. _____

15. Eyes

    a. My eyes are blue. _____
    b. My eyes are brown. _____
    c. My eyes are green. _____
    d. My eyes are gray. _____
    e. My eyes are _____.

16. Hair

    a. My hair is brown. _____
    b. My hair is black. _____
    c. My hair is red. _____
    d. My hair is white. _____
    e. My hair is blond. _____
    f. My hair is _____.

17. Size
  a. I am big. ———————

      I am not big. ———————

  b. I am little. ———————

      I am not little. ———————

  c. I am tall. ———————

      I am not tall. ———————

AUDITORY CUES

The following simple poem will help to determine whether or not the child is receiving auditory cues:

Our Five Senses

Our ears tell when
Folks are cheering.
We call this sense
The sense of ———————.

To use this sense,
As you can tell,
I need my nose.
The sense is ———————.

To use this sense
Both day and night
We need our eyes.
The sense is ———————.

When eating well
In no great haste,
We use this sense
And call it ———————.

We use our hands
To feel and clutch,
And call this one
The sense of ———————.

Now you've named the senses;
There are only five.
Hearing, smell, sight, taste, and
Touch tell us we're alive.

1. Select a number of rhythm band instruments. Encourage the children to explore the use of these and give them an opportunity to learn the sounds of each. Have the children turn their backs and hold their hands up when they recognize the sounds. Give them an opportunity to tell what they have heard.

2. Select a number of boxes, such as oatmeal or match boxes, and place small rocks in one, sand in another, and small rubber balls in another. (The contents may be varied.) Shake the boxes one at a time so that the children can learn the differences among the sounds. Then have the children turn their backs and guess at the sounds as you shake the boxes.

Note: Fifth graders will loose interest in these activities much more readily than will younger children. Still, many fifth graders do not discriminate readily among sounds. It may help to put a time limit on each game. (They must be able to tell the sound in, say, two seconds.)

3. Select eight bottles and place varying amounts of water in them. Demonstrate the different sounds by blowing over them or tapping lightly. This technique is used only to help each child become aware of different sounds. Low sounds may be demonstrated, then high sounds. Place the same amount of water in some pairs of bottles in order to have the children guess whether the sounds heard are the same or different. For this the children will have their backs turned while the teacher or some other child taps or blows on the bottles.

4. Ask the children to turn their backs, then perform the following acts and ask them to identify what you are doing by the sounds: tap pencil on desk, tap heel on floor, clap hands, knock on the desk, stomp foot slightly, snap fingers, and knock on a door. A variation of this would be for the children not only to tell what they hear but also to tell from which side of the room the sound originates.

5. Play guessing games, identifying family members by description of that member's role or responsibility in the family.

6. Tap a fairly large metal bar or old-time metal triangle with another piece of metal. Vary the taps and have the children respond with the correct number.

7. Read a story to the children—a descriptive story is very good for this. Ask the children to draw what they have heard

in the story. This not only tests the child's ability to *decode* what is said, but also his ability to *remember* what has been said.

8. Give the child a picture and ask him to find the *green house*, the *red barn*, the *yellow car*, etc. Later, more complicated directions can be given, such as *Find the tall tree without fruit*.

9. Describe one of several objects or pictures, and ask the child to select the one described from among many.

10. Ask the child to act out what is said to him.

11. Tape-record animal sounds and let the child write down what animal made the sound.

TEACHING THE DAYS AND MONTHS

Have the child underline the day of the week or the month of the year that makes the statement true.

1. Easter is always on (*Sunday, Friday, Tuesday*).
2. (*June, September, February*) is called the month of roses.
3. There is no abbreviation for the month of (*January, May, April*).
4. (*August, April, February*) is colder than September.
5. Labor Day is always on (*Tuesday, Monday, Thursday*).
6. One of the summer months is (*August, September, December*).
7. (*April, January, February*) is a spring month.
8. The day after Friday is (*Tuesday, Monday, Saturday*).
9. The seventh month of the year is (*July, January, April*).
10. The first day of the week is (*Tuesday, Sunday, Friday*).
11. The first month of the year is (*December, January, June*).
12. The last month of the year is (*December, January, June*).
13. Fall begins in (*March, September, July*).
14. Our school begins in (*October, June, September, April*).
15. (*November, May, December*) is the month we celebrate Thanksgiving.
16. We have fresh vegetables from the garden in (*March, January, July*).
17. It usually snows in (*February, July, September*).

Specific and precise vocabulary may be increased by using sentences with general verbs. Have the class suggest synonyms that would make the action more vivid. Example: The teacher in the hall said, "Slow down." The students are asked to supply several synonyms for *said* to give a better idea of the teacher's attitude toward the students in the hallway.

Discuss the differences in meaning between certain words: *strong, brave; money, cash; trip, voyage; allow, permit.*

COMPREHENSION AND STUDY SKILLS*

1. Write on the blackboard the headings *Where, When, How, Why.* Then write in a list at one side the following phrases: *in the morning, over the house, at three o'clock, for fun, one at a time, before long, on her head, to make sure.* Ask the children to put the first phrase into a sentence of their own (*I awaken in the morning*). Ask them what *in the morning* tells: where I awaken, when, how, or why? Write *in the morning* under the heading *When.* Develop each of the other phrases in the same manner.

2. Write the following on the blackboard:

as _____ as a feather	light
as _____ as wax	smooth
as _____ as lightning	graceful
as _____ as a swan	neat
as _____ as a uniform	quick
as _____ as tinsel	bright

Tell the children that these expressions are common ways of describing things. The words on the right belong in the blanks.

Have the children start with the first blank, tell what word belongs in it, and give a sentence using the whole expression (*as light as a feather*), to prove that the word does belong. This exercise may be copied by the pupils and completed by them independently after the first blank has been filled.

WORD ANALYSIS

Have the pupil who needs more practice in analyzing words find in the list of words below the word that goes with each descriptive statement, and write the number of the statement before the word.

---

* Russell *et al.*, 1961.

1. A hyphenated word
2. A compound word
3. It rhymes with *ship*.
4. Final *e* gives it a long-vowel sound.
5. It has the sound of *ou*.
6. Two words with four syllables
7. Three words with three syllables
8. This word has a double consonant before the ending *ed*.
9. This word begins the same as *squirrel*.
10. These words end with a syllable with *le*.
11. It ends with a suffix meaning *in that manner*.
12. Its first syllable is a prefix.

____plow	____pantaloons	____similar	____squibs
____cockalorum	____jigsawed	____barnacle	____pondalorum
____horse-radish	____clip	____strutted	____puzzle
____lame	____factory	____exclaimed	____promptly

UNDERSTANDING STORIES
READ ORALLY

G
R
A   6
D
E

Auditory decoding may be practiced by having the child listen to a short story read orally and then answer questions concerning the story. Short stories of appropriate difficulty may be found in S.R.A. reading labs and the *Reader's Digest* Skill Builders.

UNDERSTANDING AND FOLLOWING VERBAL DIRECTIONS

The child may profit from practice in following directions such as those he encounters in a typical day at school.

Simple Directions

1. Turn to page 143.
2. Point to the second column.
3. Find the third paragraph.
4. Read the second sentence.

Complex Commands

1. Turn to page 267 and read the first sentence in the second paragraph.
2. Copy the first problem in row four on the board and solve it.

The teacher may give step-by-step directions to the student as he completes a project or science experiment.

IDENTIFYING NONSENSE

Present the child with a series of verbal statements which contain nonsense elements. Ask him to point out the nonsense element in the statement. As the child progresses in competence, ask him to explain why a certain element is nonsense.

1. Giraffes may vote when they are 21.
2. Radios sing when you turn them on.
3. A knot appeared on the baseball after it was struck with a bat.
4. Canada and Texas are both part of the Pacific Ocean.

UNDERSTANDING VERBAL DESCRIPTIONS

The teacher attempts to get the child to recognize familiar objects from short verbal descriptions of them.

1. It is made of cloth but is not clothing.
2. It is colored red, white, and blue.
3. Stars and stripes are on it.
4. It may be found in front of the school building.

The child may also be given pictures and asked to identify the picture that the teacher is describing.

UNDERSTANDING VERBAL STATEMENTS

The student answers *yes, no,* or *maybe.*

1. A *front* is the place where a cold air mass and a warm air mass meet.

2. *Relative humidity* is the percent of water vapor which the air contains at a certain temperature compared to what it could hold at that temperature.

3. *Weather* is what happens in the sea day by day.

4. *Climate* is weather over a long period of time, such as a year.

5. *Radio sounds* are instruments sent into the upper atmosphere which send radio signals. They tell the kind of weather which is occurring high above the ground.

6. Small and large objects fall at the same rate of speed if all other conditions are the same.

7. Bread molds in the refrigerator because it was fresh when it was put in.

8. Animals do not distinguish color but see only gray objects.

9. Rattlesnakes are not afraid of human beings.

10. Flowers and vegetables can grow in water to which minerals have been added.

BUILDING A RECEPTIVE VOCABULARY

The child may receive practice in recognizing subtle differences in words when the teacher gives a sentence verbally that contains an inappropriate word. The student picks out the inappropriate word or words and substitutes the correct word for the incorrect words.

1. Mr. Wright *dove* his *par* into the service station.

2. The mother bird *blew* straight to her *test*.

3. Willie *burned* the TV to *chunnel* 13.

UNDERSTANDING STORIES
READ ORALLY

G R A D E S **7 & 8**

The child should be told to listen to the story carefully; then find out how well he has done so by having him retell the story in his own words, answer questions regarding specific occurrences and characters in the story, or complete sentences read aloud. Example:

The Greeks give us the story of the beautiful youth, Narcissus, who was loved by the nymph, Echo.

When Narcissus scorned the love of Echo, as he did the love of all lovely maidens, Echo died, leaving in the hills only her sad voice to return the last word to anyone who calls her.

Narcissus was punished for his heartlessness by Aphrodite, goddess of love, who caused him to fall in love with his own image, which he saw mirrored in the depths of a woodland pool. Thinking the reflection he saw was a beautiful water nymph, Narcissus held out his arms to her, and she, in return, held two white arms up to him; however, when he tried to touch her, water sifted through his hands and she disappeared from his sight. Again and again he tried to touch and embrace her, but always she eluded him. Finally, because he loved her so hopelessly, Narcissus died of a broken heart.

The gods, because they realized his devotion, then changed Narcissus into the sweet white or yellow flower that bears his name.

Have you ever seen it peeping over the edge of a silent pool?

Questions

1. From what nationality does the story of Narcissus come? (*Greek*)

2. What did Narcissus think his own reflection was? (*A nymph*)

3. How many times did Narcissus try to reach and embrace his reflection? (*repeatedly* or *several*)

4. What caused Narcissus to die? (*his heart was broken*)

5. Why did the gods change Narcissus into a flower? (*they realized his deep devotion*)

Completing Sentences

1. Echo was a ___(*nymph*)___ .

2. Aphrodite was the goddess of ___(*love*)___ .

3. Echo died, leaving her ___(*voice*)___ .

4. Narcissus was changed by ___(*the gods*)___ in the hills.

FOLLOWING AND UNDERSTANDING VERBAL DIRECTIONS

To test the student's ability to grasp verbal directions, play the **Simon Says** game. Or, give each student a piece of paper, a pencil, and the following instructions:

1. Put your first name on the top line of your paper near the center of the sheet.
2. Put a triangle in the lower left-hand corner of your paper.
3. Turn your paper around so that the top is now the bottom and put an *X* in the right-hand corner.
4. Turn your paper back around, and in the middle of the sheet draw an arrow pointing to your left and write *left* on this arrow. Then draw an arrow pointing to your right and write the word *right* on this arrow.
5. Put a square around your name.
6. Put a circle in the upper right-hand corner.
7. Draw a line from the last letter of your name to the circle.
8. Write the first four letters of the alphabet in the lower right-hand corner.
9. Put the number 717 above the triangle.
10. In the center of the bottom line on your paper, write your last name.

Variations of this can be done by telling the child to do activities in the room, such as: *Take the book from the table, put it in the box on the chair, and then place the box on the bookshelf.*

IDENTIFYING NONSENSE

Ask the child to identify nonsense in sentences:

1. The table fell off the fork.
2. The tire repairman just turned the wheel around, because it was only flat on one side.
3. After mowing the lawn, we jumped into it for a cool swim.
4. I was careful not to step into any water because I didn't want my shoes to melt.
5. On my way to school, I threw away my lunch because I wasn't hungry.

6. I like to eat peas with a shovel because they don't roll off as easily.

7. I like to go to bed around noon because I can't sleep when it is light.

8. One and one are three because that is how many quarters I have in my pocket.

UNDERSTANDING VERBAL DESCRIPTIONS

Games:

1. Leader: *I'm going on a trip and I'm taking something black.* (Any color of an object that should be in the room.)
   Pupil: *Is it the blackboard?*
   Leader: *No.*
   Another pupil: *Is it an umbrella?*
   Leader: *Yes, it is. What are you taking on your trip?*
   (The pupil who guesses correctly becomes the leader.)

2. A variation in the above game: *I'm going on a trip and I'm taking something beginning with the letter*   (letter of the alphabet). Again the object should be in the room.

3. Another variation: *I'm going on a trip and I'm taking a*   (sound). Examples: *meow, clip-clop,* etc.

Identifying objects described:

1. It is round and flat and when we use it we can hear music. (*record*)

2. It comes in all sizes with bark and leaves on it. (*tree*)

3. You hold me in your hand; I come in all colors and when you make a mistake, you use my head. (*pencil*)

4. I'm usually found in the country; I have one white stripe and an odor which I use to protect me. (*skunk*)

5. I'm just a straight line, but I'm found in many places— on houses, in telephone books, in grocery stores, and in your multiplication table. (*the number 1*)

IDENTIFYING FAMILIAR SOUNDS

1. Play records and have the child identify the music or singer.

2. Record familiar sounds on the tape recorder and have the child identify them. For example: horn sounds (Volkswagen, Diesel truck, etc.), musical instruments, animal sounds, footsteps (high heels, sneakers, taps, etc.).

3. Take a hike and identify the natural sounds heard in a woods, park, playground, residential or business section of town.

BUILDING RECEPTIVE VOCABULARY

Say a sentence with one word used incorrectly and see if the pupil can find it.

1. The boy saw the *quarrel* run up the tree.
2. Bob fell and hit his *heard*.
3. My mother will sweep the house out with the *groom*.
4. Please bring the bucket of *pant*.
5. The new movie was a big *sincere*.
6. I am not very good at *including* people to each other so they can meet.
7. I'm hungry. Please *six* me a *sandal*.
8. The pretty *grill* was too tired to play the piano.
9. To sweeten my breakfast cereal, I put two teaspoons of *salt* in it.
10. They put their groceries in a *pepper* bag.

Use new words in sentences and have the pupil tell you the meaning by the context.

Ask *yes-no-maybe* questions. At times it would be appropriate to ask the pupil why he gave a particular answer.

1. Five continents are shaped the same.
2. Usually medicine makes you sick.
3. All rivers curve and wind.
4. Human body cells are usually dead.
5. The boy is seven feet tall.
6. Playing sports takes a lot of time.
7. All cows have horns.
8. Doors hang on hinges.
9. The radio is the only source of music.
10. Many countries are governed by a democracy.

CB ACTIVITIES

Exercise 1

Place on cassette tape a series of 10-code questions. Instruct the student that he is to explain the meaning of each 10-code. The tape may be adjusted to allow for time to respond to the questions or the tape may be stopped after each response. You should keep a book with a good CB vocabulary handy to add material according to need. Examples of 10-code questions are as follows:

"What do the following 10-codes mean?"

1. 10-4 (OK—message received)
2. 10-20 (a person's immediate location)
3. 10-10 (standing by)
4. 10-27 (moving to another channel)
5. 10-36 (time check—what time is it?)
6. 10-77 (negative contact)
7. 10-8 (inservice—OK to call)

Exercise 2

Ask the student the meaning of the following statements. The student is asked to answer in explicit but not lengthy terms.

1. "We're clear and down." (transmission completed)
2. "Keep it on the double-nickle." (go 55 miles an hour)
3. "Have you got a copy?" (have you received my message?)
4. "Do you have your ears on?" (are you listening?)
5. "I'll be the front door." (the lead car)
6. "I'll be the back door." (the last car within a group to observe highway behind)
7. "I'm in the rocking chair." (the middle car between two cars transmitting by CB)
8. "What are you going to do, four-wheeler?" (asking question of a passenger-car driver)
9. "What about it pickem-up?" (asking for information from a pick-up truck)
10. "Break 1-9 for the eighteen-wheeler." (asking for time on channel 19 to talk to a large truck)

11. "Break 1-9 for the Foxy Lady." (request to talk on channel 19 to a person who uses the name of *Foxy Lady* on the CB)
12. "Wall to wall and tree-top tall." (many highway patrol moving about)
13. "Momfort Lane." (extreme left lane)
14. "We down, we gone, bye-bye." (transmission completed)

Exercise 3

Use exercises 1 and 2 (or similar ones), but vary the *pitch* of the spoken expressions in the following ways.

1. Talk in a high-pitched voice.
2. Talk in a low, throaty voice.
3. Talk in a wavy voice from low to high.

Exercise 4

Use exercises 1 and 2 (or similar), but vary the amplitude of the spoken expressions, i.e., from barely audible speech to a very loud voice.

Auditory Association

Auditory association refers to the ability to associate spoken words in a meaningful way, and it deals with the auditory process of interpreting relationships. Can the individual relate two segments of stated information? Does the student know, for example, that to "cut" with a saw is in the same *category* of events as chopping with an ax? To train for this skill you may supply many abstract cues and provide visual aid cues when possible.

A specific approach to aid in the development of this skill could be to train on the basis of concrete, functional, or abstract similarities. For example, to train for concrete qualities you could teach children to examine aspects of shape, such as round, circular, oval, and the absence of corners. You should then often repeat, "They are alike because they are round-like (or circular or have no corners)." Follow this procedure with comparisons to squares, rectangles, and triangles, having the child note various differences and asking the child to explain why circles and ovals are alike.

To train for functional similarities explain that some objects are to be eaten, some to be driven, some to be ridden, or some to be read. Then ask the child to name items which are to be eaten, and to explain how these named items are alike.

To train for abstract concepts explain that some items have different names. A chair is a chair, but it is also furniture; an apple is an apple, but it is also a fruit. After asking children to think of two names for items in sight: ball or toy, bat or toy, wagon or vehicle, train or vehicle, you should then ask in what way a ball and a bat are alike; a wagon and a train.

This procedure could be a beginning approach, but if the problem is one of concentration, you may need to ask the child to stand, sit, or raise his arm, as the answer is given. This causes a minor tension which could make the child more alert. The training for auditory reception should also help the training of auditory association. Kirk (1971) reports that learning is an integrative process and training for one process may help that of another.

GRADE K

FRIENDS

Ask a child to stand up before the group and to choose a friend to stand beside her. Ask her to tell one way in which she and her friend are alike. ("We are both in kindergarten; we are both wearing blue jeans; we are both in school; we both ride the bus to school; we are both five years old; we are both wearing sneakers.") A second child is then asked to tell one way in which they are different. ("He is a boy and I am a girl. Her hair is braided and my hair is short.") The first child chosen sits down and the second child chooses a friend to come up and the game is repeated. Encourage the other class members to add likenesses and differences to those given by the two children who are standing.

Since this is an auditory association game, the children must speak out clearly for others to hear and learn to understand differences heard. (This can also be used for visual association.)

BIG AND LITTLE BOX

A collection of everyday items which come in two sizes but are alike in all other respects are kept in a large, sturdy box or plastic dishpan. Examples: large and small bars of soap, a small baby cereal box and a large baby cereal box, a small and large box of Jello of the same flavor, empty cartons from large and small sizes of toothpaste (same brand), a pocket comb and a regular comb, a standard toothbrush and a child's toothbrush, an empty large vanilla bottle and a small vanilla bottle, a large spoon and a small spoon, a large safety pin and a small safety pin, a large button and a small one, etc. These items are identified and paired by the children and the concept of big and little and large and small is reiterated. The comparative form (-er) is stressed. Although the use of actual items introduces a kinesthetic visual element, there is much opportunity for auditory-vocal associations. There is also excellent opportunity for pointing out qualities of likeness— both toothbrushes are made of red plastic, but the size is different; both cereal boxes are made of green cardboard and both contain rice cereal, but the size is different.

OPPOSITES

Collect magazine pictures which illustrate opposite concepts. Reinforce these pictures by mounting them on construction paper. Store them in separate folders which are labeled *Open-Shut, Empty-Full, On-Off, Few-Many*, etc. In the Open-Shut folder show a picture of an open door and a closed door, an open window and a closed window, a refrigerator with its door open and a refrigerator with its door closed, an automobile with its door open and an automobile with its door closed, an open book and a closed book. The Few-Many folder might contain pictures of an almost deserted street and a congested street, a tree with only a few leaves and a tree with many leaves, a few blossoms and a field profuse with flowers, a few people and a large crowd. You present a statement ("When we drive the car, the door is shut. When we get out of the car, the door is _____."), and the child supplies the missing word and then finds the appropriate pair of pictures to illustrate the statement. Different statements can be used from day to day which will elicit slightly different responses and maintain interest but which will illustrate the same pair of pictures. Later, the children may be able to initiate the statements.

LIKE SOUNDS

You say a pair of sounds such as *ah-ah* and ask, "Did I make the same sounds?" Then say *ah-O,* and ask if you made the same sounds. Use nonsense sounds and letter sounds. Then progress to words as *cat-rat, man-can.* Vary this procedure by pairing sounds made with pencil tapping, or a tablet hitting on a desk. Children must close their eyes for this variation.

TAPED SOUNDS

Have a series of sounds on tape and a series of pictures. From a group of pictures have the children choose the ones that represent your request. Examples: The child is asked to find pictures of the vehicles which made the sounds she heard. She hears the following:

> horn on car and boat
> finger scratching
> train whistle

RHYMES

"Can you make a rhyme? Let's see if you can finish these sentences." (Examples follow.)

Find your nose, touch your _____ (toes).
Take a nap, put your hands in your _____ (lap).
The little mouse ran into his _____ (house).
My little cat found a funny _____ (hat).
The big black dog jumped over a _____ (log).
The little bunny looked very _____ (funny).

Use motions or picture clues to encourage responses.

ASSOCIATING WHAT IS HEARD

Read the following sentences and ask the children to fill in the proper word from the two choices. The children must wait until you read the sentence with two choices.

1. The boy *(caught* or *taught)* the ball
2. The airplane *(flies* or *cries).*
3. Mother *(cooks* or *books)* the dinner.

4. The mail carrier (*brings* or *swings*) the mail.
5. Daddy (*mows* or *sows*) with the lawnmower.
6. The children (*sing* or *ring*) the song.
7. The truck driver (*blows* or *slows*) the horn.
8. Tom (*bats* or *mats*) the ball.
9. Juan (*sleeps* or *creeps*) in a bed.
10. Maria (*eats* or *beats*) her breakfast.

CATEGORIES

You say, "I am going to say three words. Tell me which ones go together. Name them." You must speak slowly.

1. grey, black, mouse
2. chair, stool, road
3. car, truck, umbrella
4. wheels, rake, tires
5. stamps, dress, envelope
6. doctor, preacher, medicine
7. bed, sofa, chair
8. bread, meat, grass
9. pickles, candy, cake
10. ice cream, snow, swim

You may vary these and add groups that are within the experiences of the children. Pictures may be shown if they are needed.

CAUSE AND EFFECT

Cause and effect questions can be employed, such as "What would happen if you fell out of the swing?" Examples include:

"What would happen if Mother gave you some ice cream?"
"What would happen if you stepped on a piece of glass?"
"What would happen if you spilled your milk?"
"What would you do if the telephone rang?"
"What would you do if Mother called you to come and eat?"
"What would you do if Mother put you in bed?"
"What would you do if Mother gave you a cookie?"
"What would happen if you dropped a glass?"
"What would you do if your baby sister was crying?"

CLASSIFYING ITEMS

Categorizing and classifying items such as a ball, spoon, cup, block, toy farm animals, bowl, fork, glass, chair, or table. For example, ask the child to put all the things she plays with together; ask the child to put "all the items that we eat with" together.

SAME AND DIFFERENT

Build the concept of same and different by using concrete items, such as a block and a ball, a spoon and a fork, a table and a chair, a dog and a cat. Ask in what way are they alike and in what way are they different. Initially concrete likenesses are encouraged, but gradually more abstract similarities are developed.

CLASSIFICATION OF OBJECTS   G R A D E **1**

Say these words slowly and let the child answer verbally which two go together:

1. ball, cow, bat
2. bread, butter, candy
3. salt, pepper, cheese
4. shoes, hat, socks
5. knife, pencil, fork
6. cup, saucer, pan
7. pencil, light, paper

LIKENESS AND DIFFERENCE

Using the examples from the preceding exercise, build concepts of same and different by asking the child how the following things are alike:

1. apple, orange, pear, carrot
2. day, year, month, star
3. bus, train, car, house
4. hammer, saw, axe, stove
5. river, ocean, lake, mountain

RHYMING AND MATCHING

1.   Cut pictures from magazines, picture books, or out-of-date readers, and paste them on small cards. Assemble several groups of cards, each containing three or four pictures that start with the same sound, and one that is different. Give a set to a child, who comes to the front of the room and shows each card, naming the pictures and identifying the one that has a different beginning sound. Later, he may be asked to name the beginning letters and give the sounds.

2.   Make picture cards in sets of two, some having the same beginning sound and others with different beginning sounds but which rhyme. (Example: lake, lamp—alike; lake, cake—unlike.)

3.   Divide the group into two teams as in a spelling match. Play this game for team points, rather than asking the child who misses to be seated. The first child on Team One calls a word to which the first child on Team Two responds with a word of the same sound. If he can do this, Team Two gets a point. Then the first child on Team Two calls a word and the second child on Team One tries to match it. If he does, then Team One gets a point. Each child gets to call a word and to attempt a matching word. This allows him to participate twice before the turn passes.

4.   Paste many colorful pictures on a large poster board. The child identifies all pictures whose names start alike, telling the names of the letters and giving the sounds.

5.   Have two sets of picture cards, each with an equal number of like beginning sounds. Pass one set of cards among members of the class. Hold up a card. The child who has a picture that starts with the same sound brings the card to you and names both pictures. All the children help to decide if the pictures match. Continue showing the cards until all have been collected.

CLASSIFYING SOUNDS

Make a tape of sounds:

1.   scratching sounds

2.   whistles

3.   automobile horns

4.   raking leaves

5.   bird songs

Present one group of sounds at a time (include no more than three sounds each). For example, three scratching sounds made on different surfaces. Ask the children to listen to all three, associate them and then determine to what "family" the sounds belong.

LIKENESS AND DIFFERENCE　　　G R A D E 2

1. Develop the same and different concepts by asking questions such as *How are pigs and horses alike and how are they different?* (*Cars and trains? Candy and nuts? Houses and garages?*)

2. Give a series of rhyming words that change only the first letter, and let the child tell how they are alike and how they are different.

PROBLEM SOLVING

Work on anticipating needs in various situations.

1. If you were going on a trip, what would you take?
2. If you were going to clean the yard, what would you need?

Anticipating what would happen next in a certain situation is a good exercise in problem solving.

1. What would happen if you put an ice cream cone in your locker?
2. What would you do if you lost your doll?

CATEGORIZING AND CLASSIFYING

1. Tell the children to name everything they can think of that is taken on a picnic—or to school, to church, to the beach, or to the mountains.

2. Ask *How are these things alike?*

A cat, a pig, and a fish?　　　Milk, tea, and coffee?
A coat, a hat, and a dress?　　A glass, a cup, and a straw?
A jar, a vase, and a bucket?

3. Ask the child to name all the words he can think of that begin with a sound of *b, c, d,* etc.

4. Ask the child to name all the words he can think of that end with a given sound, such as *t, g,* etc.

PREDICTING THE OUTCOME OF STORIES

Begin a story about a dog and let the child supply the ending. *We have a little puppy. His name is Spot. He is a . . .*

G
R
A
D
E **3**

LOGICAL RELATIONSHIPS

To help the children identify incongruities in sentences, ask questions such as these:

1. Do you walk smoothly if you stump your toe?
2. Do you shake when you are very cold?
3. Could you carry an umbrella on your feet?
4. Would a dress made of flowers last for a month?
5. Could you fish in a swimming pool?
6. Does a bird have wings?
7. Can a fish go where there is no water?
8. Do people use glasses to eat meat?
9. If you are tired, are you ready to play?
10. Would you go to a drug store to buy sugar?

Or, read these questions and then ask the pupil to decide upon an answer.

1. Which of these has legs but cannot walk?
   a. a table   b. a chair   c. a dog
2. Which of these has eyes but cannot see?
   a. a needle   b. a nail   c. a potato
3. Which of these has a tongue but cannot talk?
   a. a man   b. a shoe   c. a radio
4. What do dogs do to rabbits?
   a. chase   b. race   c. face
5. Which of the following sings without words?
   a. girl   b. boy   c. bird

CLASSIFYING

Tape-record sounds and have the children classify them.

1. car horn, train whistle, bicycle horn (vehicles)
2. *oink* of pig, *moo* of cow, *baaa* of sheep (farm animals)
3. wind blowing hard, thunder, and rain (storm)
4. dog barking, cat *meow*ing, and canary singing (pet sounds)
5. marching, dancing or shuffling sound, and tap dancing (sounds made by feet)

Read the words in each row. Have students tell how they are alike.

1. Hammer, ax, saw   All are _____
2. Chicken, bird, goose   All are _____
3. Carrot, squash, potato   All are _____
4. Flower, tree, shrub   All are _____
5. Pig, horse, lamb   All are _____
6. Chair, table, stool   All are _____

FINDING OPPOSITES

Read these sentences for the children to complete.

1. Up is to down as out is to (*in*).
2. Over is to under as stop is to (*go*).
3. Left is to right as bottom is to (*top*).
4. Snow is to cold as rain is to (*wet*).

ANALOGY   GRADE 4

In order to help the children grasp the idea of analogy, read the following sentences to them, and ask them to fill in the blanks.

1. A ring is to a hand like a hat is to a (*head*).
2. A (*doll*) is to a little girl as a baby is to a mother.
3. A boy is to a man as a (*girl*) is to a woman.
4. A foot is to a shoe as a (*hand*) is to a glove.
5. A (*car*) is to a road as a boat is to the water.
6. A picture is to the eye as a radio is to the (*ear*).

CATEGORIZATION

Have children listen to several words and put them in the proper category.

1. Germany, Italy, France are all (*countries*).
2. Salt, stone, sulphur are all (*minerals*).
3. A table, a chair, a lamp are all (*furniture*).
4. A robin, a hen, a duck are all (*birds*).
5. Snakes, lizards, turtles, alligators are all (*reptiles*).
6. Roses, tulips, daisies are all (*flowers*).
7. Cumulus, cirrus, stratus are all (*clouds*).

PROBLEM SOLVING

Ask questions such as *What would you do if you heard the fire bell ring?* Give the child ample time to think through his answer and respond.

1. What would you do if you received fifty dollars?
2. What would you do if a stranger knocked on your door?
3. What would you do if you were riding a horse and you saw a snake?
4. What would you do if you saw a wreck?

WHAT'S THE "OBJECT"

You instruct the children to answer with the name of the *object* related to the action described in the following statements.

1. The clothes are swishing around and around wet. (washing machine)
2. The dirt is lifted up from the pile. (shovel or large road equipment)
3. The steam pops out as the clothes become pressed. (steam iron or steam presser)
4. The picture comes on when the knob is pushed or turned. (TV)
5. The grass looks smooth and there are no weeds. (lawnmower)
6. The food gets hot and is cooked. (oven or stove)

CLASSIFICATION

Tell the child to name everything he can think of that is:

1. Red   4. Soft
2. Has four legs   5. Tiny
3. Has feathers   6. Has hair

Any recent study subject may be used for this exercise.

MAKING SENTENCES

Give each student a group of words and have him use these words in a meaningful sentence. Any number of words may be used. Select words from the geography, science or reading lesson.

1. man   science   today
2. woods   water   tiny
3. spider   sun   house
4. sky   eyes   without

THE VOWEL GAME

The only thing required to play this game is a group of 3 x 5 cards with the letters of the alphabet printed on them. These cards are passed out at random to the students. After all the cards are passed out, the teacher calls out a word (a word from the spelling lesson would be good). The students having the letters in that word come to the front of the class and stand in order to spell the word. If the vowel in the word is long, the student with that letter squats down. If the vowel is "r-controlled," the student holding the R stands behind the vowel he controls, holding his R so the class can see both the R and the vowel he controls. If the vowel is silent, the student having that letter turns his back and holds his letter where the class can see the vowel but not his face.

SIMON SAYS

This familiar game may be used to improve attention span and auditory perception. Use more difficult phrases as the child responds. Be sure students understand they are to remain still unless instruction begins *Simon says*.

1. Hold left ear lobe with right hand.
2. Hop on right foot three times, left foot twice, and both feet together four times.
3. Turn around twice to the left and sit down.
4. Take three steps forward and five steps back beginning on the left foot.
5. Pat your head with your left hand and rub your stomach with your right hand.

IDENTIFYING LETTER SOUNDS

Have students place their heads on one arm on the desks, keeping the other arm free. Call out a list of words and have the student raise his hand if he hears a word without the sound he is listening for. This exercise can be used for beginning, middle and ending sounds as well. (*Example:* For beginning sound *k* (not the letter *k*)—cook, cake, kettle, mud, candy, car, cafe, elephant, telephone, cactus, circus, hamburger, canyon.

SOUNDING BEE

This game is played in the same way as a spelling bee. Divide the class into two groups. Have Pupil One on Team One call out any word. Pupil One on Team Two must call out another word that begins with the same sound. If he does then Team Two gets one point. Now Pupil One on Team Two calls out another word and Pupil Two on Team One must name another word that begins with the same sound. If he can, then Team One gets the point.

This game can be varied for the sounds of the alphabet. Begin with long *a*, then short *a*, then *b*, soft *c*, hard *c*, *d*, long *e*, short *e*, *f*, soft *g*, hard *g*, *h* . . . Continue alternating from Team One to Team Two until all the sounds of the alphabet have been used.

SOUND CLASSIFICATION

Say to the children, *Name all the things you can think of that:*

1. Begin with the *b* sound and end with the *k* sound.
2. Begin with an *h* sound and end with a *d* sound.

3. Begin with the *r* sound and end with *b* sound.

4. Have the *m* sound in the middle.

After the teacher has found the sounds that are difficult, these can be stressed in this exercise.

LISTENING

Ask the question *What do you hear?* Let students really use their ears to hear all the sounds that may be heard in their classroom. They may have become so accustomed to hearing these sounds that they have to think about it a few minutes. See if each one can name something different.

LIKENESS AND DIFFERENCE   G R A D E 5

Develop same-different concepts by showing objects which can be compared as to likeness and difference. (Examples: chair, stool; coke bottle, catsup bottle; scissors, knife; spoon, fork; horse, cow; bracelet, necklace; shoe, boot; radio, TV; block, ball; milk, orange juice; dog, cat.) For more alert children, ask *In what way is a football team like a baseball team? How are they different?*

For practice in finding common characteristics, ask the children to tell how these things are alike:

1.	book, newspaper	6.	jungle, swamp
2.	rocket, airplane	7.	tree, bush
3.	house, house trailer	8.	lettuce, cabbage
4.	lake, river	9.	circus, carnival
5.	motor boat, steamer	10.	steak, pork chops

Ask the child to name all the words he can think of that *begin* with a given sound. Then ask him to name all the words he can think of that *end* with a given sound.

Ask him to tell how things are different and similar, using the preceding list for examples. Move from the concrete to the abstract.

Present problem-solving situations to the child and let him relate his ideas on the solution. Examples:

1. What would you do if you found a rattlesnake in your yard?
2. What would you do if a tiger chased you?
3. What would you take on a three-day vacation to a warm place?
4. What would you do if you hurt yourself while your mother was at the store?
5. What would you take on a picnic?

CAUSE AND EFFECT

Ask questions such as:

1. What would happen if you were going on a picnic and it began to rain?
2. What would happen if you clapped your hands?
3. What would happen if you dropped an egg on the floor?
4. What would happen if your mother forgot to get gasoline for the car?
5. What would happen if it should snow all night and all day?

PREDICTING OUTCOMES

Tell a story and, as you tell it, have the child guess the possible ending or what could have happened if certain other events had taken place; or, begin a story and let the child supply the ending.

John's father took him to the drag races and he saw that one car had a problem with the left front wheel. In the pit the mechanic . . .

RELATIONSHIPS AND ASSOCIATIONS

1. To help the child see relationships, name two items and have him tell you in what category they belong. (Examples: rudder, propeller; plum, apricot; transmission, muffler; home run, base; rings, bracelets.)

2. Say a word and ask the child what it makes him think of and what expression he associates with the word.

1.	fear	5.	laughing	9.	triumph
2.	anger	6.	hurry	10.	sullen
3.	pride	7.	threatening	11.	patience
4.	homesick	8.	snarling		

CATEGORIES

List three categories, then give a description and ask the child to tell which category it fits and to name it, if possible.

1. The three categories are: school, state, ship. I am thinking of something that is the second largest in America. It has cattle, cotton, wheat, oil and many other things. (*state: Texas*)

Let children name which category certain animals belong in— reptiles, mammals, birds, fish, amphibians, etc.

LOGICAL RELATIONSHIPS

Ask the child to choose the one incongruous word in each of the following groups:

1. newspaper, magazine, book, broom
2. stove, refrigerator, sink, bed
3. rose, turnip, onion, radish
4. shoes, blanket, dress, blouse
5. car, truck, ball, train
6. bowl, pitcher, plate, crayon
7. crayon, paper, door, pencil
8. multiply, word, divide, subtract
9. barn, fence, sugar, cow
10. map, graph, horse, chart

Ask these questions to help the children identify incongruous elements:

1. When you sleep late, do you get up early?
2. Could you put eggs in a bucket?
3. Could you find shoes growing on a bush?
4. Is a chicken undressed when its feathers are taken off?

5. Would you go to a bakery to buy potatoes?
6. If you are doing nothing, are you busy?
7. Do people use glasses to hold milk?

Or, read these questions and ask the child to choose one answer:

1. What unkind thing do farmers do to corn?

    a. grow it   b. pull its ears   c. look at it

2. Which of these uses a pen but cannot write?

    a. pencil   b. patch   c. pig

3. Which of these has a head but cannot think with it?

    a. a needle   b. a nail   c. a napkin

4. Which of these has hands, but cannot clap them?

    a. clock   b. a clown   c. a chain

Ask which sentence does not belong in this paragraph.

As John was playing ball in his back yard, he saw the new boy in his neighborhood going slowly down the street. John's sister was in the eighth grade. John called to the new boy and asked him to come to play. (*John's sister was in the eighth grade.*)

After the child achieves mastery of short paragraphs, use longer ones with more abstract ideas.

FACTS AND OPINIONS

After reading a short story, ask questions and let the children tell which answers are fact and which are opinion.

Bart's father builds racing cars in his spare time. His father is really a school teacher, but he likes cars for a hobby. On weekends he races his car in Amarillo, Lubbock, and Oklahoma City, and he goes to Florida during the summer for the races. Some people think that his car is the best in this area. He has built the car with the help of a friend. Many people do not like the car races, and others like them as a spectator sport. I would not like to drive a racer. Would you?

TAPE RECORDER

A tape recorder may be used for exercises in choral reading, speaking, and to encourage imitation.

Ferry Me across the River

Ferry me across the river
Do, Boatman, do.
"If you've a penny in your purse
I'll ferry you."
I have a penny in my purse
And my eyes are blue.
So ferry me across the water
Do, Boatman, do.
"Step into my ferry boat.
Be they black or blue—
For the penny in your purse
I'll ferry you."

SIGHT VOCABULARY

There are many ways of teaching word recognition. Select a word scale such as Dolch's 220. Games may be effective here. Word Bingo is an example; it can be bought or made by using sight words on cards and proceeding as in a regular bingo game.

Sight words can be put on black Flash X disks and the child may hold open the slot for study and examination. (This is more for motivation.)

Using sight words for spelling words can be effective.

COMMON CHARACTERISTICS

Provide the student with a list of words (shown in the following list).

1. Ask how many categories can be found from this grouping and ask for a listing to be made under one category.

2. Ask the children to write the name of each object under the proper category. (The categories may be animals, transportation, household items, or farm implements.)

Word List

elephant	sheep	combine	wagon
kangaroo	bed	ditch-digger	ship
refrigerator	plow	planter	horse
lamp	airplane	bicycle	train

chair   cow   stove   rabbit

truck   table   bus   tractor

dresser

PERFORMING BEFORE THE GROUP

1. Many students like to perform orally. Others who are shy need encouragement. We need to give them clues and "crutches," wait longer for their responses, and help them to make complete sentences. (Question: *How are a car and an airplane alike?* Answer: *A car can . . . ; A plane can . . . ; Both can . . .*)

A concrete answer, which is the easiest, is that they both have wheels, windows, etc. An abstract answer which shows deeper thinking is that they are both means of transportation.

2. Let two students carry on a telephone conversation. Select two shy students to duplicate the conversation. The class listens carefully to see if any points are omitted. (Possible topics: the latest space exploration, the weather report, the history assignment.)

News stories or announcements could be used in the same way. These are to be given orally with specific details as to time, place, and events.

3. Give the children practice in storytelling. Write a list of characters on the board—such as a girl, baby, father, old man, dog, and parrot. Select the first four students to tell a story. The first student sets the stage using only the little girl as the main character. As the story develops, each student adds another character from the list.

FOLLOWING DIRECTIONS

Being able to follow directions is most important to the child. Have the student repeat the directions and then carry them out. This involves auditory-motor coordination also.

a. Sharpen your pencil, erase the board, and pick up the paper.

b. Draw a circle on the board, go to the southeast corner of the room and count to 100 by tens, and then place a number in the circle.

c. Skip to the door, turn around, and hop on your right foot to your seat.

CLASSIFYING OBJECTS

   1.   Read a list of words and ask the children to classify them in such categories as:

1.	Business world	4.	Country
2.	Home	5.	City
3.	School	6.	Aviation

ACTIVITIES AND EXERCISES   GRADE **7**

   1.   Ask the students to describe an object and tell a story about it. Let them pick something in the room, tell where it was made, from what, the process involved in making it, and how they think the object made its way into the classroom from the factory.

   2.   Have students classify objects in the classroom according to the material of which they are made (wood, metal, plastic, fiberglass, rubber, glass, etc.).

   3.   Put a mixed list of animals on the board and let the students group them according to their characteristics, then tell how they are alike and how they are different.

a.	salamander	a.	snake	a.	rat	a.	sparrow
b.	toad	b.	lizard	b.	guinea pig	b.	hawk
c.	frog	c.	turtle	c.	mouse	c.	blue-jay
d.	newt	d.	alligator	d.	squirrel	d.	crow

   4.   Let the students teach the lesson in geography. Assume they are going on a trip. Let them show where the place is on the map or globe. *How far is the place? Which direction is it? How are you going to travel? How long will it take to get there? What type of clothing will you need to take with you? What will you find when you get there? What type of food do the people eat? What are some of the customs of these people?*

   5.   Ask cause-and-effect questions.

   a.   Why do our bodies need food and water? What would happen to them if they did not get this food and water?

   b.   What causes bread to rise at the bakery?

   c.   What happens to a burning candle in a jar when we put the lid on the jar?

   d.   What causes the tide to come in and go out?

6. Ask thoughtful questions and let the students explain and associate their ideas.

a. What is life?
b. What is right?
c. What is wrong?
d. How far is north?

7. Have the student tell which does not belong in the list of words and why:

a. car	a. tire	a. horse	a. oxygen
b. train	b. steering wheel	b. hay	b. sulphur
c. airplane	c. windshield	c. goat	c. helium
d. driver	d. road	d. sheep	d. hydrogen

8. Ask the student to name all the things he can think of when you say the word *electricity, tornado, boat, farm,* etc.

9. Say a word and let the students give an antonym (*tall, down, eastward, ceiling, light,* etc.)

10. Let the students put their heads on their desks with their eyes closed and listen intently for fifteen seconds. Ask them to relate each sound they heard during this period to its source.

11. Have the child pretend to explain in detail to a stranger how to get to the nearest drugstore.

12. Tell a story on a specific topic and let each student contribute one sentence.

13. Let students complete sentences and supply the ends of sentences to show the function of word signals.

a. My sister and I planned to go to the movies last night but . . .

b. We went on our vacation last year; we saw . . .

c. The last time I went fishing . . .

d. This morning on the way to school, I saw . . .

14. List verbally the items the students can classify and let them write the items in appropriate spaces on a previously prepared outline form.

a. Foods
1. bread
2. steak
3. milk
4. cake

b. Animals
1. cat
2. raccoon
3. prairie dog
4. anteater

c.	Types	1. boat	d.	Plants	1. cottonwood
	of	2. train			2. sunflower
	trans-	3. airplane			3. grass
	porta-	4. automobile			4. tumbleweed
	tion				

15. Ask the students to use these words correctly in sentences:

a. another	a. measure	a. expense
b. increase	b. weight	b. worth
c. part	c. acre	c. spend
d. smaller	d. quarter	d. earn

MAKING COMPARISONS
IN AN AURAL MESSAGE

G R A D E **8**

1. Have the students listen as you read the names of several objects. They are to select the one that is different in function or category.

   1. Stomach, small intestine, brain, large intestine.

   2. Pulley, screw, wedge, jug.

   3. Noun, sentence, pronoun, verb.

   4. Trumpet, trombone, cornet, clarinet.

2. Ask the student to explain the differences between different types of animals.

   1. Fish and birds

   2. Amphibians and reptiles

   3. Mammals and crustaceans

MAKING INFERENCES AND DRAWING CONCLUSIONS

A series of short paragraphs or selections may be read to the students, with concluding statements to be completed by their responses.

   1. The birds were singing and the grass was beginning to turn green. I was preoccupied with the beauty of the day and bumped into the corral gate.

      The season is . . .

      The speaker lives on a . . .

2. Jane watched the airplane circle lower and lower until it finally ...

3. The Eagles and the Tigers football teams were tied 6-6. The Eagles kicked the ball through the uprights.
   Who won the game?
   What was the final score?

4. The boys had planned to go camping, but ...

5. A man walked one mile south, one mile east, and one mile north, arriving at the place where he started and shot a bear.
   Where was the man when he started?
   What color was the bear?

DISTINGUISHING RELEVANT AND IRRELEVANT INFORMATION

1. Read sentences which contain one word which is poorly chosen—perhaps an inappropriate adjective, noun, or verb. Ask the student to call out the word which does not belong and substitute a better word.

1. The boy went to the bakery to buy some *corn*.

2. We packed our fishing gear and headed for the *circus*.

3. As the car reached the top of the mountain, we *seen* the valley below.

4. John *run* the race in the meet yesterday.

2. Read aloud a paragraph in which one sentence does not belong. Ask the student to identify the sentence that does not fit the topic.

One key to Country A's swift victory over Country B in a six-day war was its near-perfect maintenance of combat planes. The ships sailed at dawn. Military intelligence sources disclose that the day the fighting began, 96% of Country A's planes were combat-ready. Only 50% of Country B's planes were ready.

AUDIO-VISUAL AIDS

Tape recorders may be used to record oral expressions. The expressions are then analyzed and criticized. This training produces a significant improvement in language usage.

The Bell & Howell Language Master can be used to a great advantage because the prepared materials allow the student to see and hear the words, phrases, or sentences spoken. He can then respond and make his own voice recording of what he has heard. Finally, he can compare his response with the original. Blank cards are available and the teacher can prepare his own master unit to be used in any area of learning.

CB ACTIVITIES

Exercise 1

Ask this question: "If most large cities being approached by CB operators are identified by their beginning letters, what are the following cities called?"

1.	Atlanta, Georgia	(Big A)
2.	Dallas, Texas	(Big D)
3.	Columbus, Ohio	(Big C)
4.	Denver, Colorado	(Big D)
5.	Seattle, Washington	(Big S)
6.	Portland, Oregon	(Big P)

Exercise 2

Sometimes cities are named because of something that happens in the cities. Why would:

1. Los Angeles, California be called the *Shakey City?* (earthquakes)
2. Boston be called the *Bean Town?* (Boston baked beans)
3. Chattanooga, Tennessee be the *Choo Choo town?* (the song "Chattanooga Choo Choo")
4. Chicago, Illinois be called the *Windy City?* (because of strong winds blowing in from Lake Michigan)
6. Indianapolis, Indiana be called the *Circle City?* (because of car races)
6. Las Vegas be called the *Gambling Town?* (because it is a city of gambling tables and slot machines)
7. Long Island be called *Shark Town?* (because of proximity to ocean)
8. Nashville, Tennessee be called *Music Town?* (because it is the major city where country music is published)
9. San Francisco be called *Shaky Town* or *Hill Town?* (because it is located on a hill and also on the San Andreas Fault)
10. St. Louis, Missouri be called the *Golden Archway?* (because of the great arch standing over the city)

Grammatic and Auditory Closure

Grammatic closure, or *auditory-vocal automatic,* refers to the ability to predict future linguistic events from past experience. This processing skill involves the acquisition of automatic habits of handling syntax and grammatic inflections. Oral language training presented in games and activities which allow the child/youth to respond aid in the development of this skill. The student in training should (*a*) be encouraged to imitate the teacher's use of correct grammar, (*b*) encouraged to memorize phrases and short poems from recordings, and (*c*) engage in sound blending exercises.

SOUND BLENDING   G R A D E **K**

Auditory sound blending is a closure function. Make flannel-backed pictures of a baby, cat, dog, horse, bus, slide, ball, apple, candy, bread, milk. Place pictures (two or three at first) on the flannel board. Say *b-us, sl-ide, b-all*, etc. Have the child go to the board and take the picture off if he knows it. Say and have the child repeat those unknown ones until he can identify them. (It may take a long time.) Act as if you have all the time in the world to get "nowhere." Later, when the child learns to recognize some of the pictures, let him hold them in his hand or spread them on his desk. As you note the syllables, have the pupil place them on the flannel board. Gradually remove all visual clues and have the child say the name.

LEARNING NAMES

Teach the child to memorize part of a sentence: "This is a _____," "Este es una _____." Then have him finish the sentence with *boy* (*muchacho*) or *girl* (*muchacha*). The pupil must have all the familiar reinforcement possible. Point indiscriminately to a boy or girl. Names of classmates are usually learned quite quickly in the first days of school. Say "This is _____," as someone points to a child. The children may help in this activity. Put stars on a chart by the child's name for each correct identification. Give stars for every success. If there is a reward at the end of the semester for the one with the most stars, there will be noticeable effort put forth. There must also be lesser rewards for next best, etc., all down the line until each child gets some small token.

Place headbands with the child's name on each child. Let them wear these in the classroom several days. Try removing them and let one child at a time see how many he can identify by placing them on the heads to which they belong. Visual motor skill is also obtained in the process. Objects in the schoolroom can be used in the same way. A good idea is to label such objects at the first of the term as: *desk, chair, piano, table, books, plants*. Teach the child to give a specific response to stimulus words. Use such pairs as: *drink, water; hall, bathroom*. Much later the words may be interchanged as: *drink, hall; water, bathroom*. Much, *much* later these sentences may be learned as responses: "We get a drink in the hall." "There is water in the bathroom."

To get first responses in learning names of objects, an example from the Miami Linguistic Series, developed by D. C. Heath

Company, is a good teaching technique and is described as follows:

The teacher models for the entire group first. The teacher will point to a desk while stating "This is a desk." The *entire class* repeats first, then *groups of three* repeat. Following this *each individual student* repeats "This is a desk." As a last procedure, the children are guided in responding to communication situations, e.g., by talking among each other and saying "Do you have a desk?" "Yes, I have a desk. It is a small desk." "(*Teacher*) has a large desk."

Pictures from magazines could be prepared for use on the flannel board to utilize in this technique. Other stimulus-response pairs are: *piano, sing; music, march; pencil, write; color, picture; hair, comb; soap, clean; broom, sweep; desk, chair; scissors, cut; paper, draw; recess, play; ball, bat.*

THE TEACHER LISTENS

You should become alert to the incorrect grammar usage of children and should plan a means of correcting *specific mistakes* of the children without undue emphasis on the wrong way. Since some children do not hear all sounds, it is good to vary the pitch, the amplification and the rhythm of correct sentences to provide speech to be heard under varied conditions. An example of varied rhythm is to repeat sentences with *emphasis* on the *italicize*d words as follows:

The *man* comes to *town* and he *buys* some *bread*. (Speed up the words *not* italicized and this will create a different rhythm.) Say the sentence at a high pitch and then repeat it a little louder until it is beyond the normal speech amplification. The children love the fun of changing rhythm and sound.

ADDITION I

Ask the children to put the sound of *s* on the ends of the following words:

bake, play, go, sit, sing, make, bat, come, swing, take

ADDITION II

Ask the children to put the sound of *ed* on the end of the following words. (Always provide an example.)

play, walk, open, cook, saw, bat, talk, close, paint, mow

WHICH SOUNDS BEST

Explain to the children that there are some words which do not have the *ed* sound added—instead, other words are used. Do not go into detail. Simply state that some words sound better without the *ed* sound. Give them choices as to which word takes an *ed* sound. Some children may be saying *drived* instead of *drove*. Do not emphasize individual mistakes. *Do emphasize* correct usage and say, "This is the way we say it." Give the children the choices of the following pairs of words, and say, "Which one sounds all right with *ed* on the word?"

drive, sing, take, sit, walk, talk, bake, lean, hold, move

FINISH MY RHYME

No knowledge of letters is required. You say, "I will tell you a rhyme but I will leave out the last word. Can you guess what it is? Listen!"

I made a *mess* when I spilled chocolate on my (*dress*). "Yes, (*child's name*), *dress* is correct. Now guess these."

The little black *dog* sat on a (*log*).
My finger hurts, but I will *try* not to (*cry*).
I will *stop* to watch the bunny (*hop*).
My mother said, "*oh!*" when she stubbed her (*toe*).
The teacher *sat* on her new (*hat*)!
When I *call*, throw me the (*ball*).
When it is *night*, there's not much (*light*).

COMPLETION I

Select a group of activity pictures: skiing, skating, swimming, driving, and others. Make statements about each and allow children to add words to make statements into complete sentences. Examples:

1. The man is (*skiing*).
    Yesterday he (*skied*).
    Tomorrow he will go (*skiing*).
    The man can (*ski*).

2. The girl's name is Maria. She is (*skating*).
    She can (*skate*).
    She has on (*skates*).

Allow the children to make up sentences to say about the pictures.

Make up a series of sentences and ask children to supply the proper words to go in the sentences. Examples are:

1. Yesterday I (*go, went*) to town.
2. Tomorrow I (*will go, went*) to town.
3. I (*am not, ain't*) eating at school today.
4. The (*men, mans*) went to the ball game.
5. These cookies are the (*best, goodest*).
6. Mary's hands are (*cleaner, cleanest*) than her friend's.
7. The sunshines (*brighter, brightest*) on cloudless days.
8. On Fridays we (*eat, ate*) hamburgers.
9. On Saturdays Daddy (*mows, mowed*) the lawn.
10. Ice cream (*melts, melted*) in the sun.

SENTENCE RESPONSE

You ask questions and the child is to answer in complete sentences with proper grammar. Examples:

1. "Who has baby brothers or baby sisters?" ("I have a baby brother"; or, "I have two baby brothers.")
2. "How old is your baby brother?" ("He is two years old.")

Explain fully and then continue:

1. What does your baby eat?
2. When does your baby brother sleep?
3. How many people in your family?
4. Where do you live?
5. Who is your closest friend?
6. What do you do at home to help your parents?
7. When do you hang up your clothes?
8. Did you put your toys away yesterday?
9. When will you go to the store?
10. Think of something you did yesterday and tell me.

You should not correct in front of the group but you can explain that there are many ways people put words together and emphasize the correct way diplomatically. It is good to say sentences correctly in unison with the group after you have heard an incorrect usage.

GRAMMATIC CLOSURE
ACTIVITIES

1. Tell the child an incomplete sentence such as, *The color of this dress is* . . . Ask the child to point to a dress worn by the teacher or girls in the class, using the proper color word in the sentence.

2. Teach the child to repeat and complete a sentence after the teacher. If he needs extra assistance, pictures may be used to provide the cues. The teacher could say:

    a.   I go to the store to buy . . .

    b.   We go to the lunch room to eat . . .

    c.   The color of the wall is . . .

3. To give further practice in auditory closure the following rhymes can be used, since the anticipated rhyme is rather obvious. Again, when necessary appropriate pictures may be used.

    a.   The fuzzy cat chased the (*rat*).

    b.   Jimmy Paul threw the (*ball*).

    c.   The children sang until the bell (*rang*).

4. A child with disability in closure processes has difficulty in using the correct verb forms. Try this: Display two words, *is* and *are*. Say the following sentences, asking the child to fill in with either *is* or *are* and to repeat the entire sentence. Corresponding pictures are helpful.

    a.   Jane _____ in the room.

    b.   Jane and Bill _____ in the room.

    c.   Jane and Bill _____ big.

    d.   Timmy _____ at his desk.

    e.   Ann and Timmy _____ working.

    f.   David _____ in the lunch room.

    g.   He and Bill _____ hungry.

5. To encourage the child to answer in complete sentences, use pictures on the flannelboard or chart holder. Children can listen to what the teacher says, then answer the riddle in a *complete sentence*.

Picture:	apple, flag, fence	**Picture:**	boy, bed, chair
Riddle:	I grow on trees.	**Riddle:**	I am soft.
	I am good to eat.		I am large.
	I have a peeling.		I need sheets.
	What am I?		What am I?
Answer:	You are an apple.	**Answer:**	You are a bed.

6. To give the child further practice in auditory closure, help him develop the skill of determining what "goes with" a given word.

bread and (*butter*)   man and (*woman*)
hat and (*coat*)   paper and (*pencil*)

7. Display pictures of familiar objects for the child—a hat, a can, a car, a flower. Then give him the ending of a word: __at. Let him choose the picture to complete the word hat. This type of exercise could be used where the *beginning* of the word is given and the child chooses the picture to complete it.

Pictures: cat, dog, table, bat
Beginning of words: ca__, do__, ta____, ba__

8. Choral reading and games are good practice for a child with this problem, and they also give him an opportunity to feel successful in a group. Use reading material from the basic text.

G
R
A   2
D
E

LANGUAGE MASTER

Large Language Master cards can be laminated, so a china marking pencil may be used and erased for different lessons. One way to use these is to draw or paste a picture at the left side, then print a sentence, leaving out a word. Of course, the teacher says it first, but the child is expected to look at and say the complete sentence himself.

This is a little pink _____.

I have a red _____.

I have a drip-dry _____.

I have four _____.

Clippings of words and phrases from readiness books may be fastened to the top edge of the Language Master for the child to repeat.

Another useful technique is to put a piece of flannel on the card, attaching a small envelope to the back in which to store stick-on pieces. The teacher records such instructions as, *Take the circle out of the pocket*. The child follows the instructions and places the piece on the flannel. Beginning sounds and words for sound blending may be used to advantage on the Language Master. There are also many commercially prepared cards available.

UNDERSTANDING INHERENT
RELATIONSHIPS BETWEEN WORDS

Beginning Sounds

Have the child circle the beginning, missing sound:

1.   The clown was very ___unny. (*f,   c,   t*)
2.   The family went on a ___icnic. (*n,   p,   b*)

Ask him to fill in the blank with a word that starts with the same sound:

(must   lost   him   ball)

1.   letter _____   3.   milk _____
2.   hear _____   4.   bark _____

Ending Sounds

Ask the child to fill in the same ending sounds:

1.   This boo___ helps me coo___.
2.   Wear a ha___ when you ba___.

Rhyming Words

Tell the child to fill in the missing letter of the rhyming word:

1.   A bag of toys is by my bed.
     The ball I have is big and ___ed.

Here, tell the child the missing word rhymes with *fall:*

1.   Steve can play with a ___all.
2.   Uncle Dave is a ___all man.

Give the child a word and let him find objects in the room which rhyme with the word.

Word	Object
block	clock
cook	book
tall	ball
hen	pen

Same and Different

Ask the child to tell you which pair of words are alike and which are different.

chalk - talk	blew - blue
ball - balls	pet - pet
come - come	was - saw

Evoking Paired Response

Teach the child to make automatic responses by presenting stimulus words. First teach him the pairs, then mix them. After these are learned, present a new set of words.

hammer - nail	school - study
sleep - bed	toys - play
man - woman	eat - breakfast

CLOSURE

Story

Tell the child that every seventh word is left out. He is to find the answers from above the story and fill them in.

(*said, he, got, as, himself, he, when, to*)

The Black Bear

When Jim went to the zoo, _____ saw a black bear. He watched _____ the bear took a swim. When he _____ out of the pond, he shook _____. He stood on his hind legs _____ the zoo keeper gave him some meat. Jim _____ goodbye to the black bear when _____ left the zoo to go back _____ his home.

Sentences

Read the complete sentence to a child first and have him repeat it. Then read it several times, omitting a different word each time, and have the child complete it each time.

1. Bob wanted to go out to play with Lassie.
2. Bob _____ to go out to play with Lassie.
3. Bob wanted to go ___ to play with Lassie.
4. Bob wanted to go out to _____ with Lassie.
5. Bob wanted to go out to play with _____.

Concluding Prelearned Sentence Segments

Give a child an incomplete sentence and let him respond with the complete sentence. (Example: *Our classroom has a _____.* The child might say, *Our classroom has a door.*)

RECOGNIZING CORRECT FORMS OF WORDS

Singular and Plural

Have the child cross out the group of words that does not sound right:

1. a doll   3. four day
    a dolls   four days

2. one coat   4. two wagon
    one coats   two wagons

Using Correct Tense

Ask the child to cross out the incorrect word:

1. Ricky came when Sheila called.
                            call.

2. Sheila will worked for Mother.
                  work

Test his use of *s, ed,* or *ing:*

1. Lassie is watch_____ me.
2. He need_____ a bath.
3. Oh! He bark_____ and ran away.

Teach proper use of the future tense:

1. Teacher: *I will go to school.*
    Child: *I will go to school, too.*
2. Teacher: *I will go Christmas shopping.*
    Child: *I will go Christmas shopping with you.*

Teach proper use of the past tense:

1. Teacher: *I went to town. I bought a new hat.*
   Child: *I went to town. I bought a toy.*
2. Teacher: *I went to the fair. I rode on a merry-go-round.*
   Child: *I went to the fair. I rode on a roller coaster.*

Have the child supply the appropriate tense of a given verb:

1. *Today I will run. Yesterday I ran.*
2. *Last week I sang. Today I will sing.*

OTHER TECHNIQUES

1. Take a sheet of manila paper, fold it, and print a beginning sound at the top of the front page. Have at least two or three "booklets" for each beginning sound. Paste a picture inside the booklet—for example, for the letter *t* you could find pictures of a tiger, toys, and toast. Give the children clues and the beginning sound and let them take turns guessing which picture is inside. Whoever guesses it, gets to hold the booklet. The first one to hold three booklets may give the clues and show the booklets. Later, this game can be extended to consonant blends.

2. Choral reading and rhyming puzzles are also effective in developing the skill of grammatic closure.

3. Use this jingle aid. Children who have had different language and culture experiences may have difficulty learning the proper grammar structure. For example, expressions such as, "He *come* to my house," may be heard. For these children, jingles may be very beneficial. Making these in jump rope rhythm could be simple. First, the errors or misuses should be determined, then the jingle may be made up. An example could be:

> He came
> She came
> You came to school

> We came
> They came
> Just to mind the rules

GRADE **3**

AUTOMATIC CLOSURE

1. Completing words: Have the child say the name of each picture and listen for the missing consonant sounds, then complete each word.

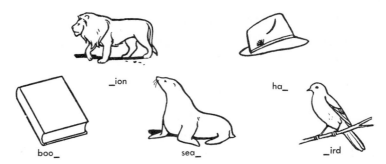

_ion

ha_

boo_   sea_   _ird

2. Ask the child to complete each sentence by writing *ar*, *er*, *ir*, *or*, or *ur* in the blanks:

    a. I heard a b___d sing his song.

    b. The tig___ is a member of the cat family.

    c. The t___key spread its wings.

    d. The h___se is in the b___nyard.

3. Read or tape this story and have the child fill in the suffix *ly*, *ing*, *ment*, or *able* after each root word in the story.

Sally's Story

Sally had gone to the store to buy a pound of cheese for her aunt, who was always particular about her food. She said very strict_____, "Now don't get any kind except bleu cheese."

Sally skipped light_____ along the pave_____. The sun was shin_____ bright_____ and Sally was sing_____ soft_____. When she got to the store, she walked in slow_____ and asked the grocer for the bleu cheese.

When he started to cut the cheese, Sal_____ said, "That's white! I have to have *blue* cheese. My aunt will say, 'That's unus_____!'"

The grocer smiled and said, "Bleu cheese is white but since you didn't know that, it is excus_____." Sally shook her head and said, "That's unbeliev_____."

She quiet_____ walked out of the store say_____, "*Blue* cheese is white! That's what he said, but surely that is debat_____."

4. Auditory sound blending is a closure function. Present a word with syllables or letters separated by a short time interval (*b-a-by*, *c-a-t*) and have the children identify it. Introduce sound-blending words that represent objects in the room: *Find*

something in this room with the name b-oo-k. Or, sound blending may be introduced using pictures as visual clues.

5. Forming automatic plurals: Read the first sentence to the child and let him fill in the plurals for the second sentence.

a. The *boy* found a *dog.*
The _____ found some _____.

b. He has one *pencil.*
He has two _____.

c. The *man* caught a *skunk.*
The _____ caught some _____.

6. Teach the child an incomplete sentence such as, *This is a very nice* . . . When the child has memorized this, walk about the room and point out objects, saying, *This is a very nice* (and he identifies whatever you have pointed out).

7. Rhyming words: Read the rhyme below. The child supplies a color word which rhymes with the underlined word.

> What color rhymes with bed?
> With ink you like to write?
> What color rhymes with shoe,
> And muff and fan and kite?
> What color rhymes with Jack
> That's easy to put down?
> What rhymes with tray and queen
> And with a funny clown?

The rhyming element may be introduced to the children by recalling some familiar nursery rhymes. Say two lines of a rhyming couplet and let the children supply the missing word that rhymes.

> Hickory, dickory, dock,
> The mouse ran up the _____.
>
> Jack and Jill
> Went up the _____.
>
> The north wind doth blow
> And we shall have _____.

Play a riddle game. Say, *I am thinking of a word that rhymes with cake.* Let the child respond with a word that rhymes with cake, such as *bake.*

8. There are certain automatic responses the child should produce when given a specific word stimulus.

Stimuli	*Possible Responses*
moon	stars
school	books
skirt	blouse
teacher	study
tulip	flower

AUDITORY SOUND BLENDING

1. Introduce sound-blending words which represent objects in the classroom. *Find something on my desk with the name b-oo-k.* Refer to things in the room, such as:

box	ball	ruler	window	chalk
door	light	girl	boy	chair
pencil	tablet	rope	flower	globe
desk	floor	map		

2. A related sound-blending activity utilizes a sentence with one word sound-blending—*The owl sits in a _____ (tree).* Examples:

a. The cat catches the _____ (*rat*). The cat _____ (*catches*) the rat. The _____ catches the rat.

b. A witch has a long _____ (*nose*). The _____ (*witch*) has a long nose.

c. The girls play with _____ (*dolls*). The girls _____ (*play*) with dolls. The _____ play with dolls.

d. The boys ran _____ (*races*). The boys _____ (*ran*) races. The _____ ran races.

e. Johnny has a new _____ (*ball*). Johnny has a _____ (*new*) ball. _____ has a new ball.

f. The children jump _____ (*rope*). The children _____ (*jump*) rope. The _____ jump rope.

3. Find common characteristics of words in sentences:

a. A hammer and a saw are both (*tools*).

b. A bed and a chair are both (*furniture*).

c. Bread and butter are both (*food*).

d. Dogs and cats are both (*animals*).

4. Worksheets can be made of any variety of words with which the child may be having trouble. Examples* of the procedure to follow is as follows:

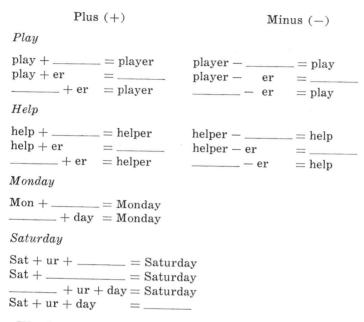

Plus (+)

Minus (−)

Play

play + _____ = player	player − _____ = play
play + er = _____	player − er = _____
_____ + er = player	_____ − er = play

Help

help + _____ = helper	helper − _____ = help
help + er = _____	helper − er = _____
_____ + er = helper	_____ − er = help

Monday

Mon + _____ = Monday
_____ + day = Monday

Saturday

Sat + ur + _____ = Saturday
Sat + _____ = Saturday
_____ + ur + day = Saturday
Sat + ur + day   = _____

5. Word association by rhyming: The child is presented with a stimulus word and asked to think of a word which has the same sound ending.

Stimulus	*Response*
call	ball
ring	sing
top	hop
fish	dish
sail	tail
book	look

Short rhymes in poems may be used:

a. He caught the ball when it bounced off the *(wall)*.

b. She hit the cat with the *(bat)*.

c. The train ran through the *(rain)*.

d. Don't cry; I'll give you some *(pie)*.

e. We found Bill near the *(hill)*.

f. Don't let the goat get your *(coat)*.

g. The children like to play with the *(clay)*.

*From *Linguistic Equations* by Claud "R". Zevely, West Texas State University, Canyon, Texas.

AUTOMATIC CLOSURE

G
R
A
D
E

4

Here is a technique to teach children to hear and recognize the difference in endings: *I am going to read a sentence, leaving out a word, and I want you to fill in the word, using the correct ending.*

    a. I have a swing in my yard. This afternoon my friend and I will be   *(swinging)* .

    b. I ate one apple out of the bushel of *(apples)* .

    c. I have many dresses but I only have one blue *(dress)* .

    d. Yesterday we played ball; today we will *(play)* ball.

    e. Only one child can swing at a time but many *(children)* can play on the merry-go-round.

    f. The blue Ford is my favorite car model but I have ten car *(models)* .

    g. I like to jump rope but after I have been *(jumping)* for a while, I get tired.

    h. The last time I went fishing I caught one *(fish)* .

    i. The horse ran across the pasture to catch the other *(horses)* .

    j. It takes one ball to play basketball but it takes several *(balls)* to play croquet.

  2. Here the teacher reads the sentences and has the child fill in the correct singular or plural form of the missing word.

    a. We went to the fire station to see a fireman, but instead we saw three fire_____.

    b. The mother mouse had five baby _____.

    c. We have one man teacher and four _____ teachers.

    d. My uncle bought another calf, so now he has two _____.

    e. The teacher told each child to put on his cap before all the _____ went out to play.

    f. The mother deer always has two baby _____.

    g. Did the shoemaker have one elf or many _____?

    h. We saw some wild geese on the lake but we only shot one wild _____.

    i. I have two feet, one right _____ and one left _____.

    j. How many sheep are there in that flock of _____?

    k. We have a red roof on our house but all of the other houses have white _____.

    l. I like the fall when the leaves turn. I would like to have a red _____ for my book.

3. This game teaches a child to pattern after the teacher, using the correct tense:

    a.   Teacher: *This morning on the way to school I saw* _____.
          Child: *This morning on the way to school I saw* _____.
    b.   Teacher: *The boys I saw on the playground were* _____.
          Child: *The boys I saw on the playground were* _____.
    c.   Teacher: *After school I will* _____.
          Child: *After school I will* _____.
    d.   Teacher: *Last Sunday I* _____.
          Child: *Last Sunday I* _____.

4. In this exercise, as the teacher says the word, the child responds with as many different words as he can make by changing the word endings. If he has trouble, put a list of endings on the board. (Examples: *ed, ing, s, age, or, tain, tion, feel, less, ness.*)

    a.   rob – robbed – robbing – robs
    b.   pad – pads – padding – padded
    c.   chat – chatting – chats – chatted
    d.   control – controls – controlled – controlling
    e.   forbid – forbids – forbidding
    f.   bag – bags – bagged – bagging – baggage
    g.   act – acting – actor – acted – acts
    h.   brief – briefest – briefing – briefs
    i.   smile – smiles – smiled – smiling
    j.   care – careless – cared – cares – caring – careful

5. The teacher gives, orally, a word or stimulus and the child gives a certain response until that response becomes automatic.

Opposites: hot – cold   black – white
              day – night   happy – angry
              good – evil   cheerful – sad
              sky – earth   short – long

This exercise can also be done with words which have the same meanings. As children gain confidence in this skill and the response becomes automatic, the teacher may introduce new concepts based on social studies, science, etc.

6. This is a game to give the children practice in hearing a word and saying a rhyming word. Divide the children into two groups. Have a child on one side say a word and point to a child on the other side to say a rhyming word. Start by using one-syllable words. As the children build this skill, go on to two-syllable words which end in the same sound. (Examples: brook – hook, mountain – fountain, bake – make, moon – soon.)

7. As you say these words, tell the children to listen for the endings and tell which word is different.

  a.   started – stopped – played – *ran*
  b.   running – playing – *start* – stopping
  c.   runs – stops – starts – *plug*
  d.   education – vacation – plantation – *freedom*
  e.   television – recreation – *produce* – graduation
  f.   refreshment – agreement – government – *governor*
  g.   fountain – mountain – *family*
  h.   bottle – tackle – marble – *lovely*
  i.   wilderness – *forest* – kindness – happiness
  j.   *happy* – cheerful – bashful – joyful
  k.   lovely – poorly – *sweet* – badly
  l.   fastest – slowest – *mean* – strangest
  m.   careless – *caution* – lifeless – useless
  n.   conductor – educator – *teacher* – realtor

CLASSIFYING   G R A D E **5**

The teacher calls out a group of words or phrases that can be placed in categories or classifications. The different categories or classifications to be used can be placed on paper or on the chalkboard, so as to give the child a visual clue.

  1. baseball, tennis, soccer, hide-and-go-seek
      These things are all   *(games)*   .

  2. cold, snow, sleet, ice
      These things are seen in the   *(winter)*   .

  3. circle, wheel, tire, dime
      These are all   *(round)*   things.

This game might also be used with words from other subject areas, such as social studies or science. Such classifications as minerals, bodies of water, cities, or states might be used.

THE COMMERCIAL GAME

Use well-known TV commercials. The teacher gives the first few words. The child then completes the commercial with the correct word.

1. You should brush after every _(meal)_ .
2. Don't be a litter _(bug)_ .
3. Only you can prevent forest _(fires)_ .

Words or phrases from social studies or science might also be used:

1. The Atlantic _(Ocean)_
2. The Appalachian _(Mountains)_
3. New York _(City)_
4. Lyndon Baines _(Johnson)_

These are only examples of words picked at random. If the game were being used to effect closure on a certain concept in science or social studies, one would stick to that subject or classification.

RHYMING WORDS

Read groups of words to the student, who will listen for the word that is different from all the rest.

1. time, climb, same, line
   The word that did not rhyme was _(same)_ .
2. room, rabbit, bounce, round
   The word that did not begin the same is _(bounce)_ .
3. talking, bending, helped, walking
   The word that does not end the same is _(helped)_ .

Use poems with which children are familiar. A clue for the child to remember is that the word he needs to say will rhyme with one at the end of the line just before.

PLURALS

Give the student a copy of the following (or similar) sentences. The teacher should read the first sentence of each group. The student reads the second, using the plural of the word underlined in the first sentence to fill the blank.

1. The _frog_ jumped into the pond.
   Five _____ jumped into the pond.
2. Sue is my _classmate_.
   Joe and Sue are my _____.

3. The *key* is in the lock.
   The _____ are in the locks.
4. My baby brother enjoys playing with a *toy.*
   My baby brother enjoys playing with the _____.
5. A *turkey* is an interesting bird.
   _____ are interesting birds.

Or use words where the plural is formed by changing *y* to *i* and adding *es.*

1. America is a country.
   England and America are   *(countries)* .
2. The pony galloped away.
   Six of the *(ponies)* galloped away.
3. The lady walked through the door.
   Five *(ladies)* walked through the door.
4. Los Angeles is a city in California.
   Los Angeles and San Francisco are *(cities)* in California.

STORIES

Give the student a copy of a story or a paragraph from a story. Every third or fifth word should be deleted from his copy, leaving a blank. List the deleted words at random at the top of the student's copy. He should fill the blanks with the correct word.

Squirrels *

country	white	gray	they	its	reddish
winter	jump	that	eat	limb	seeds
squirrel	in	of	and	watch	
common	to	friend	is	the	

The western gray *(squirrel)* is one of the most *(common)* squirrels *(in)* the United States. It *(is)* a cousin *(to)* the eastern *(gray)* squirrel which has a *(reddish)* head and reddish feet. Both *(of)* these bury nuts, acorn, and *(seeds)* . They *(eat)* these during the *(winter)* time. The red *(squirrel)* is another common *(squirrel)* . It has a *(white)* stomach *(and)* chin. It *(is)* smaller than *(the)* gray squirrel. This squirrel likes *(to)* live *(in)* the pine trees. It can *(jump)* easily from limb to *(limb)* and it uses *(its)* tail to keep balance *(in)* case it falls *(to)* the ground. The Kaibab *(squirrel)* is one *(of)* the rare squirrels in this

* This story was by Annette Clevenger, Andrews, Texas.

(*country*) and it lives near (*the*) Grand Canyon. The largest (*squirrel*) is found (*in*) the south. It is so heavy (*that*) it can't (*climb*) trees very well. Squirrels are fun to (*watch*) if you are quiet (*and*) wait until (*they*) learn that you are a (*friend*) .

G
R
A
D
E 6 CHORAL READING OR SPEAKING

Choral reading or speaking has been found to be very helpful in improving the fluency of reading, regardless of the preferred modality in learning (visual or auditory). Selections should be of the child's interest and ability levels. Particularly recommended is the *Neurological Impress System,** a system of unison reading whereby the teacher and the student read aloud, simultaneously, at a rapid rate. No corrections are made, and the reading continues for at least 15 minutes per session. One of its purposes is to imbed patterns of language that involve both morphophonemic units and syntactic structure.

GRAMMATICAL CONSTRUCTION

Many types of sentences must be given to the child to improve grammatical sense. The sentences should be read silently by the child. Practice should be done mainly through the visual sense and vocal response should be short and simple. Read short, interest-catching sentences to the child. Let the vocal application of what is learned through reading and listening progress at the child's rate of understanding. Use sentences such as these:

1. Three men have gone fishing.
2. Mother has bought four potatoes.
3. We boys borrowed two skateboards.
4. The astronauts have been seeing many interesting formations.
5. Teeth grind animal's food.
6. Sally and I have new swim suits.

Use short, informal chats to check the child's progress.

---

* Heckelman, R. C., Merced County Schools, California.

SHORT STORY COMPLETION

Have the child read a short story which has no ending, and then write an ending to complete the story. Ask him to explain orally, but briefly, his ending. Again, use selections that will appeal to the child's interest and ability levels.

FLASH CARD VOCABULARY

Choose words of the child's interest and ability levels. Work as a partner with the child in selecting the words and making flash cards. This will give the child the opportunity to hear the word, to see the word, to say the word, and to write the word. (Some of the words suggested in the next section may be used to stimulate interest.)

SENTENCE COMPLETION

1. Have the child memorize a sentence like, *This morning I saw* ... After he has memorized the sentence to be completed, use pictures from any source to stimulate a response. The following are words for which pictures must be obtained which should be of sixth grade interest level: *dragster, space capsule, Stingray (a bicycle), surfer, surfboard, slotcar, Batman, Robin, The Man from Uncle, football, baseball, basketball, ping pong ball, fur coat, The Beatles (George, Paul, John, and Ringo), diamond ring, Keds, loafers.*

2. Read the first sentence; then have the child complete the second sentence.

    a. The boy found a stick.
        All the boys found _____.

    b. I see one row of chairs.
        You see five _____ of chairs.

    c. I have one tack.
        They have a box of _____.

    d. The little boy threw a rock.
        All the boys threw _____.

    e. Mr. Jones drives a bus.
        Mr. Jones and Mr. Smith drive the _____.

SUFFIXES

Explain that a suffix is a short syllable added to the end of a word. (Example: Wonder-ful is wonderful; play-ful is playful.) Then have the child complete these sentences, using the words *playful, useful,* and *helpful.*

1. His dog was very _____.
2. The little girl was very _____.
3. The paper can be very _____.

Examples of other kinds of suffixes—*talking, crying, playing, driving:*

1. The children were _____.
2. The baby is _____.
3. The dog is _____.
4. The man is _____ his car.

G
R
A
D **7&8**
E
S   EVOKING
AUTOMATIC RESPONSES

1. The television game of **Password** can be played using a basic word list compiled by the teacher. Include words from the students' speaking vocabulary, but only those suitable for this type of game. Divide the class into two teams with two members from one team opposing two members from another team.

2. This exercise could be used following a study of antonyms. The teacher gives a stimulus word, and the student replies with a word that is its opposite. (Example: stimulus word, *empty;* possible answer, *full.*)

3. The same type of exercise could be done with synonyms.

4. Following a study of compound words, the teacher could use this same exercise. After the word is called, the student adds another word to form a compound word.

Stimulus Word	Possible Answer
any	body one
book	case cover card
table	cloth top
class	room mate time
play	ground room
door	way bell stop
school	mate ground
street	car light
every	body one
grand	mother father

SUPPLYING THE MISSING WORD

1. This exercise could be used after a study of poetry enjoyed by this age group. Tape selections of the poetry, omitting some of the rhyming words. As the students listen to the recording, they supply the missing word on their papers.

2. Review how words change their form according to the way they are used in speech. Have an individual student supply the missing words in groups of sentences such as the ones below. He may read them into a tape recorder and later listen to himself.

    a. My grandfather has cherry, peach, and pear _____ in his orchard. I picked a bushel of _____ from his cherry tree. I also _____ a bushel of _____. I would like to _____ some more bushels tomorrow. There are several good things one can make from fresh fruit, but my grandmother _____ some pies and _____ several jars of _____.

    b. Football, basketball, and baseball are favorite _____ in America. Every boy on our basketball team is tall, but Terry is the _____ boy on the team. We _____ to play sports the year around, but we usually _____ football in the fall, while baseball is _____ in the summer.

3. To help the student understand further the construction of words, an exercise built around the root word might be done.

    a. The root word of hobbies is hobby.
       The root word of libraries is _____.

    b. The root word of shelves is shelf.
       The root word of knives is _____.

    c. The root word of dresses is dress.
       The root word of glasses is _____.

    d.   The root word of toys is toy.
        The root word of kings is _____.
    e.   The root word of parties is party.
        The root word of jellies is _____.
    f.   The root word of wolves is wolf.
        The root word of leaves is _____.

CLOSURE

1. Using the prefix and root clue, have the students build words. For the stimulus, call the prefix with its meaning and the root word followed by the definition. The student then calls the word in response.

(Prefix *un* means *not*)

Prefix plus root	*Student response*
not common	uncommon
not sure	unsure
not happy	unhappy
not able	unable
not broken	unbroken

(Prefix *dis* mean *not*)

not trust	distrust
not agree	disagree
not honest	dishonest
not loyal	disloyal

2. Read the following sentences one at a time to the student. After each sentence has been read, the student repeats the sentence making the correction that is needed.*

    a.   The United States is my native *county*.
    b.   This morning I planted *parrots* in my garden.
    c.   He went to the store to buy a *brook* to sweep the floor.
    d.   Tom Fields is the star *picture* on the baseball team.
    e.   My birthday is next *mouth*.
    f.   Karen ordered a *stick* at the restaurant.
    g.   She asked Bill to *sign* in the choir.
    h.   Mary took the baked *beams* out of the oven.
    i.   The store had a *For Scale* sign on the door.
    j.   Louis went to the henhouse to fill the *biscuit* with eggs.

---

* Parts of this material are from Robinson *et al.*, 1963.

CB ACTIVITIES

Exercise 1

Instructions: Read a part of a sentence and ask student to complete the sentence with a suitable word.

1. Shake the (*trees*) and rake the (*leaves*).
2. If I agree I (*answer* or *ask*) *affirmative*.
3. A beanstore (*is* or *are*) a restaurant.
4. When you receive a "big" message, you say "That (*is* or *are*) a big 10-4."
5. A passing bicycle is said to be "(*blowing*) a door off."
6. To (*copy*) is to hear and understand message.
7. *Eights* is a word *mean* (*ing*) goodbye.
8. A person's turn (*to talk*) is expressed by the words *come back*.
9. To have a "fat load" is to have too (*much*) weight.
10. *Good Buddy* is a term meaning (*helpful*) person.

Exercise 2

Instructions: Fill in the proper form of the word from the list below in the following story about CB.

In a small town a car was _____ fast through the _____. A call came through on the _____. A voice was _____ and asking the directions to the hospital.

In moments other_____were_____. The_____ very _____ gave the directions to the hospital.

street	CB	move
answer	modulate	respond
good buddy	quick	

Exercise 3

Instructions: Place the proper ending on the words in the story below:

A child was stay __(ing)__ at home when he heard his father' __(s)__ CB. A voice was say __(ing)__, "Break 1-9 for local information." Another Break __(er)__ came on and offer __(ed)__ to help. The second Breaker did not have the answer. The child recogniz __(ed)__ the urgency in the first Breaker' __(s)__ voice. He ran to get his mother. She (*came* or *come*) to the CB and was able to help the first Breaker.

5

Auditory Memory

Auditory memory refers to the ability to remember the words, sounds, or sentences one has heard. Some children/youth cannot attend and thus cannot respond because they are not aware of what they hear. Others cannot remember because they find it difficult to retrieve information of which they have been aware. Memory is an important aspect of the learning process since following instructions and communicating what one knows is necessary in academic endeavors. Training for the auditory memory processing skills should include:

1.　The use of many visual cues.
2.　Writing information that has been heard.

3. Information that has been organized as in parsing,* e.g., in telephone numbers, 767-4321.

4. Teaching to overachievement.

5. Daily review of the most pertinent information.

SEQUENCING MEMORY

To develop memory of ideas in logical sequence, tell stories to the children. Ask them to retell the story in their own words. In the initial stages, the stories should be short with only a few ideas, but as the children grow the stories can be increased in length. A flannel board can be used to great advantage at the beginning. Also, animal stories are best to use as the human is sometimes a threatening figure. Pictures of the three bears or the three little pigs can be cut out of worn story books or dime store paperbacks. At first, characters "Papa Bear," "Mama Bear," and "Baby Bear" should be named and in that order. The child is allowed to place these on the board in that order. The same procedure is used for other stories, "The Three Little Pigs," "The Little Red Hen," and others. Look for new stories with simple sequential order.

SONGS AND RHYMES

Learning songs and rhymes also aids auditory memory. "Ten Little Indians," "Alphabet Song," and tuned resonator bells could be used to play the scale up and down. First the children should sit in order until the tune is learned. Later their positions could be changed to see whether the pupils could remember by sound which note came next. Note letters could be printed with a magic marker to make them stand out boldly. These could be attached to the resonator and the pupil could be "bombarded" with the alphabet.

STORY EXPERIENCES

Stories of actual experiences develop auditory memory. An example is, "John went to the store to buy some bread, meat, and

---

* Segments of a group of numbers or words emphasized by being separated in parts.

milk. When he returned, he had bread and milk. What did he forget?" Or, "When Alberto gets ready for school each morning, he puts on his shirt, pants, socks, shoes, and jacket. One morning he slept late and had to hurry. He put on pants, shoes, and jacket. What did he forget to put on before he went out to the bus?"

DO WHAT I SAY

Choose a child and whisper a set of instructions to him. "Go to the door, open it, close it, and come back to your chair." Verbal responses are involved when you ask the other children to describe what the chosen child did. The child who can name all of the activities performed is chosen next. This game can be effective if you suggest rather interesting and unusual things: "sit on the table, peek through your legs," etc. The children want to perform next and, therefore, watch carefully so they can do a good job of describing what they have seen.

PRETEND ANIMAL

"Today we are going to be farm animals. We need a farmer to take care of us. Who wants to be the farmer? All right, _____, you will be the farmer. I'll come around the table and you whisper which animal you are going to be and the sound that animal makes. Good. Everybody knows which animal he is. Now let's pretend we are hungry and we want the farmer to feed us. We will use our animal voices to call him. The farmer will walk around the table and you 'moo' or 'cackle.' The farmer will call your name and say, 'Here is your food.' All right, farmer, you had better feed your animals!"

ADDRESS AND PHONE NUMBER

Discuss with children the need to know their address and telephone number. You may cut out patterns of a house and a telephone for the children to trace around and cut from colored construction paper. As a student watches, write his address and telephone number on his finished product and allow him to place it on a bulletin board. When he has learned his address, let him place a chimney on the housetop. After memorizing his telephone number, he could attach a yarn telephone line from the telephone to his house. After most children have succeeded in this activity, attach both house and telephone to another piece of construction paper to be taken home. Most parents will be glad to reinforce this activity at home. Place no stress on those who do not know their address or telephone number.

FOLLOW THE SIGN

Materials needed are green, yellow, and red construction paper, a flashlight, small toy car or motorcycle (or a picture of one) for each child. Place colored papers on board. The *green* means the car goes fast. *Yellow* means the car goes slow. *Red* means the car stops. Flash the light on a color. The child makes his car do what the color means. Other colors can be added. *Blue* means bumpy road. *Orange* means curvy road. The child must remember what the signal means.

SILLY RELAY

Three or four children are adequate for a relay row. Place everyday items (a chair, hat, mitten, eraser) in a line ahead of the relay row. Give the first child in the row a command series: "Sit on the chair. Put on the cap. Take off the cap." After he completes the series he runs back to his team, taps the next player in line, and goes to the end of the line. Give the second child a different command series which involves the same objects: "Walk around the chair. Jump over the cap. Put on the mitten." Continue until each child has had an opportunity to perform a command series. Gradually increase the complexity of the commands, but begin with only three for the first games.

FUNNY SENTENCES

"Who can remember what I say?"

I sat on a tack and jumped straight up.
I stumped my toe and said "oh-oh!"
I like to swim when it's pouring rain.
I can't drive until I'm older than five.
I like boys who like toys.
I like girls and I like curls.
Today is sunny and I feel funny.
Who's the best in the whole wide west?
I can say "hello" 'cause I like Jello.
Who can say, it's a "googaly" day?

CHIN, CHIN, CHIN

Seat the children in a group facing you. Point to your chin and say, "Chin, chin, chin." Then switch and point to another feature such as your eye but continue to say *chin*. The children must point to what you say and not to where you point.

NUMBER FUN

Say this poem.

> One, two, three, the bee stung me!
> Two, three, four, helicopters soar!
> Three, four, five—I can't drive!
> Four, five, six, the donkey kicks!
> Five, six, seven, I (we) like Kevin!
> Six, seven, eight, the fish ate the bait!
> Eight, nine, ten, let's count again.

Vary this in twos and fours and fives. Example:

One, two, buckle my shoe.
One, two, three, four, please don't be a bore.
One, two, three, four, five—in the swimming pool we dive.

Use rhyming schemes typical of the experience of the children.

SPEED GAME

After the children have learned their (*a*) names, (*b*) telephone number, or (*c*) street addresses, time them with a stop watch on how fast each one can recall the information requested. Divide the room into two or three groups and check to see which group was the fastest to remember.

ALERT GAME

Direct a child to sit upright in a chair and begin to say a series of sounds. The child is to stand when he hears a *b* and a *c* sound. He is not helped after a complete explanation of the sounds. He must remember to listen for the *b* and *c* sounds. Say these words about a half second apart.

1. jump   bump   hump
2. bat   rat   cat
3. book   cook   took
4. bear   tear   care

Continue with this same group until each child has learned to pay close attention to the sounds and is able to distinguish between them. Other sound groups may be added after the child has completed these.

ACTIVITIES FOR
AUDITORY MEMORY

G
R
A   **1**
D
E
GRADE

Alphabetical Sequencing

Start with three letters and increase until the subject cannot repeat.

a, b, c — a, b, c, d — b, d, f, a
g, h, l, j, k, j — p, q, r, g, h

Give letters out of order and ask the subject to repeat them in order.

b, c, a — e, d, f — i, h, g
o, p, n — y, w, y, u, t, s — r, q, s

Numbering Sequencing

Same procedure as above.

1, 2, 3 — 1, 2, 3, 4 — 1, 2, 3, 4, 5 — 5, 4, 3, 2, 1 — 6, 3, 5, 7 —
7, 4, 7, 6, 5 — 10, 20, 30 — 30, 50, 60 — 60, 70, 60, 40 — 90,
50, 70, 40 — 15, 17, 19, 11 — 25, 35, 45, 55 — 21, 61, 71, 18 —
2, 4, 6, 8 — 8, 6, 4, 2 — 22, 24, 26, 46

Word Sequencing

Same procedure as above.

boy, cat, dog — dog, cat, boy — run, hop, skip — skip, hop, run, jump — run, hop, skip, jump, swim — was, saw, went — was, saw, went, for

Instruction Sequencing

Have the child repeat the instruction and then follow it.

Go to the chalkboard. — Go to the chalkboard; get a piece of chalk. — Go to the chalkboard; get a piece of chalk; bring the chalk to me. — Walk to the door; tap three times; come to your seat. — Tap your desk; stand up. — Sit down; tap your desk three times. — Touch your nose; touch your ear; touch your eyes. — Clap your hands three times. — Stamp your feet four times. — Clap your hands three times; stamp your feet four times. — Fold your right hand; fold your left hand. — Lift your right foot; lift your left foot. — Lift your left foot; lift your right arm. — Shake your right foot; shake your right hand; lift your left foot. — Wink your eye; rub your nose; touch your toes.

Rhymes

Repeat the rhyme line-by-line until the child can say all four lines. Let each child carry something different to town in his basket as the activity progresses.

> I must go down,
> Down to the town,
> Down to the town
> With my basket.

Examples: With my basket of eggs—With my basket of nuts. The game may become increasingly difficult as it progresses.

1st child: I must go down,
Down to the town,
Down to the town
With my basket of eggs.

2nd child: I must go down,
Down to the town,
Down to the town
With my basket of eggs and nuts.

3rd child: I must go down,
Down to the town,
Down to the town
With my basket of eggs, nuts and corn.

The game may continue in this manner until the last line gets too long to remember. Reward the child who is able to say the longest line by allowing him to be first in the game the next time.

Short poems can be used to encourage listening and vocal sequencing. Aileen Fisher's poem, "The Coffee-Pot Face," may be used effectively.

Motivation: Have children look in a mirror. Talk about other places they have seen their faces. Let them look in other pieces of bright metal such as a coffee pot, tray, sauce pan lid, or lamp base. Call attention to the distorted features. Read the poem. Read it a second time to see if it reflects their own experience with the objects you have given them. On the third reading they say the poem with you.

The Coffee-Pot Face

(1) I saw
    my face
    in the coffee-pot

(2) Imagine!
    a COFFEE-POT FACE!

(3) My eyes
    were small
    but my nose was NOT

(4) And my mouth
    was . . . every place!

Enrichment: The teacher may say one line and let the children say another line, or one child may say a line and point to another child to say the next line. On the last line, let the children stretch their mouths for different expressions. Allow them to look in the mirror to see their own expression. This poem is an excellent one to use to stress natural expression as well as vocal sequencing.

Rhyming Words in Sequencing

Let the children say the words and add another rhyming word, as in:

go, so (no)   sat, mat, pat, cat (hat)
now, bow, (cow)   light, sight, bright (might)
run, fun, sun (gun)   get, let, bet, (pet)

Increase words as ability indicates.

The Tape Recorder in Number Sequencing

Ten Little Indians: Display paper cut-outs of ten Indians. (These may be made by the children.) Play a tape on which you have previously recorded the counting rhyme of *Ten Little Indians*. Be sure that ample time is allowed on the tape for the child to repeat each line. Move the pictures in a sequential pattern as the child repeats the lines.

Enrichment

Fingers may be used in counting. Pictures may be used on the flannelboard or on the overhead projector. Children may manipulate the pictures for stimulating interest after they are able to repeat in sequence.

CONCENTRATION

You may choose a particular sound with which the child has been having difficulty. This sound should be included within a selected number of words that are to be presented in a series.

The child is requested to sit upright in the chair, hands extended in front of chest and clinched fists pressed together. When the child hears the sound as you read, the child lifts her thumbs up but keeps her fists together. This sitting stance helps to keep the child alert and attentive to the sounds she has heard. After a 5-minute session, the child is asked to name as many words as can be remembered that were presented in the session.*

G
R
A
D
E
2

SEQUENCING

Have the child reproduce letters, words, numbers and sounds by repeating them in the sequence in which you gave them.

   a. *B, D, F, A, Z*
   b. *A, E, I, O, U*
   c. 5, 7, 3, 2, 8
   d. Bow-wow, meow-meow, moo-moo, neigh-neigh, oink-oink
   e. Dog, cat, cow, horse, pig

Teach rote counting by 1's, 2's, 5's, and 10's. And teach the day of the week, months of the year by oral repetition.

More Complicated Versions

   a. The teacher says letter names, *s, l, m, n, r*. The child says the sounds of these letters in proper sequence.

   b. The teacher says the sounds of letters. The child repeats the names of the letters.

   c. The teacher says the names of animals, *cat, dog, horse, pig, cow*. The child says the sounds the animals make—in proper sequence.

   d. The teacher says the letters of the alphabet in order, repeating only part of them at a time. The groups of letters get longer as the children can remember them.

   e. The teacher says a telephone number which is a combination of letters and numbers: DR 3-3725. The child repeats it.

   f. The teacher spells a word and then says it: *m-a-n, man*. The child repeats after her. The words increase in difficulty.

---

* This technique may be used for visual memory. Instead of an oral presentation, print the words on cards and present the cards to the child for reading and searching for particular sounds.

REPETITION OF SENTENCES

1. Begin by saying a simple sentence, then make it progressively more complicated, asking the child to repeat after you each time. *I saw a rabbit. I saw a little white rabbit. I saw a little white rabbit hop into the bushes.* Continue until the sentence becomes too difficult.

2. Repetition in sentences may be used in playing a game. The first child says *I am going to New York. I am going to take my* **toothbrush** *with me.* The next child repeats the statement and adds something of his own. *I am going to New York. I am going to take my* **toothbrush**, *my* **billfold**, *and my* **book**. This is continued until a child is unable to repeat everything in the proper sequence. The game may be started over again with different children participating.

REPETITION OF SOUNDS IN THE ENVIRONMENT

Have the children close their eyes for this exercise. Then perform the suggested tasks and have them tell what they hear, in the proper sequence.

    a. Sharpen pencil, knock on door, rap on table.
    b. Bounce a ball, clap hands, tap foot.
    c. Write on board, open window, walk across floor and drop book.
    d. Tear a paper, open a drawer, slide chair across floor, hum a few notes.

MUSIC AND RHYTHM

1. Perform rhythms which the child is to duplicate.

    a. Clap hands in a simple rhythm, as *Clap, clap, clap.*
    b. Clap a more complicated rhythm, *Clap, clap-clap-clap, clap-clap.*
    c. Use drum beats in a simple rhythm, *Beat, beat, beat.*
    d. Use drum beats in a more complicated rhythm, *Beat-beat, Beat-beat-beat, Beat-beat-beat, Beat-beat.*
    e. Combine two types of rhythms. *Clap-clap, Beat-beat-beat, Clap, Beat.*

2. Sing a song with repetitions. Use *John Brown's Baby,* to the tune of *John Brown's Body*. First the song is sung through as it stands.

John Brown's baby had a cold upon his chest,
John Brown's baby had a cold upon his chest,
John Brown's baby had a cold upon his chest,
And they rubbed it with camphorated oil.

The second time the song is sung, the word *baby* is omitted each time it occurs, and a pantomime of rocking a baby is substituted. The third time, the pantomime of rocking a baby continues to replace the word *baby*, and in addition the word *cold* is omitted each time it occurs and a sneeze or a cough is substituted. By the last time through, actions have been substituted for words wherever possible.

Or, use the song *I Am a Gay Musician*. The children sing and pantomime the playing of each instrument. They may make their own verses for other instruments.

3.   Have the children sing and jump rope to nonsense rhymes.

Cinderella dressed in yellow
Went upstairs to see her fellow
How many kisses did she get?
One, two, three, four.

Teddy Bear, Teddy Bear, turn around,
Teddy Bear, Teddy Bear, touch the ground,
Teddy Bear, Teddy Bear, shine your shoe,
Teddy Bear, Teddy Bear, that will do.

Teddy Bear, Teddy Bear, walk upstairs,
Teddy Bear, Teddy Bear, say your prayers,
Teddy Bear, Teddy Bear, switch off your light,
Teddy Bear, Teddy Bear, say good-night.

NURSERY RHYMES

One, two—buckle my shoe;
Three, four—open the door;
Five, six—pick up sticks;
Seven, eight—lay them straight;
Nine, ten—a big fat hen;
Eleven, twelve—I hope you're well;
Thirteen, fourteen—draw the curtain;
Fifteen, sixteen—the maid's in the kitchen;
Seventeen, eighteen—she's in waiting;
Nineteen, twenty—my stomach's empty.

Polly, put the kettle on,
Polly, put the kettle on,
Polly, put the kettle on,
We'll all have tea.

Sukey, take it off again,
Sukey, take it off again,
Sukey, take it off again,
They're all gone away.

A dillar, a dollar,
A ten o'clock scholar;
What makes you come so soon?
You used to come at ten o'clock,
But now you come at noon!

SPELLING AID

After it is determined which word is extremely difficult for a child to remember, he is requested to trace that word on any rough surface: textured walls, textured bedspreads, or in the sand. Tracing for each word should be accompanied by sounding out the spelling, and should be repeated for a minimum of 10 spellings for each word.

Each "difficult" word should be reviewed by the child each morning until *test* time.

SUGGESTED ACTIVITIES G R A D E 3

1. Have the child repeat sentences verbatim—each word in the proper order.

1. A small mountain is a hill.
2. We seed the lawn to grow.
3. The windows are made of glass.
4. The girl wore a pretty dress.
5. School starts when a bell rings.
6. You smell with your nose.
7. Look when you cross the street.
8. Ten boys are in our class.

9. The teacher will tell a story.
10. A school is made of brick.
11. A tie goes around the neck.
12. Frost will kill a plant.
13. You are now learning to read.
14. The sun ran after the moon.
15. Making money is fun.
16. Please pass me the bread.
17. The man told tall tales.
18. Today is my birthday.
19. I live in a red house.
20. The cat sat in the chair.

2. Present related and unrelated words for verbatim repetition. This activity may produce auditory, visual, and vocal outcomes. The child repeats the sequence and then describes the relationship.

Related words (Series A)

1. turkey, duck, chicken, pigeon
2. cow, horse, monkey, ape
3. run, gallop, slide, jump
4. hand, eyes, nose, ears
5. car, bus, train, plane
6. boy, lady, man, girl
7. rain, hail, sleet, snow
8. socks, tie, belt, hat
9. talk, yell, whisper, cry
10. meat, bread, beverage, dessert

Unrelated words (Series B)

1. watch, block, post-office, clock
2. Kennedy, airport, carpenter, horse
3. large, book, small, tree
4. cowboy, blue, booth, animal
5. street, jacket, paper, sheet
6. calendar, road, soldier, paint
7. panther, streetcar, smile, Tuesday
8. goat, baby, cat, stocking
9. shoe, kid, four, moon
10. sun, boot, month, study

3. The story is read to the child. He may answer questions regarding the content or retell the story in his own words.

*Riding Shotgun**

Out on a large grassy pasture, in the Colorado foothills of the Western Rocky Mountains, lives a white Shetland pony named Shotgun. He lives with three other horses, Duke, Dawn, and Cleopatra on Rancher Bob's pasture.

Every Saturday morning, Rancher Bob walks deep into the pasture carrying a leather bridle in his hand. When he gets close to Shotgun and Duke, he lets them see the yellow corn he has for them to eat. After they enjoy their treat, Rancher Bob rides Duke and leads Shotgun up to the ranch house.

Shotgun is glad to come with Rancher Bob because he knows he will see his two little friends, Sheila and Steve, who are waiting for a ride.

Steve helps his dad put the red leather saddle on Shotgun's back. "Girls first," shouts his sister, and with that Sheila and Shotgun are off on another exciting ride around the ranch.

Shotgun loves to run and jump when the children ride. Sometimes he jumps so high, Steve and Sheila slide off. It doesn't hurt them though—it makes the ride more fun.

1. This story is about (a) a calf; (b) a dog; (c) a pony; (d) a cow.

2. The story tells about life on a (a) farm; (b) houseboat; (c) spaceship; (d) ranch.

3. The horses' pasture is in the (a) foothills of Colorado; (b) hills of Wyoming; (c) Eastern Pennsylvania; (d) Kentucky.

4. The number of horses on the ranch is (a) two; (b) four; (c) twelve; (d) six.

5. Rancher Bob treats Shotgun with (a) a bridle; (b) an apple; (c) yellow corn; (d) a saddle.

6. On the way to the house, Rancher Bob rides (a) Cleopatra; (b) Duke; (c) Dawn; (d) Shotgun.

7. Shotgun is always glad to see his (a) master, (b) mother; (c) friends; (d) saddle.

8. Steve helps his dad put on the (a) corn; (b) bridle; (c) blanket; (d) saddle.

---

* By Marian T. Giles.

9. Sheila rides Shotgun (a) into Johnstown; (b) around the ranch; (c) to the mountains; (d) to the barn.

10. Sometimes Shotgun jumps so high, the children (a) are afraid; (b) slide off; (c) hurt themselves; (d) run away.

GRADE 4

TAPPING RHYTHM

With the use of pencils or of short segments of dowel pins (8 to 12 inches), beat out rhythm patterns on a table top. The child is asked to repeat each pattern. In the beginning the patterns should be simple, then become more difficult. Examples:

1. Tap Tap   Tap Tap
2. Tap Tap   Tap Tap Tap
3. Tap   Tap Tap   Tap   Tap
4. Tap Tap Tap   Tap Tap Tap Tap.

You should have your patterns clearly noted on a paper to check the child's responses. It also is suggested that the child be told to remember one pattern of the group which will be presented or repeated as the last of the group. The child should then be sent to get a drink and upon return be asked to repeat this last pattern.

Repetition of Unrelated Words

Drill the child in reproducing series of unrelated words.

1. house, train, boat, grass
2. pillow, ship, light, chair
3. car, school, ball, angry
4. floor, fast, love, between

Following Directions

Give lengthy directions and then have the student repeat the directions and follow them. (*Go to the door, close the door, face the class, hop on your left foot to the teacher's desk, wave your left hand in a circle, walk on tip-toe to your desk, sit down.*)

Reporting News

A student reports a news item, giving a few facts. Then other members of the class are asked to repeat the news. Example:

The president of the United States met in New Jersey with the Prime Minister of England to discuss world problems. They discussed countries in Africa, Kenya, Rhodesia, and Republic of South Africa."

The news item should be kept short for fourth graders.

Rhymes

Memorizing songs and rhymes is helpful in this area. Two songs that are especially good are *The Twelve Days of Christmas* and *Somewhere over the Rainbow.*

Rhymes to be said while jumping rope are also excellent:

> Cinderella went upstairs to kiss her fellow,
> Made a mistake and kissed a snake.
> How many doctors did it take?
> 1, 2, 3, 4, 5, 6, etc.

> Not last night, but the night before
> Twenty-four robbers came knocking at my door.
> I ran out, they ran in,
> Spanish dancer turn around,
> Spanish dancer touch the ground,
> Spanish dancer show your shoes,
> Spanish dancer that will do.

> Teddy Bear, Teddy Bear, turn around.
> Teddy Bear, Teddy Bear, touch the ground.
> Teddy Bear, Teddy Bear, show your shoes.
> Teddy Bear, Teddy Bear, that will do.

Repetition of Digits

Ask the child to repeat digits backwards. Example:

Teacher:	Student:
2, 4, 6, 8, 10	10, 8, 6, 4, 2
1, 3, 5, 7, 9	9, 7, 5, 3, 1
8, 2	2, 8
9, 5, 6	6, 5, 9
4, 8, 3, 1	1, 3, 8, 4

Explanations

Let the children tell how to do something, such as how to drive a car, how to bale hay, how to bake cookies, etc. Then, let others repeat the explanation in exact order.

Memory Retention

Read an unfamiliar story to the class. Let one child recall it, then have others fill in the details he may have forgotten.

Tongue Twisters

The children should repeat these after the teacher.

1. Betty Batter made some butter.
   Now, if Betty Batter made butter,
   Where is the butter that Betty Batter made?
2. She sells sea shells by the sea shore.
3. A big black bug bit a black bear.
4. Rubber baby buggy bumper.

Informal Dramatizations

Commercially written plays are being replaced by informal dramatization or creative dramatics. Here the children develop a general notion of the sequence of events in the story and then ad-lib their way through the presentation.

G
R
A
D
E
5

SUGGESTED ACTIVITIES

Repetition in Sequence

The child listens so as to repeat verbatim items in a sequence. Stand a few feet from him and turn your head so that he will be unable to read your lips. The child covers his right ear and repeats the sequence after you. Start the sequence with a normal voice and gradually fall into lower tones. (Example: 21, 17, 12, 71, 18, 81; 14, 41, 32, 23; 2, 4, 6; 13, 1, 3, 5; 3, 6, 9; 4, 8, 12.) The child then covers his left ear and repeats words. (Can, car; was, saw; hear, dear; boy, toy; they, hay; he, be.)

Memory Training Games

Say-It-Take-It: Put a variety of objects on a table, the names of which contain sounds being studied by the child. Say a sound—*ut*, for example. The child has thirty seconds to find an object on the table which has the *ut* sound in it. After he has found the object, he must repeat the sound given, then name the object. If the child is unable to find the item after thirty seconds, give him another chance or go to another word.

Sounds	Objects
at	bat, hat, mat
ap	apple, cap, map
et	letter
en	pencil, pen
ar	car, star, jar
ip	clip, zipper
an	candy, fan, can
ut	button, nut
in	pin, tin
op	top, pop

Let's Get Acquainted: In the game, the student must listen in order to recall specific information about his classmate. First, have each child introduce himself to the class, telling his name *and address*. The teacher starts the game by repeating the first child's name and address. The first child must repeat the second child's name and address. This procedure continues to the last child. This child repeats the teacher's name and address. The second day, add telephone numbers to the sequence.

Dial-A-Phone

Give numbers orally to the child for him to dial on a play telephone. The child must repeat them orally, verbatim, as he dials.

Single digits: 3-2-3-7-3-4   4-5-1-6-6-4
                       6-9-1-4-4-0   7-1-2-2-4-6
Double digits: 42-28-24-32   12-24-36
                       37-42-16   89-63-44-56
Triple digits: 196-321-024   042-346-894

Consonant Ending Sounds

Here is a game for one or more children working with the final consonant sounds in words. The teacher gives a direction and then a word. The child repeats the direction and begins his word with the last consonant sound of her word.

Teacher: I will spell a word that begins like *tub* ends. *B-a-l-l.*
Child: I will spell a word that begins like *ball* ends. *L-o-g.*
Teacher: I will spell a word that begins like *log* ends. *G-a-l-l-o-n.*

This procedure continues as long as the pupil is able to spell his word within the time limit.

Hearing Syllables

Pronounce a word, and have the child use his pencil to tap out the number of syllables he hears. He then repeats the word in syllables, telling the number of syllables he heard. After he becomes familiar with common words, use words from specific areas —geography, science, etc.

Listen-and-Say Puzzle

The teacher tells a puzzle to the child. The child listens, repeats, and tells the answer to the puzzle. The purpose of this game is to place things in the correct category.

1. Coffee, milk, bread, and tea—
   One does not belong. Which can it be?

2. A rose, a dandelion, a daisy, a face—
   One could never be put in a vase.

3. A tiger, lion, dog, or kangaroo—
   Which one wouldn't you find in a zoo?

4. A fish, robin, crow, or parakeet—
   Which one travels without any feet?

5. Carrots, potatoes, tomatoes, a hoe—
   One of these will never grow.

6. A fly, a bee, a cricket, a toad—
   One doesn't belong on the insect road.

7. Airplane, scooter, train or car—
   Which one will not take you far?

8. A table, a dog, a lamp, a chair—
   Take one out to make it fair.

Action Games

Use action games in which the child must listen in order to repeat the action described.

Winnie-the-Pooh was walking, (*children pretend to walk*) in the woods one day. He looked for food (*children shade eyes and look about them*). He stretched himself tall to reach some berries. He ate the berries, and so on.

Hearing News

This game can be played with an individual or a group. Its purpose is to test listening and recall. How well can the child repeat what he hears? Have the first pupil read a short news item to another pupil. The second listens and repeats the item to the third, etc. When the fifth child has heard the news, have him repeat it to the entire class.

Tongue Twisters

Tongue twisters provide a good exercise to use with consonant digraphs and consonant blends, and they also improve diction. Read the twister only one time, speaking distinctly and clearly, and at a constant rate of speed. Let the child repeat the twister rapidly three times.

1. Chester chucked the chestnuts and chucked the shucks.
2. Sheila snickered as she slowly shrugged her shoulders.
3. Shelley slowly shut the summer shutters.
4. Flags freely fluttered from the floating frigate.
5. She herself shook the salt shaker.
6. Bravely Brenda broke the blackened blister.
7. Grace glanced greedily at the glistening growing grapes.

Concentration Games

The teacher gives directions, and the children repeat the directions verbatim, then perform the activity in sequence.

1. Walk to the door, turn around twice, write the numeral 81 on the board, hop three times, and walk to your seat.
2. Go to the chalkboard, draw two large boxes. Make one square and one triangle in the first box. Put an X on the square. Put a line under the triangle. Move to the next box, draw a circle, clap your hands twice and return to your seat.

Word-O

This is an auditory-vocal sequencing game with a visual clue (similar to Bingo). It can be used with an individual child or with a group.

Give the child a card with words from a fifth-grade vocabulary list. Give a short oral definition for one of the words on his card. He repeats the definition, then finds the word on the card. When he finds the word, he places a little square on the word. He then signals for another definition.

Alphabetizing

Read several words and ask the child to repeat the words in correct alphabetical order.

1. Simple level: Teacher says, *Ate, all, are.*
   Child says, *All, are, ate.*

2. Advanced level: Teacher says, *Apple, able, aim.*
   Child says, *Able, aim, apple.*

3. Complex level: Teacher says, *Attend, attack, attach.*
   Child says, *Attach, attack, attend.*

GRADE 6

SUGGESTED ACTIVITIES

Repetition in Sequence

1. There are quite a few exercises designed to help the student reproduce letters and numbers in sequence.

   a. Teacher: *I shall say several letters in alphabetical order, omitting some. Repeat the letters I have omitted: a, b, c* (pause) *e, f, g* (pause) *i, j, k* (pause) *m, n, o, p.* Child: *d, h, l.*

   b. Give numbers in a series. The student must give the number that will complete the series: *1, 4, 7, ___.* The student says, *1, 4, 7, 10.* Teacher: *3, 6, ___, 12.* Student: *3, 6, 9, 12.* Teacher: *8, ___, 24, 32. Student: 8, 16, 24, 32.*

   c. Teacher: *Listen to this series of numbers and repeat all but the first one: 3, 5, 8, 9.* Student: *5, 8, 9.*

   d. Teacher: *Listen to these numbers and say the one in the series that is closest to the number five: 1, 4, 7, 8.* Child: *Four.*

   e. Teacher: *Listen to these letters and tell me the one closest to m: d, j, x.* Student: *j.*

2. Use poetry to demonstrate a sequence of noises. For instance, read some lines of poetry from *Noise* by Jessie Page:

   The whoop of a boy, the thud of a hoof,
   The rattle of rain on a galvanized roof—

The student recalls: *The whoop of a boy, the thud of a hoof, the rattle of rain on a galvanized roof.*

3.   Have the children practice following directions in sequence. (*Walk to the board. Write your name. Point to a friend. Go sit in your chair.*) The student repeats the directions as he follows them.

4.   Spell words orally—*s-i-m-p-l-e, simple*—and have the child repeat them.

5.   Say nonsense words or syllables in sequence: *bot, it, oot, id.* Have the student repeat them. Increase the number of words as quickly as he is able to do them. (*Ad, ade, em, ist, ell, et.*)

6.   Alphabetizing words in a sequence should take no more than ten seconds.

 a. Teacher: *Happen, hopped, hitting*
   Child: *Happen, hitting, hopped*

 b. Teacher: *Ban, barrel, back*
   Child: *Back, ban, barrel*

 c. Teacher: *Chose, choice, chat*
   Child: *Chat, choice, chose*

Rhymes

1.   Use the repetition of rhymes to help the student remember certain facts. For social studies: *In fourteen hundred ninety-two, Columbus sailed the ocean blue.*

2.   Have the class listen to rhyming riddles. They should repeat the riddles and guess the answers. Students may make up their own riddles.

Teacher: It starts with B and ends with K. I will read a good one today.

Student: It starts with B and ends with K. I will read a good one today. The answer is book.

Teacher: I start with A and end with E. Many people ride in me.

Student: (repeats riddle and answers automobile or airplane)

Tongue Twisters

This is a good activity to use with consonant digraphs and consonant blends. State the twister only once, at a constant rate of speed. Have the child repeat the twister rapidly three times. Refer to the list of tongue twisters found on page 136.

Absurdities

Have the child listen to catch the absurd sentence in a group of sentences.

1. I went to the movie with Bill. We saw a tragedy. We laughed a lot. It was very sad.
2. Mary lives on a ranch in Texas. She has no close neighbors. Many wild animals, such as elephants and tigers, live there. She has to ride miles to visit her friend.

Parts of Speech

Tell the students to listen and repeat descriptive words, naming words, or telling words.

1. Here are some words that are descriptive. Which one means cruel? Kind, fierce, agreeable, barbarous, savage.
2. Some of these words name something (are nouns). Others do not. Repeat the words that are nouns: Mountain, magnificent, molecule, marriage.
3. Some of these words tell something or denote action (are verbs). Which ones? Hop, skip, house, read.
4. Some words are descriptive. Some are not. Repeat the descriptive words: Beautiful, ugly, magnificent. (The child repeats them all.)

Geographical Names

Teach the names of the states and their capitals in alphabetical order. Pronounce the name of the state and its capital, then have the student repeat it. Do only five or six, test, then add some more. This activity can be pre-taped so that the child can work by himself.

GRADES **7&8** SUGGESTED ACTIVITIES

Repetition in Sequence

1. Call out numbers or letters of the alphabet in a series and have the student repeat them verbatim. Or, give a series of related words and tell the student to repeat the series and add a word that shows how they are related.

1. Teacher, principal, student (*school*)
2. Hamburger, potato chips, cokes (*food*)
3. Tackle, quarterback, receiver (*football*)
4. Mustang, Cougar, Thunderbird, GTO (*cars*)

These activities can be taped for the student's later use. Leave enough blank tape between each exercise for the student responses. The entire tape can be replayed after completion.

Repetition of Sentences

Dictate these sentences and have the students repeat them verbatim.

1. Johnny and his brother will play in the band.
2. Let's go to the party Saturday.
3. All eighth graders are allowed to take choir this year.
4. Please pass the cereal to Grandma.
5. Ed is taking a date to the game.
6. Our baseball team won the last seven games.
7. Good listening is very important.
8. The late show was a re-run.
9. Will you apply for a job next summer?
10. We use the tape recorder in our reading class.

Songs

Teach the students a patriotic song using this method: Tape the song with music and lyrics, then lyrics alone. Play the tape until the child is familiar enough with the song that he can dictate the lyrics into the recorder. Use *The Star-Spangled Banner, America, America the Beautiful, God Bless America,* etc.

States and Capitals

Teach the names of the states and their capitals in alphabetical order. Pronounce the name of the state and of its capital city, and ask the student to repeat it. Teach only five or six at a time. Make sure the children pronounce them carefully and distinctly. The tape recorder can be used to pre-record this activity.

Following Directions

Have the student listen to directions and repeat them as he follows them.

1. Go to the board and write your full name, address, and telephone number.
2. Skip quietly to the library table and select a book.
3. Erase the board and put your materials on the shelf.
4. Set up the tape recorder, put on your head set, and listen to this tape.
5. Read this story and answer the questions.
6. Walk slowly to the door and close it.
7. Open the window.

Alphabetizing by Memory

Make a list of words/names from some subject matter in grades seven or eight. These words/names are to be presented out of alphabetical order and are to be repeated in the correct order by the student. Example (from history) :

> Roosevelt, Teddy
> Roosevelt, Franklin
> Tyler, John
> Taylor, Zachary

Building Sentences

The teacher or leader begins a sentence. Each person must add something to the sentence after repeating what has been said. The last person must end the sentence. (*I am going. I am going to Paris. I am going to Paris next week with my best friend.*) Suggested leads:

1. The worst time
2. Tomorrow I will
3. The movie
4. My favorite sport
5. The vegetable I like best
6. My brother
7. Teachers really
8. The game

Initial Consonants

One student, or the teacher, pronounces a word; then the next student pronounces it and gives another word that begins with the same consonant sound. This practice continues until the teacher feels it is necessary to end or until all the children have had a chance. (Example: teacher, *good;* student, *good girl.* Suggested words:

rain	cream	track	jump
New York	put	ghost	kitten

dictionary	drag	visit	complete
frog	football	wagon	zig-zag
young	radio		

Top Ten

Secure the "Top Ten" song list from a local teen-age radio station. Select, maybe, songs 1 through 5, giving the name and the artist. Have the child repeat these in order. The list will have to be a current one because the ratings of these popular songs change every week.

Pass-Along

One student, or the teacher, whispers a short sentence or phrase in the ear of the person sitting next to him. This message is passed along until it reaches the last person. Each person repeats the message only once, so the children have to listen carefully. The last person repeats the message aloud so that the first person can determine if it is the message he sent.

It Happened Like This

This game is used to help students recognize a sequence of events. The children are to arrange cards in the order in which certain events happened. Among the things which the cards could have on them are dates of historical events, processes, steps in the manufacture of products, happenings, or other things decided on by the teacher and the class. To check the answers, write a small number on the back of each card to indicate its correct placement in the series. The pupil with the greatest number of correct responses wins the game.

(*Note:* This activity deals more with motor training, but it does teach sequential order. However, the teacher can adapt this to auditory-vocal by repeating the events and having the children work in pairs, one dictating the answers to his partner, who writes them down to be checked.)

1. Vowels: *a e i o u*
2. Arrangement of words in alphabetical order
3. Parts of the letter (friendly and business)
4. Steps in writing book reports

CB ACTIVITIES

Exercise 1

Give the following directions : "Quickly give me the meaning of the following 10-codes."

1. 10-08 (standing by)
2. 10-04 (OK, message received)
3. 10-20 (location)
4. 10-77 (negative contact)
5. 10-36 (time check)
6. 10-27 (moving to another channel)
7. 10-10 (listening in)

Ask for others for variety. Consult any CB manual for more.

Exercise 2

Reverse the procedure in Exercise 1 and ask the student to give the 10-code numbers in response to the stated meanings.

Exercise 3

State a list of 10-code numbers and ask students to repeat verbatim. Begin with only three 10-codes, then add more to provide greater challenge as needed. Present the codes in different orders.

Exercise 4

Ask the following question : "Quickly give me the CB name for these."

> accelerate (put the pedal to the metal)
> all clear ahead (clean and green)
> short antenna (little mama)
> talk (modulate)
> fog (ground clouds, thick stuff)
> gas (motion lotion)
> empty load (post holes)
> name (handle)

Part III

Visual Modality

Marian T. Giles

The visual modality, as it relates to learning, includes the active processes of receiving, integrating, interpreting, and retrieving visual stimuli. The need for activities to aid in the acquisition of these skills cannot be overemphasized. If children are to learn to read, write, spell, and calculate, they must be afforded opportunity to engage in activities which provide visual stimulation (unless they have specialized training as for the blind). This part of the text provides a variety of such activities under the psycholinguistic headings of visual reception, visual association, visual closure, and visual memory. These topics are introduced and discussed separately as follows.

VISUAL RECEPTION

Visual reception commonly refers to the ability of a person to comprehend the meaning of symbols, written "sight words," pictures, or concrete objects. Visual acuity (the sharpness of detail) plays an important role, since visual perceptions are developed from what one sees. The central nervous system must attend and initially decode this sensory information. (Myklebust, 1975a).

In this chapter, many of the activities involve nonverbal learning tasks stimulated through the visual modality. These activities will help teach children who cannot readily understand visual material and oral directions at the same time. Other aids to those children who learn better visually are charts, the chalkboard, overhead projector, printed material, and manipulative three-

145

dimensional materials. Such children may rely a great deal on tactile sense integrated with the visual.

Thus it is evident that when a child has a deficit in visual reception ability, she can be observed relying on multiple cues from the other sense modalities. She usually becomes insecure when faced with visual tasks unaccompanied by auditory-verbal or tactile cues. A good example of this is illustrated by the frozen expression on the face of a child when she is confronted with a word on a flashcard which is devoid of pictures, context, or sound. Deficits in nonverbal processes lead to distortion of meaning and inner experience and become more debilitating than verbal disabilities (Myklebust, 1975b).

A child should be encouraged to look at a picture, a word, or an object and then close her eyes and see the item in her "mind's eye." This strategy aids in developing the visual imagery which will be critical in the retention and later recall of the information received. Care must be taken to blend these activities into the student's basic curriculum so that this new learning will readily transfer to other content being taught.

VISUAL ASSOCIATION

Visual association commonly refers to the ability of a person to relate incoming visual stimuli to other visualizations which have been previously learned. This process is critical in the comprehension of vocabulary, math, or other nonverbal information.

Visual association is a connecting process. Past experiences are researched by the brain and similarities or differences are perceived.

Hunter (1971) states, "knowledge about one thing can transfer to another if one of our sensory modes perceives it as the same and sends us the same signal." We can then discover relationships which increase the learning of new information.

When a person uses visual association skills, she is using true thinking skills. This technique requires the immediate visual reception of stimuli to connect with an old visualization. This reperceiving action causes a reconstruction of the image in relationship to the new input. Thus, memory may be strengthened because of the associations.

VISUAL CLOSURE

Visual closure refers to a person's ability to create whole pictures or images in the mind after seeing only portions of the stimuli. This skill requires abilities to see total configurations.

Developing visual closure skills increases perceptual speed. When a person can move rapidly from item to item in her visual field without having to take time to analyze each detail of the item visually or auditorally (i.e., sounding out words in reading), she will comprehend the information at a much higher level. Closure ability aids the student in organizing a disparate visual field into a unified percept or concept.

When a child has difficulty visualizing the information she has already been taught, such a problem may be due to a disability in figure-ground perception or visual closure. A child who is visually distractible, hyperactive, or who has cerebral palsy or epilepsy usually has a difficult time developing adequate closure skills. This process requires smooth eye-tracking ability, adequate fusion and depth perception, and clear spatial perceptions. A child must calmly attend to the appointed stimulus while unconsciously screening out the background or peripheral information which is not useful to the particular task. This skill requires clear perceptions in the reception and association processes, as well as visual imagery and memory retention, before it can be highly developed.

VISUAL MEMORY

Visual memory refers to the person's ability to recall visually presented items. This ability may occur immediately after the stimulus is presented, or after a short-term delay consisting of a few seconds or minutes, or a long-term delay consisting of days, weeks, or months. To achieve mastery of skills requiring memory, such as spelling, reading, math computation, or poetry recitation, a person must be relaxed, calm, confident, and well-trained through consistent drill or practice. Fear, anger, anxiety, or excitement disturb visual memory ability. Children who are visually distractible usually do poorly on memory tasks.

In remediating this type of disability, care must be taken to constantly use the regular content in close association with these activities so that the practice and drill will increase the achievement and eventually the mastery of the subjects required in school. Practice on unrelated activities, no matter how interesting, may not transfer to the desired information required by schools. Teaching must be done in such a way that retention occurs. "Retention may be increased through meaning, degree of original learning, presence of feeling tone, positive and negative transfer, and the schedule of practice" (Hunter, 1967). Teachers are not teachers when they become monitors. They must present the information vividly in a positive and reinforcing manner.

REFERENCES

Hunter, M. *Retention*. El Segundo, Calif. TIP Publications, 1967.

Hunter, M. *Teach for transfer*. El Segundo, Calif. TIP Publications, 1971.

Myklebust, H. R. *Progress in learning disabilities*, Vol. III, from Ch. I, James R. Killen. New York: Grune & Stratton, 1975. (*a*)

Myklebust, H. R. *Progress in learning disabilities*, Vol. III, from Ch. V, James R. Killen. New York: Grune & Stratton, 1975. (*b*)

6

Visual Reception

Visual reception, or visual decoding, refers to the ability of the child to understand or interpret what is seen, that is, the ability to comprehend the meaning of symbols, written words, or pictures. There may be many reasons for this difficulty in visual comprehension. In some cases interpretation may be difficult because of visual form perception, visual figure-ground, and visual spatial problems. The teacher should consider placement in the room when the student is required to read written material from the board. The teacher should also encourage the student to take time to process what is being viewed. Vocabulary drill paired with representative objects is a beneficial technique as is the heavy use of auditory cues.

When remediation is needed, you should *provide broad experiences* in reading stories of interest to students. Group activities structured to have students exchange ideas, discuss detail in pictures, identify items, and trace shapes of different sizes with the fingers are beneficial. Often it is necessary for a student to study detail carefully in order to process the stimulus. Allow time for this and encourage the child to be cautious and discerning of the details of letters, words, and events. Verbal expression activities provide opportunity for the child to attempt explanations of what is being seen. Interpretation of facial expressions and gestures also makes what is observed more meaningful. Description of what has been seen, what one imagines, and what one has heard provides opportunities for decoding visual stimuli.

COLOR IDENTIFICATION

Place on a tray (or in a flat box lid) objects of many different colors. For example, the objects might be a red toy car, a yellow whistle, a green lollipop, or a brown ribbon. Say, "On this tray are objects of many different colors. Can you find something yellow, _____?" Have the child choose the object and place it on a table beside the tray. "Can you find something brown, _____?" Continue until all objects have been taken from the tray. "Now there is nothing on my tray. Will you help me put things away again? Will you put something white on my tray, _____? Will you put something orange on my tray, _____?" Continue until all objects are replaced on the tray.

TELL ME WHAT YOU HAVE

Give each child several small pictures cut from magazines, mounted on cardboard, and laminated. Ask leading identification questions which will help the child identify the picture card you have in mind. "Who has a picture of a red car?" After the correct picture has been located, ask specific questions of the child who holds it. "How many children are in the car? Who is driving? Are they driving in the city or in the country? How do you know?"

OBJECT IDENTIFICATION

Provide a large catalog. Each child takes turns opening it at random and pointing to an object. She then identifies that object (chair, dishes, hat, shoes, lamps). She is encouraged to identify objects very quickly.

PICTURES

Use meaningful pictures. Say, "Tell me about the picture. Have you ever seen a place like this? What would you do if you were there? How many children do you see? Wonder why the children came to this place? What kind of weather are they having? What made you think so? What time of the day do you think it was? Why did you say that? Wonder what the children will do next? Wonder what will happen next?" Continue with questions until the children show that they understand what they are seeing.

TRACKING

Materials required are a sand table or a plastic dishpan filled with damp sand and a collection of objects with which to make "tracks" (pop bottle cap, pencil, cup, small cookie cutters, fork). Direct the children to close their eyes while you make tracks with one of the objects in the sand. The children must then decide which object was used to leave the trail. (This activity can be elaborated upon during storytime with some of the excellent children's books available on animal footprints.)

UNDERSTANDING FEELINGS

Show a simple picture to the child; for example, a crying baby in a playpen. Ask leading questions: "Is the baby happy? How can you tell? What do you think made him cry?" Pictures can increase in complexity as the child's ability to generate interpretations increases. The object is to help the child understand feelings through visual stimuli.

SHAPES

Draw a square on the board. Ask the children to find any object in the room that might be shaped like a square: a square desk top, a square window, a book approximating a square, a square file cabinet drawer. Ask one child at a time to go to board and draw a square. Follow this same procedure with other geometric designs, circles, and rectangles. Ask the children to try to remember any such shapes outside of the schoolroom. Continue daily until each child understands the concept of shape and can recognize the common shapes.

NUMBERS

Train the children to recognize numbers up to 5, then up to 10 while looking at numbers on the board. The numbers should be spaced as follows: 1   2   3   4   5   6   7   8   9   10. Present only the first five until all children have learned to recognize these, then present the other group. Allow the children to say in unison each single number, then move up to saying them in groups of five. Always point to the number as it is being said. Allow time for children to visually process each number. The object is to help develop, in keeping with the metric system, the concept of grouping by fives.

LETTERS

Train the children to recognize letters of the alphabet. Show uppercase and lowercase letters separately and then paired. Allow each child to trace letters on board with fingers as they say the letters. Variations are as follows:

1.   Give each child a set of cards with a small number of letters (for example, *aA, Oo, Cc, Bb*) both in uppercase and lowercase. Write one letter at a time on the board and have children find the matching letter. The child raises her hand when she finds the letter. Allow the child to say, "I have found the letter (*a*)." The child is allowed to show you another letter of *her* choice for you to write on the board. The game continues until all children have recognized the small letter studied that day. Review each day until all children recognize the letters readily.

2.   Make a large card (5 x 8) for each of a sample group of letters (both uppercase and lowercase). Place them on the floor; arrange them about 12 inches or 30 cm apart.

$$\frac{A}{O} \qquad \frac{a}{o} \qquad \frac{C}{B} \qquad \frac{c}{b}$$

Write letters on the board and ask one child at a time to stand beside letter on the floor. Give each child a chance to find the letter.

ENVIRONMENTAL AWARENESS

Small groups of children can go to the window and come back and tell of things that show fall is here. Plan to take a walk around the block. Talk about leaves falling and why they change colors. Show pictures of cocoons, leaves, and shells. Discuss their looks, where they are found, and what has happened to make them as they are. Discuss raking leaves. Children will enjoy pretending to rake, to push wheelbarrows of leaves, and to actually be falling, twirling leaves.

NEIGHBORHOOD NATURE WALK

Walk around the block and discuss signs of fall: leaves, trees, birds, gardens, and grass. What is happening to the trees? What are acorns? Are they of any use? Have the children draw a picture of the things they saw on the walk? Ask the children to bring leaves to school. Use the newly fallen ones for art activities. The crisp ones can be placed in a "crunch" box for the pure delight of feeling and hearing them crunched between little hands. The neighborhood nature walk can be repeated in the springtime.

WINTER ANIMALS

Show beautiful pictures of animals in the fall season. Allow children to name the animals. Plan to watch for birds going south and animals that may be preparing to hibernate. Look up the word *hibernation* in the dictionary. Children will then realize where we may look up words that we do not know.

CHANGING WEATHER

Suggest that the children might draw pictures of themselves and let the others guess the kind of weather by the clothes they are wearing. Plan to bring pictures of boys and girls from magazines, and let the class guess the time of year by their clothes. Discuss weather and how we read the thermometer. Plan to listen to the weather reports. What are the types of weather: rain, snow, windy, cloudy, sunny, cold. Plan to make a weather chart. Have available large round objects, such as can covers or wastebaskets, for children to draw around for circle. Divide the circle into quarters. Suggest that pupils be Jack Frost with their crayons and make beautiful colored designs to take home. Draw in each section a weather story: rain, sun, clouds. Cut out for children to take home for use in their own rooms.

SEEDS

Arrange fall flowers and place them around the room. Discuss their colors, their petals, and where they were grown. Look closely at the flower blossom for petals and centers. Discuss the importance of not picking flowers that are on someone else's lawn or that have a fragile life cycle. Do not disturb the roots of the plant. Pick long stems. As children bring seeds, talk about how the seed travels: carried by people or animals, pop seeds, flyaway seeds, and stick-to seeds. Plan to do experiments as soon as they have gathered enough different kinds of seeds. Bring cattails for the science table. Discuss and plan to read a science book concerning them. Plan to find out what kinds of seeds fly. Pull seeds from an opened milkweed. Have the children take turns at blowing them. Discuss importance of this type of travel. Compare apple seeds and acorns. Plan to make booklets about seeds.

ANIMAL CHANGE

Bring tadpoles in a jar to school. Place the jar on the science table. Lead a discussion about frog eggs. Plan to watch the tadpoles and tell a story about a frog at storytime.

Bring a caterpillar to class. Place it in the science center along with the cocoon. Lead class in discussion of what will happen. Show pictures of the different stages of change. You can print on a large chart what children dictate. Make drawings of each new development. Read and show pictures of what will happen to the cocoon.

VALENTINES

Plan to look in magazines at valentines. Ask, "How are they shaped? Do we see a circle in them? Do we see a triangle? Does everything have a shape?" Plan to make valentines. Give each child a symbol:

Place one of these symbols on the back of each valentine a child makes. Each child places a valentine (with symbol on back) in a "mailbox." One child acts as the mail carrier and delivers valentines to the individual desks by matching symbols. Allow each child to be the mail carrier over a period of several days before Valentine's Day.

ACTION IDENTIFICATION

Draw a series of actions portrayed through stick figures. Ask the children to identify the actions. Examples:

 jumping   waving   bending

OBJECT IDENTIFICATION

1.   Cut out pictures from magazines, catalogues, and old books, and make scrapbooks of pictures that begin with a single sound. Place a single picture at the top of the page with the beginning-sound letter. Have the child find other pictures that begin with the same sound and paste them on the page. Have one page for each individual sound.

2.   Take the children for a walk, and ask each one to draw a picture of something he has seen. This can be a seasonal manifestation, such as new leaves, snow, or birds' nests. Or walk to the site of a building under construction, to a new road being built, etc. Field trips to a local store, post office, fire station, or bakery are good. After they have drawn a picture, give the children an opportunity to tell about what they have drawn.

3.   Give the child a piece of paper with one consonant sound written on it. Have him draw a picture of something that begins with the sound. Increase difficulty by writing on the back a second beginning sound to be illustrated. Later, have the child fold the paper into fourths and write in each square a separate beginning sound to be illustrated.

4.   On a large piece of paper write a verbal description of what the child is to illustrate. (*Draw a large red barn with a little door.*

Draw a big green tree with a blue bird on a limb.) As the child develops, increase the difficulty of instruction.

5. **Write two different** beginning sounds on the blackboard. Pronounce a word with one of the beginning sounds, and have the child identify it correctly on the board.

6. Make sandpaper letters and put one on a flannelboard. Have the child feel and trace the letter. Have a selection of pictures from which he can choose the ones that begin with the sound on the flannelboard, and ask him to place the pictures on the board.

7. Mount pictures attractively on cardboard and have the child point out and name all the things that begin with a certain sound.

8. Make flashcards with a different beginning sound on each. Hold a card up and ask the child to name something that begins with the sound on the card.

9. Mark single pictures with two different sounds and have the child select the correct beginning sound.

10. Paste pictures of familiar objects that begin or end with the same sound on a single page, and write the sound at the top. Under each picture place two short lines. The child is to decide whether a picture begins or ends with the sound and place the letter on the correct line—the first line being used if the letter is the beginning sound, and the second line if the letter is the ending sound.

11. Provide a box of toys and have the child select those that begin with the same sounds.

12. Provide pictures or objects in books, catalogues, or magazines. The child describes the object or pictures and their function.

13. Ask the child to look at a picture. Tell him what to look for. (*Find the large tree. Find the dog under the porch*, etc.)

14. Have the child sort objects or pictures and categorize them. Then have him tell why certain things go together. (Desk, table, chair are furniture. Apple, orange, banana are fruits.)

15. In viewing a filmstrip, have the child identify objects or actions seen.

16. Ask the child to describe an ongoing activity, such as an action performed by another child.

17. Cut construction paper of various colors into squares, triangles, circles, and oblongs. Paste small strips of felt on the backs of the shapes. The child may then use the flannelboard to group the shapes according to color, size, or form.

18. Paste related items on cardboard, such as table-chair, pillow case-sheet, button-shirt, knife-fork, etc. Cut in two irregular pieces. Have the child match items that go together. Increase difficulty later by cutting into more pieces.

19. Place some articles in a box. They could be a toy car, a red ribbon, a paper clip, and an eraser. Show the articles to the child for a minute and ask him what he saw. He may be able to name just one thing. Try again. Repeat this several times each day until he is able to name all of the articles. Change the contents of the box and continue this as long as it is effective (Garton, 1961).

20. Letters that are spatially confusing for children with poor up-and-down or left-to-right directional sense (*m*, *w*, *n*, and *u*, for instance) are mastered through repeated tracing, coloring and cutouts. Rolling and shaping letters of clay is also helpful. The color, depth, and texture of the clay produces visually vivid forms that can be identified easily.

21. Have the child make letters from pipe cleaners. These letters can be used to make words.

22. Make a lightweight wooden frame with shelves deep and tall enough for a shoe box and wide enough for five shoe boxes on each shelf. On the end of each box write a letter of the alphabet and the four diagraphs—*ch*, *sh*, *th*, and *wh*. Add a picture representing each sound. Into each box place familiar miniature objects whose names contain initial sounds that match the sound of the picture on the front. Identifying the drawer representing a given sound and associating with the sound the objects in the box hastens recognition and strengthens the memory.

23. *Weber Musicall Technique*. Spatial orientation and form constancy can be helped by using this technique. Music books provide all the information needed to show how to match letters or forms of different designs. These letters and forms are placed on the piano keyboard (or small toy electric organ). They match other letters or forms which have been stuck on a sheet of paper (or paste board) in an order to simulate the spacing and arrangement of the notes on a music score. The child will be playing a tune but the object is visual discrimination. The Musicall books provide a large number of tunes applicable to this technique. This activity may also be used for older retarded children.

IDENTIFYING OBJECTS
AND PICTURES

G
R
A
D
E

2

1.   Use old workbooks from which to cut pictures of like objects. Mount them on tag board, and ask the children to match them.

2.   Cut family pictures from magazines and have the children identify the members of the family and the activity that is taking place in the picture.

3.   Make animal identification games from color-book and magazine pictures.

4.   To promote recognition of words and their meanings, use picture-word cards, phrase cards, and vocabulary lists. Also, you can use a daily weather chart—cut out words describing all types of weather to go on the chart.

5.   Make a food game from pictures, and have the child identify the food and an "appropriate" meal at which it is eaten.

6.   Ask the child to trace geometric forms, designs, words, or his own name.

7.   Dot-to-dot games and pictures with numbers and alphabet are both very good for practice in recognition.

IDENTIFYING COLOR, LETTERS, NUMBERS, AND GEOMETRIC FORMS

1.   Matching objects: Provide colored objects in pairs to be matched (red apple, blue kite, green turtle). Assign a number to each color and write the appropriate color number on each picture. In matching these, the child combines study of objects, numbers, and colors.

2.   Identifying letters: Cut letters from sandpaper for the children to trace with their fingers and then trace in the air. This can also be done with numbers. Use alphabet cards. Ask the child to find and circle capital letters, or circle small letters that appear more than once in a list of words.

3.   Letter banks: Letter banks are useful to help identify letters for the day. Each child has a small box (a match box) and in it new letters for the day. All letters that have not been identified at the end of the day are called *withdrawals*. The same can be done with words and called *word bank*. When the words are

checked at the end of the day or week, all forgotten words are called withdrawals. The children like this for several weeks.

4. Reading signs: Ask the children to notice all the signs along the way to school. Then make signs with the words they saw. (*For Sale, For Rent, Beware of Dogs, Keep Off the Grass, Men Working*, etc.) Begin this from the board; then print on tag board. From sign reading the children begin to identify objects in cans and boxes by the labels, and to increase vocabulary.

5. Geometric forms: From heavy cardboard, make large geometric forms that can be easily traced.

6. Sharp eyes: The children form two teams, facing each other about four feet apart. At a given signal each person looks carefully at the player opposite him. At another signal, both lines turn around so they face in opposite directions. Each person then alters two items in his appearance (unties shoes, takes off glasses, etc.). On the third signal, each child tries to tell what the person did to change his appearance. Repeat several times.

7. Eye-openers: How well can the child visualize? Here are five items for him to answer on paper.
   a. Which is larger, a dime or a cent? (cent)
   b. How many wheels on a freight car? (eight)
   c. On which side does a policeman wear his badge? (left)
   d. Which end of a horse gets up first? (front)
   e. Which end of a man gets up first? (head)

8. Memory test: Test the visual memory of the children. Place ten different objects in a paper bag. Take them out one at a time, hold them up for a few seconds, and replace them in the bag. Then ask the children to list the objects they saw in the order they saw them. Use simple objects. (Variations: use all vegetables, all flowers; use a tray instead of a bag.)

9. **I See a Color:** This game is sort of visual treasure hunt. One child looks around the area and selects some object in sight. He says *I see something blue,* or whatever. The others take turns trying to guess it. The first to guess correctly chooses the next object to be guessed.

VISUAL ACHIEVEMENT FORMS

The following are excellent sources of material for improving the child's visual perception.

1. Marianne Frostig, *The Frostig Program for the Development of Visual Perception* (Chicago, Ill.: Follett Educational Corporation, 1964). The work sheets are in her program.

2. Perceptual Copy Forms, Winter Haven Lions Publication, Box 1045, Winter Haven, Florida 33880.

3. Newell C. Kephart, *The Slow Learner in the Classroom,* "Ocular Pursuits," p. 146 (Columbus, Ohio: Charles E. Merrill Publishing Co., 1960).

FINDING LIKENESS AND DIFFERENCE

1. Geometric exercises of likeness and difference can be found in S.R.A. Math, kindergarten level.

Activity Example

Put a red mark on the two squares.

2. S.R.A. Math can be used for greater and lesser numbers in both the first- and second-grade levels.

3. *A Picture-Word Book*, A Bonus Coloring Book, Whitman Publishing Company, can be used for likeness and difference.

REMEDIATION OF VISUAL DECODING

Drill and game:

1. **Uncle Wiggley Game,** The Milton Bradley Co., Springfield, Ohio.

2. *Simple Objects to Color*, Whitman Publishing Co.

IDENTIFYING FEELINGS AND ACTIONS

1. Show cartoon faces, smiling, laughing, crying, angry, and sad. Ask the children to describe what they think the individuals are feeling.

2. Cut out pictures of individuals in action shots, individuals with crutches, or in sleeping or sitting positions. Ask the children to describe what is happening.

CONCEPTS

1. *Large, larger, largest* can be taught by drawing circles.

Activity Example

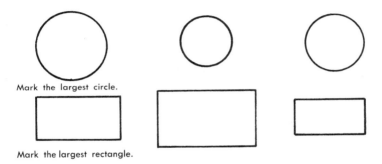

Mark the largest circle.

Mark the largest rectangle.

2. Color can be taught here by asking that geometric figures be reproduced in form and size with color added.

3. Left-to-right can be taught by using the forms that are alike and making an *X* on some of them. If a child has a vision-and-hand coordination problem, to mark *X* on a certain object becomes difficult. It may also be difficult for him to circle forms and letters.

G
R
A
D
E

IDENTIFYING OBJECTS

Workbooks may be used to advantage in identifying and collecting pictures of objects.

1. *Using Phonics First* (Miller, 1966) asks the teacher to match key cards with corresponding workbook pages. As the child identifies the words with the help of a picture, the teacher reads the word, jingles, and rhymes found on the backs of the key cards. After the association is made between picture and word, the teacher may demonstrate the physical production of the sounds while the child repeats the words after her. On the workbook page, a sentence printed in red ink contains the selected word. As the teacher reads the sentence, the child's comprehension of the word is further reinforced.

During subsequent sessions, the child traces the letters in his workbook with his finger as he pronounces the names of the letters after the teacher. At this time the child is learning to work from left to right, to look for likeness and difference, and to listen for phonetic sounds while involved in the process of visual decoding.

2. *Pictionaries* are useful when made by the child. Pictures may be cut out of old workbooks or magazines and matched with words and sentences. These may be glued into a scrapbook and finally indexed in alphabetical order at the end of the book. They may be indexed in specific classifications (i.e., pets, foods, clothing, transportation, shelter, communication, nature, occupations, holidays, etc.) This activity is easily correlated with the social studies units used in the regular class.

3. It is essential that maximum rapport be established and maintained with students of this age. Motivation must also be kept at a high level. In order to accomplish these objectives, activities should be planned for short, intense periods of time. Rewards and encouragement should be given freely and spontaneously. The following is one method of reinforcement found to work quite well with children of this interest level.

Ask the student's mother to send some loose trading stamps to you at the next session. Put the loose stamps into a cigar box marked *Bank*. Provide the student with an empty saver book and the gift catalogue furnished by the stamp company. During activities where the child needs to identify or classify objects, the loose stamps are given to him as a concrete reward to reinforce meaningful and correct responses. The stamps should be pasted into the saver book at the moment of reinforcement for maximum effect.

Using his left hand, the child flips through the gift catalogue slowly. When the teacher says *stop*, the child puts his right hand over the page. The child then opens the catalogue and, beginning at the top left corner, names as many pictures as he is able, describing their uses, or showing by gesture or pantomime that he understands what he sees. Later on, the objects may be put into word form, and may even be used in sentences and paragraphs in an interesting way.

Reinforcement should be geared to the individual situation and not used to the extent that the pasting of stamps into the saver book becomes the main objective.

As the saver book fills, the child gets much pleasure from searching the catalogue and selecting the toy or game to be acquired in exchange for his own book of stamps. Almost immediately, the task of careful searching becomes meaningful in the remediation of a visual decoding disability. When the saver book is completely filled, the child should be allowed to purchase the selected gift as soon as possible. The gift may be brought to the next lesson if the child desires.

IDENTIFYING COLORS, LETTERS,
NUMBERS, AND GEOMETRIC FORMS

1. Here is an activity combining the color and number concepts by using the *Cuisenaire Rods.**

First, take two blue (9 cm) rods, and between them put a dark green (6 cm) rod, so that between the two blue rods and above the dark green one there is an empty space 3 cm long. Ask the child to look at this arrangement and make one just like it on his table. After this is accomplished, say to the child, *Now find the rod that will just fill up that empty space.* It may take several trials in the beginning for the child with a visual decoding deficit to find that a light green (3 cm) rod will fill the space exactly. Next, remove the dark green (6 cm) rod and turn the rods over so that there will be a 6-cm space where the dark green rod had been. Repeat the question.

To vary the activity, use different sizes and colors of rods. After a few lessons the child should be able to see that there is regularity and orderliness in the relationships of the rods. Soon the child will need only one cycle to convince himself that a certain rod is the one he needs for a certain size space.

These rods are excellent tools to use in teaching the concept of how one thing is half of another. Many variations of this activity are possible.

The rods may also be used in making the outlines of many geometric forms. Construct a square out of the orange (10 cm) rods and then ask the child to make one like it. The white (1 cm) rods are small enough to use in constructing circles and ovals. Even letters and other symbols may be designed with the rods, thus giving the child a much better sense of space and direction, as well as strengthening the process of visual decoding.

---

* Available from Cuisenaire Corp. of America, 12 Church St., New Rochelle, N.Y. Named after their inventor, a Belgian school teacher, they are a set of wooden rods, or sticks, one centimeter (cm) wide and one cm high, about the thickness of one's little finger; they vary in length from 1 cm to 10 cm (1 cm is about ⅜ of an inch). Each length of rod is painted its own color: 1 cm, white; 2 cm, red; 3 cm, light green; 4 cm, crimson (pink); 5 cm, yellow; 6 cm, dark green; 7 cm, black; 8 cm, brown; 9 cm, blue; 10 cm, orange.

2.   Identifying colors, numbers, letters, forms and objects can be facilitated by using flannelgraph cutouts and a large wooden tray divided into sections. Have the child match the colors of the objects, letters, numbers and forms (put the orange ones together in one of the sections, the blue in another section, and so on). The names of all cutouts could be said by the child, and descriptions or uses given at the same time.

Recognizing vowels and consonants may be reinforced by using green flannelgraph in making the vowels and yellow flannelgraph in making the consonants. The child uses the sections in the wooden tray for one letter at a time; thus, four sections would be used in making a four-letter word like *home*.

REMEDIAL TECHNIQUES   G R A D E 4

Identification

1.   Mount large pastoral or action scenes on poster board. Engage the students in identifying aspects of the pictures. For example, if the scene is a seascape, ask the following questions to determine whether students understand what they are seeing.
a.   What do we call the dark green spots on the rocks near the water lines?
b.   What is this white part of the wave called?
c.   Why do the trees bend inward toward the inner land?
d.   Could boats dock in near the shore? Why?

2.   Mount large pictures of objects and items on small poster cards, 8½ by 11. Engage the students in naming the objects and discussing how and for what they are used. Use "families" of objects, such as:

Large Machinery Equipment   Electronic Equipment

a. tractors   a. radios (AM)
b. forklifts   b. clocks
c. trenchers   c. tape recorders
d. bulldozers   d. radios (citizens' band)
e. graders   e. aerials
f. cranes   f. stereos

The object is to train for understanding what one sees, which includes pictorial vocabulary. Other areas from which to choose "families" of objects are: sports, automobiles, yard equipment, rock formations, artists' tools, dancing, theater, shopping stores, community buildings, household tools, and household objects.

Concrete Activity

The child often learns better if he has a concrete activity upon which to focus his attention. Rather than showing a child two blocks and saying *this one is big* and *this one is little*, let the child handle the blocks. Such activity focuses the child's attention and emphasizes the sensory training he is receiving.

Moving Toys

Particular attention should be given to toys that move. The child can be motivated to improve his perception through toys that he can see moving, such as tops, balloons, balls, and pull toys.

Colors before Abstracts

Sorting and matching of colors precedes sorting and matching of abstract forms. The child will learn his ball is blue before he learns it is round. After color perception is developed, the colors can be used as cues to help in assimilating other qualities. If a child needs help in perceiving corners, a color may be used to outline each corner.

Characteristics of Objects

It is important to present one characteristic of an object at a time. In teaching a child a certain shape, you will confuse him if he is exposed to a variety of other characteristics at the same time. If he is learning two shapes, such as a triangle and a circle, both objects should be of the same color. (He *may* sort these objects according to shapes instead of colors.)

Contrasting Objects

The child can be helped to learn one distinct color, size, or shape by contrasting it with another. If the color *blue* is to be taught, show not only *blue*, but *yellow* and *blue*, one immediately after the other.

Qualities before Names

An intermediate step between simple sorting or matching and understanding the meaning of qualities is that of attaching the correct meaning to the name when it is spoken. A child will probably be able to follow the direction *Point to the yellow one* before he can answer the question *What color is this?*

Different Percepts

A teacher who reminds herself that a child may not perceive things as she does will be able to give him better training. For example, teach awareness of *top, bottom, under,* and *over*.

Parts before Wholes

A child may be more interested in shiny door knobs than in the colorful toys so carefully selected for him. The teacher should eliminate as many of these distractions as she can from the classroom, thus helping the child to concentrate. Some children will fool you into believing that they understand the whole picture when they are actually conceiving only a portion of that picture or some minor detail.

Confusing Background with Foreground

A clear-cut boundary between figure and ground can be achieved by reinforcing the outline of a form with a black crayon. This is also helpful when the child cuts out pictures, colors inside a form, or saws a figure from wood.

Significance of Action Pictures

Ask the child to describe an action he saw in a filmstrip or an action performed by another child. If the filmstrip showed a farmer milking a cow, the child could discuss what is occurring and why, and what products we get from the cow.

ACTIVITIES

Size, Form, Color

Have the child match colored blocks of various shapes to cards portraying the same shapes and colors. The teacher can make simple cards with only one or a few block shapes on them at first. The shapes can be black silhouettes, so the child will need to think only about the form; or they can be colored, in which case the child has to think of both form and color.

Pictures

1.   The child can be asked to match black-and-white pictures of objects with real objects, or to name pictures, thus showing recognition of them.

2. He can sort pictures into categories, such as boys' clothes and girls' clothes. (A set can be made using two ladies' hosiery boxes. Paste a picture of a boy on one cover, a girl on the other. Mount on cardboard and cut out clothes for a boy and a girl, then store in the boxes.) The child opens them, removes all the pieces, and sorts them by placing the appropriate ones in each box cover.

3. Ask the child to assemble more difficult picture-form inset puzzles, in which pieces represent recognizable parts of objects or of people.

Noises and Sounds

The child can do the following:

1. Listen to sound, with or without seeing person making the sound, and identify it or find where it came from.
2. After hearing a sound, select a picture of the thing or animal that makes the sound.

Number Activities

Tell the child to:

1. Count slowly, along with teacher, the number of children, balls, or crayons.
2. Count pennies while moving them from left to right.
3. Match and sort cards with dominoes or dots.

Quantity

Have the child:

1. Play store using a few pennies.
2. Sort and match small coins.
3. Buy balloons, stamps, or candy at a real store.

Time

Ask the child to determine the time of day by seeing pictures of morning, noon, and afternoon scenes. Such indicators could be depicted in the scenes:

1. Rooster crowing in morning with the sun rising.
2. Children going or leaving school building.
3. Lunch in the cafeteria with the clock on the wall.
4. Breakfast with book satchel near by.
5. Father or mother coming home with signs of *evening* depicted.

PERCEPTION OF POSITION IN SPACE

   This exercise trains the children in following more complicated
directions and in developing the concepts of *same* and *different*.
Using Fig. 6.1, have the children mark an *X* on the figure that is
different from the one at the left.

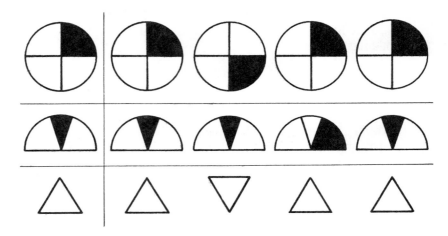

FIGURE 6–1

UNDERSTANDING PICTURES
—A SPEED GAME

G
R
A   5
D
E

   Cut pictures from magazines and old catalogues. Group them in
sets of ten, each set made up of two classifications. An example
would be five houses and five garages, or any combination of the
same objects, such as three houses and seven garages.
   Tell the child that you will give him *five seconds* to find as many
houses (or garages) as he can. These may be placed face up on a
table so he can see them all at once when the teacher gives him
the *Go* signal. The main purpose is to help develop quick and correct judgment about what is seen.
   Other possible classifications of objects are listed below:

   1.   Wood garages and tin garages
   2.   Wood houses and brick houses
   3.   Trees and bushes
   4.   Weeds and flowers

5. Truck vans and highway maintenance trucks
6. Cows and sheep
7. Claw hammers and shingle hammers
8. Tacks and short nails (the real objects could be used here)

This list could be enlarged upon and planned around the child's experiences. The main purpose is to aid perception. The game could also be used for auditory decoding (reception) where the names are similar.

MATCHING WORDS

The teacher has a box of cards with different shapes and on which words are written. The cards should be cut out to cover the linear design of the word. For example, if the word is *house,* the shape should follow the lines of the word in this fashion:

house

The child is given the directions to match as many cards as he can within thirty to sixty seconds. The teacher may vary the number of cards with the time allotted. It is strongly suggested that the teacher choose particular words from the child's reading, spelling or geography books. Specifically included should be the ones which have been difficult for the child to learn.

OPERATIONAL PERCEPTION—A NUMBER GAME

On small flash cards, write problems with designated operations such as addition, subtraction, multiplication, and division. These should be varied in this manner:

$$
\begin{array}{llll}
\begin{array}{r} 2 \\ +\,2 \\ \hline \end{array} & 2+2= & \begin{array}{r} 2 \\ \times\,2 \\ \hline \end{array} & 2\times 2= \\[2ex]
\begin{array}{r} 2 \\ -\,1 \\ \hline \end{array} & 2-1= & 2\overline{)4}= & 4\div 2=
\end{array}
$$

Flash the cards at one-second intervals. The child is to perceive quickly *what should be done.* The same pattern as $2+2=$ may be varied by use of different numerals. The student should respond by giving the correct mathematical process—*add, subtract, multiply,* or *divide.*

USE PICTURES TO LABEL,
DESCRIBE AND CATEGORIZE

G
R
A
D
E

6

1.   Show several pictures. The child decides how the pictures are similar.

2.   Use the above procedure, but have him look for things that are different.

3.   Use a group of pictures. Let the child put them in the right category. For example, categories such as life in China, life in Germany, life in Nigeria can be used.

4.   Show a picture and have the children as a group write three different sentences about it.

5.   Use pictures with a mistake in them. Let the children find what is wrong. These can be found in old workbooks and various children's magazines.

6.   Find illustrative pictures and write sayings to match the picture. Scramble the sayings and pictures. Let the children unscramble them.

7.   Use a picture with several things in it. List and number the items in the picture in random order. Have the children mark the corresponding number on the item in the picture.

8.   Find pictures which can be used for position and location. List the words under the picture. (Example: *outside the house, under the chair.*) Match the pictures with the phrases.

9.   Use a picture with the opaque projector. Let the children see the picture for about ten seconds. Have them recall what they saw.

10.   Mail-order and stamp catalogues can be used to find categories and cost of items.

11.   Use magazine pictures to find phonetic examples and examples of kinds of words. For instance, a picture illustrating a two-syllable word, or a picture illustrating a silent *e* word.

TECHNIQUES TO DEVELOP SEQUENCING ABILITY

1.   Make a *time line*. This might include the year the children were born, the year they started to school, and the year they were

in each grade. This can progress to more difficult things after they are familiar with the years.

2.   Make a calendar for each month of the school year. Put each child's name on his birthdate. School and classroom activities may also be included.

3.   Make analogies such as: *car is to transportation, chair is to furniture.*

4.   Use a map of the school building and grounds, or of the city. Write a paragraph including various places on the map. The children can follow the events on the map as they read the paragraph.

5.   Make a simple outline form. Partially fill it in, and let the children complete it.

6.   Write sentences on a set of cards or chart. Scramble the sentences. Have the children unscramble them.

7.   Use the Sunday comics. Cut out comic strips such as *Dennis the Menace, Blondie, Peanuts* and *Nancy*. Cut into squares, and scramble them. After the children unscramble them, stick in an extra square from a different date. Comic books can also be used. Use the entire page instead of the squares. A duplicate book may be necessary for comparison the first few times.

ACTIVITIES TO DEVELOP DIRECTIONAL CONCEPTS

1.   Girls can use recipes to learn to follow directions. Or they could make marionettes.

2.   Boys can make simple toys, including model airplanes and cars. The Boy Scout Handbook may be useful.

3.   Use various kinds of reference materials, such as an encyclopedia, dictionary, atlas and magazine. Have a picture of these references at the top of the student's paper. Ask questions pertaining to the best use of each. (Example: *Where would you look to find several maps of Virginia?*) The child draws a line from the question to the appropriate pictured references.

4.   Play the age old game of **Simon Says.** Write the directions on the board or on sentence strips and let the children read the directions and carry them out.

5.   Use the opaque or overhead projector. Write a direction on the screen and let the child follow through. (Example: *Write your name in the middle of the page,* etc.)

ACTIVITIES FOR READING IMPROVEMENT

    1.   Use independent reading materials. Let the children paraphrase the author's idea.

    2.   Copy a paragraph leaving a blank for every sixth word. Let the child fill in the missing words.

    3.   Make Bingo cards using phrases such as *under the table, beyond the yard, on the desk, outside the house,* etc.

    4.   Use short sentences with comprehension questions immediately following. (Example: *A mustang can go fast. What can a mustang do?*)

    5.   Let the children write a telegram, choosing the main ideas from a paragraph or two of reading material.

ACTIVITIES FOR MATH CONCEPTS

    1.   For measuring quantities, use an abacus, counting discs, domino cards or telephone dial; for size, use square-inch, foot and yard cards; for volume, use pint, quart, and gallon jars, bottles, spoons, and cups. Charts illustrating these measurements can also be made (by the teacher).

    2.   Cuisenaire rods are useful for learning fractions. These begin with a cube and are different colors for different sizes. The cube stands for *one* (cm). A rod which stands for *two* would be the same size as two cubes put together, etc.

MISCELLANEOUS ACTIVITIES

    1.   Use interest centers where things can be labeled. (Example: Sea life—all animals would be labeled.)

    2.   Put several items into a sack. Sewing notions could be used for girls and carpenter tools for boys. Have the items written on the board and let them match the label with what they find. A variation: Put something in the sack which does not belong.

    3.   Read the newspaper. Girls can look at grocery ads and make out grocery bills. Boys can look for tools they would like to buy and figure how much the bill would be. A study of weather and general news can also be used.

    4.   Use the television schedule. Let children find the programs they enjoy watching, and the day and time they are shown.

5. Use the telephone directory. Let the children find the addresses and phone numbers of classmates.

G
R
A
D
E
S
7 & 8

IDENTIFYING PICTURES
AND OBJECTS

1. Have the student describe pictures from books or bulletin board, or paintings on the walls. He may tell a story about it.

2. Ask the student to describe action seen in film strips.

3. Take out every eighth word of a paragraph. The student tries to put them back in appropriate places.

4. Have geometric forms made of wood for use in math. (For example: square, rectangle, circle, triangle, cube, cylinder, sphere, cone, etc.)

5. Use charts, graphs, pictographs, maps, and building plans. Ask the student to interpret them.

6. Have the student watch experiments in science. Let him describe the germination of a seed, and its growth.

7. With the students, observe objects and events in their natural environment on field trips (shades of color in the sky, clouds, trees, etc.)

8. Devise matching exercises, such as finding leaves of particular shapes and asking the student to find others that match.

9. Have students put shapes of various colors on pictures that have the same shape and color (color lotto).

PROJECTS

Occupations

The student cuts pictures of as many different occupations as possible from magazines and newspapers to make an illustrated notebook, writing appropriate comments. He might spend more time and research on the ones in which he is most interested.

Driver Education

This is similar to the preceding, except the student cuts out small pictures of cars and uses them in making diagrams to illustrate rules and regulations of safe driving. Teach him to read road maps.

Home Economics

The student can secure models from catalogues to illustrate clothes that are appropriate and in good taste for different places and functions—church, school, office, play, parties.

Collections

Making and labeling collections of insects, butterflies, rocks, coins, pictures of airplanes, or pictures of cars will be instructive for the student at this level.

Poetry

Use drawings or secure pictures to illustrate each poem in a poetry notebook.

GAMES

1.   The student looks at a map as the teacher calls out a capital or principal city. The student then writes the city and state.

2.   Use a flannelboard outline map of states in the United States. Capitals on cards are given to the student. When the teacher calls a certain state, the student places a capital card in that state.

3.   The flannelboard can also be used for word-matching games.

4.   Use flash cards for fundamentals in arithmetic: addition, subtraction, multiplication, division.

5.   Write a long word from the lesson on the board—such as *Constantinople*. The student writes as many short words as he can, using letters of the word on the board.

6.   Use jigsaw puzzles of maps and pictures related to stories in literature.

READING

Since all reading develops visual decoding, be sure to make available a variety of library books and materials along the student's line of interest and, especially, on a level easy for him to read. (A student in Grades 7 and 8 may be able to read only at 5th grade level.) *Use books that do not have the grade level designated.*

CB ACTIVITIES

Exercise 1

Make cards with 10-codes written on one side; ask student to give the meaning of each 10-code.

10-4 (message received)	10-20 (location)
10-8 (standing by)	10-36 (time)
10-10 (listening in)	10-32 (radio check)
10-13 (road/weather conditions)	10-39 (message delivered)

Exercise 2

Use magazines and newspapers to cut out pictures of the following:

accidents (10-42)
person dialing a telephone (10-21)
person yelling with caption *help* (10-34)
person looking in mailbox (10-65)

It is not easy to find pictures depicting the 10-code messages, but it is recommended that teachers study these for creative ways of presenting meaningful pictorial representations.

Exercise 3

Place on flash cards the following words and ask the student to *decode quickly.*

1. mercy (general exclamation)
2. come back (repeat message)
3. handle (CB name)
4. Windy City (Chicago)
5. hundred-mile coffee
    (strong cup of coffee)
6. Big Mama (9-foot whip
    antenna)
7. Little Mama (short antenna)
8. threes (good wishes)

    9. tags (licenses)

  10. Smokey (patrol)

  11. pictures (radar)

Exercise 4

Ask the student to write the words in Exercise 3 (and other words) in the sand and in the air.

Exercise 5

Write any CB terms in bright, bold letters, 3 inches high, and with proper syllables marked on white paper. Place the written words on the floor, spaced 1 foot apart in column fashion. Ask the student to stand before each one, say the word, spell the word, and say the word again.

Visual Association

Visual association refers to the ability to associate visual symbols in a meaningful way; thus it deals with the visual process of interpreting relationships. Is the individual capable of relating events seen in pictures or in writing? Does the student recognize that, e.g., the glove he is viewing goes on a hand? Does he recognize that a ball and a bat can be in the same category as a ball and a tennis racket? To train for this skill you may provide auditory cues when possible and appropriate.

An example for remediation is: if a child begins to "block" when attempting to relate similarities between a person working in a garage and a person working on pipes in a kitchen, you may ask questions concerning what the individuals are doing. If the child does not respond, you may say, "One is working on cars and the other person is working on pipes. What words are the same?"

Continue such questioning until the word *working* is identified as the common factor. This procedure also aids auditory association. (A main principle is that any testing [questioning] should be facilitated by clues through other forms of questioning.) Reinforcement of the concept should be done by repeated statements such as, "Both individuals are working."

OBJECT-PICTURE MATCH   _{GRADE} K

Collect everyday items (a shoe, belt, knife, pair of glasses, pencil, comb, etc.) in a box. "We will pass this box around the table. Each of you take one thing and then tell us what it is. Now I'm going to pass around another box with pictures in it. Find the picture that has the same thing on it as you have just picked out of the other box."

SILENT COUNTERS

Materials needed are nine potholders and nine cards. Allow the children to line up and count these. Also stack and arrange the potholders in order as follows:

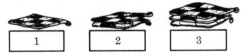

Vary these for the children to make associations of a number with a stack of potholders.

TABLE SETTING

Set up a model table setting with mat, plate, knife, fork, spoon. Give each child the necessary items. "Set your table like mine." Cups, glasses, or napkins may be added later. Doll dishes and play silverware may be used.

CANDY DESIGNS

Make a row with four colored candies: red, green, red, yellow. Give each child an assortment of candies to choose from. Can he make the same pattern under yours? Make a simple design with five candies. Give the child the exact number of items he needs to copy it. Can he reproduce the figure? Later, give each child more candies than he needs to copy the design. Does he copy the pattern one for one, or does he attempt to reproduce the pattern using all of the candies? Activities similar to those above can be structured from a variety of materials: wooden beads, oyster crackers, or felt pieces and a felt board.

FINDING IDENTICAL PICTURES

Prepare simple, mimeographed sheets which show an array of similar objects. Instruct each child to find two which are the same. Example: two identical fish among six assorted spotted and striped fish; two identical birthday cakes among the assortment with different decorations and number of candles; two identical flowers among an assortment of flowers.

OBJECT SORTING

Use muffin pans, egg cartons, small plastic containers, small aluminum pie pans, or paper cups for sorting activities. Dried seeds make an excellent early sorting activity. The seed assortment might contain kidney beans, lima beans, calico beans, northern beans, and popcorn (unpopped). Safety pins, nails, and screws of different sizes may also be sorted. Buttons may be sorted by size and color. Wooden beads may be sorted by shape and color. Advanced sorting may require the child to put one bead (for whatever is being sorted) in the first muffin cup, two in the second, etc., up to six.

ALIKE AND DIFFERENT

Materials needed are gummed paper stamps arranged in lines on cardboard. Have child find the one picture that is different on each line. Name the objects. The stamps may be old stamps from Christmas or commemorative stamps.

COPYING DESIGNS IN BEAD STRINGING

Give each child beads and lace in a small container. "Can you make a necklace just like mine? Watch me. A red bead, a yellow bead. Can you do that? Good. Let's try it again. A red bead, a yellow bead." Later, prepare a different bead pattern on a piece of lace (knotted at both ends) for each child. Can he copy this pattern by himself, checking for accuracy as he performs the task?

PICTURE SHAPE PUZZLES

Mount small catalog and magazine pictures which show an everyday object with a familiar geometric shape. Examples: a cracker, clock, or cushion in a circle shape; a window or table in a rectangular shape. Direct the child to sort these pictures by shape. Each child may monitor a specific shape, or the sorting may be done in piles in the center of the table.

THINGS THAT GO TOGETHER

Materials could be any objects that "go together": cup, saucer; brush, comb, mirror; knife, fork. "Name the objects. Place the ones that belong together. How are they used? In which room at your home would you find these articles?"

DIFFERENCES AND LIKENESSES

Collect items in related pairs: two balls—one big ball, one little ball; two clothespins—one pinch and one snap on; two shoelaces—one plaid and one brown, or one long and one short. Question: "What do you have?" Answer: "Two balls." Question: "How are they different?" Answer: "One is big." Vary the questions according to the items and increase the specific detail requested.

BOOKS

Allow the children to observe varieties of boats, trucks, and trains from books. As the children go through the books, they can take turns telling about one particular kind of truck, train, or boat. The McGraw-Hill Panorama books are useful for similar activities. These books are made of very heavy cardboard and fold outward and stand up by themselves. The children may take turns telling about each page. The Bowman Manipulative Books are another excellent source.

CHALKBOARD COPYING

Materials needed are overhead projector and transparencies. Have a pattern made of figures on a transparency. Have the child extend the pattern by drawing on the board.

MATCHING

Give the child pictures of two pets and two household items on flashcards. Let him go to the toy box and pick out these items in toys; this activity makes learning concrete. Ask him to group and name them.

LETTERS

Letters of the alphabet, both lowercase and uppercase, can be presented. The letters can be scrambled and the child picks out the lowercase and uppercase of the same letter.

GRADE **1**

VISUAL CLASSIFICATION

1. Make cards (about 9 x 12) from tagboard. Cut pictures from catalogues or magazines and mount six on each card. Choose pictures of interest to young children, such as animals, birds, toys, etc. Duplicate these pictures separately on cover cards (3 x 4). These should be almost like the pictures on the large cards. Have the child choose the smaller card and cover the picture on the large card that matches it.

2. **Who gets it?** This activity can be made into a game. Picture cards are distributed to the children. A stimulus picture is shown to the group. The child who has a picture to match it, may have it. The child matches not just pictures of objects exactly alike, but pictures of two different types of the same object (e.g., pictures of two kinds of chairs, two kinds of coats, two kinds of hats or shoes, etc.)

3. Have the child cut from magazines, catalogues, or old workbooks pictures that fit into different categories: things that we wear, good things to eat, animals that we find on a farm, things we can ride on, and so on.

VISUAL RELATIONSHIPS

1. Present a set of pictures to the child. Three of the pictures are related; one is not. Have the child identify the picture that does not seem to be related to the other three. (See Fig. 7.1).

WHAT IS OUT OF PLACE?

Eeny, meeny, miny, mo
What should *not* be in the row?

FIGURE 7–1

2. **Find the Shadows:** Divide a large sheet of paper into two sections. On the left side draw a group of recognizable objects in detail. On the right side draw the same objects in different positions and blacked in like shadows. Instruct the child to draw a line from the object on the left side to its shadow on the right. (See Fig. 7.2).

3. Relating numbers of figures by sight (game): Make a group of cards about 8 x 12. Draw lines or objects on one card; on another card draw the same number, but different, lines or objects. The game may be called **Match Mine**. Two children can play, or the teacher can play with the child. Put all the cards out where they can be seen. One of the players takes a card. He may say, *I have five crosses. Can you match mine?* The other player must choose a card with the corresponding number of objects but in different forms (five stars or five balls).

4. Pattern completion exercises are found in *Instructional Materials for Exceptional Children,* Visual Readiness Skills, Level I (Eichler and Snyder, 1958). Have the child complete patterns by drawing lines. The easiest ones have dots to use as guides. Later, as the child progresses, the dots are left out.

FIND THE SHADOWS

FIGURE 7–2

5. Ask the child to find similarities and differences in details:

   a. Here are a lot of kites with different patterns on them. Can you find the one that has the same pattern as the one in the box on the left? If you can, put a red mark on it. Can you find two others that are exactly alike? Mark them with your blue crayon.

   b. Here is a picture of cows in a field. All the cows except two have different patterns on them. Two of the cows look just alike. Can you find the two cows that look alike and put a mark on each of them?

6. Finding objects that are different—ask the children to find:

   a. A square button in a box of round ones.
   b. A large block in a box of smaller ones.
   c. A green marble in a sack of blue ones.
   d. A rough piece of paper among smooth ones.
   e. A pink flower among blue ones.

INCONGRUITIES IN PICTURES

1. Here is an exercise from the *Frostig Program for the Development of Visual Perception* (Frostig, 1964): *Here you see at the top left a picture of a fish in a bowl. But the other pictures show each fish with only the top of a bowl. See if you can draw the rest of the bowl in each picture. Try to do it with one line without stopping or going back. Make all the pictures look like the top left one.*

2. Present the child with a page of pictures where something has been left out of each picture:

   1. A door without a door knob.
   2. A glove with a missing finger.
   3. A wagon minus a wheel.
   4. A tricycle with only one pedal.

   Have the child draw in the missing part.

3. Give the child an envelope containing cutouts of ears and tails of different animals, such as rabbits, squirrels, horses, pigs, and so on. At the same time give him pictures of the various animals minus ears and tails. The object is to put the right ears and tails on the animals.

OPPOSITES

Secure magazines or catalogs that have faces of children who are happy and who are sad. Cut out several happy faces and an equal number of sad faces. Ask the children to pair the opposites. Each time a sad face is picked, an opposite must be chosen.

G
R
A   **2**
D
E

TRAINING THE

ABILITY TO CLASSIFY

Use small pictures in groups of any four things with one or two unrelated and to be designated in some way.

1. Put a line under the ones Mother uses to clean the house. (Lawnmower, wet mop, broom, car; vacuum cleaner, books, feather duster, rake.)
2. Put a line under each boy (group of stick-figure boys and girls).
3. Color with red the things we would eat (Fig. 7.3).

FIGURE 7–3

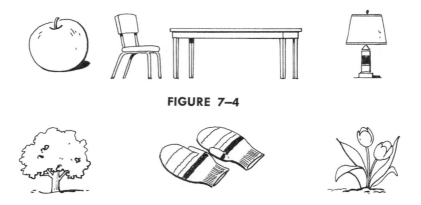

FIGURE 7–4

FIGURE 7–5

4. Color the bananas yellow (a flat basket of mixed fruit).

5. Make an X on the one that does not go with the others. (Snow-covered tree, sled, hammer; book, pot of ivy, evergreen tree; daisy, telephone, grass. See also Figs 7.4 and 7.5).

Pictures from magazines may be utilized. Ask the children to look for and bring to school specified pictures. The consonant, vowel, and sound-blending pictures from the Ideal Company are good, and are available in most dime stores.

Several *games* may be played with sets of four separate pictures, each containing one unrelated to the other three. Have the child select the unrelated pictures and put them in a separate stack. Extend the game with one or two players by placing the unrelated pictures face-up in a horizontal line between the two players. They choose from the unrelated pictures to make "books" of four related pictures, taking turns. To complicate the game, you could have some extra pictures which cannot be grouped in the classifications selected.

SORTING OBJECTS

Use small pictures or line drawings; read the directions for the pupils.

1. Put a ring around the things that can run (chair, boy, dog, lamp).

2. Put a line under the things that have straight lines. (See Fig. 7.6).

FIGURE 7–6

3. Color the big ones red (one large, two small squares; one small, one large triangle; three small, two large circles).

4. Put a ring around the ones we can ride (tricycle, horse, table, bicycle).

5. Color with blue the ones we can wear (tree, shirt, light bulb, shoes).

6. Draw a line from each one to its home. See also Fig. 7.7.

horse	nest
dog	barn
bird	tepee
Indian	chicken coop
hen	dog house

7. This large box has many things in it. Put everything we use in our school work on this desk. (Pencil, sock, chalk, apple, eraser, umbrella, tablet.)

8. This large box has many things in it. Put all the things with *straight edges* on this side of the desk. Put all the things with *rounded sides* on this side of the desk. See if you can tell us where it goes before you pick it up. (Chalk, rule, ball, chalk eraser, orange, reader.)

FIGURE 7–7

ASSOCIATION PARTS IN SEQUENCE

Use line drawings pasted onto cardboard (laminated, if possible) and cut into approximately three-inch squares.

1. This is a car in three pieces. You make it right.

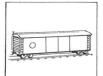 

FIGURE 7–8

2. This is a three-part train. You make it right. (See Fig. 7.8).

3. We are shopping for groceries. What happens first, what happens next, and what happens last? (Full sack of groceries, empty cart, partially filled cart.)

4. There are four people in this family. Put the baby first, then the next biggest or oldest, then the next, then the oldest. (Baby, high-school brother, second grader, grandmother.)

Have the child listen very carefully to a story and then, on a large sheet of paper, draw a picture story of what he has just heard.

1. John skipped happily down the road to the lake with his fishing pole over his shoulder. His dog, Spotty, tagged right behind him.

2. "Grandfather is here!" shouted Suzy. "Look at the pretty red wagon he brought us."

Simple, four-unit funny-paper stories could be used for this. Illustrations cut from old readers and mounted on cardboard also make good stories for the child to arrange in sequence.

INCONGRUITIES IN PICTURES

Use line drawings such as the following and ask the child to tell what is wrong.

1. Faces—with one eye, with no mouth, with one ear, with open mouth and no teeth.

2. Two feet, one with shoe and sock and one with shoe only.

3. Side view of car with no door handles.

4. Bicycle with part of handle bar missing.

5. Birthday cake with candles, three with flames and four without flames.

6. House with no roof.

7. Outdoor picture with the sun, moon, and a star in the sky.

8. Car with one wheel missing.

9. Stylized flowers with tulip-like leaves and some of the blooms absent.

10. Stylized sun, circle with rays out; incomplete circle and a quadrant of rays missing.

GRADE 3 — CLASSIFYING PICTURES VISUALLY

1. To combine visual-motor drill with training in the ability to classify, have the child practice arranging in correct categories such things as toy furniture, pictures of people and their occupations, transportation modes, sports (baseball, football, track, bowling, swimming), seasonal scenes, clothing apparel, foods, etc.

2. Play word-picture matching games which teach opposites by analogies (hard is to soft as sour is to sweet; short is to tall as high is to low, etc.).

3. Use Ideal *Magic Cards* illustrating classification, opposites and sequences. (Note: Order these from any catalogue of teaching aids which lists materials from The Ideal Company; cost is nominal.)

4. Show art blobs, evocative art, spring paintings, etc., and train the child for quick spontaneous responses of *It looks like* . . .

PERCEIVING RELATIONSHIPS

1. Plan group-discussion periods in which children are to recognize what is wrong, or what does not belong, in a picture. Allow discussions on how to change "what is wrong" to "what is right." This is especially effective when pictures deal with character-building ideas such as truthfulness, cleanliness, honesty, courtesy, patriotism, loyalty, etc.

2. Give drill in following the steps in a story by arranging pictures in proper order.

3. Use puzzles and games:

a. **Wordo**, like Bingo, requires individual cards divided into sixteen or twenty-five squares. Each square has a noun or verb printed in it. The teacher or leader flashes picture cards and the child places a bottle cap or button over the matching word. The winner calls *wordo* and must read the word and select the correct picture before earning a point.

b. **Teach-Me** dominoes are available from all school-supply catalogues. Made out of heavy cardboard, each domino is 3 x 5 and painted black with white dots. They are very durable, and there are many uses for these dominoes.

c. Arrange three related pictures on a single card. The child chooses a fourth related picture from another set. For example, a picture of a wagon would match the boat, car and train. Other group sets might be road, runway, sidewalk—street; bird, duck, hen—turkey; nose, eye, mouth—head; Indian, teepee, arrow—buffalo.

PEGBOARD GAMES

You may secure two peg boards (two squares of acoustic tile are also excellent). Place pegs of any kind, preferably different colored ones, in each board to make different designs.

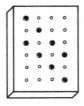 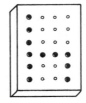

Ask the child if the designs are alike or different. In what way? Then ask the child to make a design of his own choosing; first, alike; second, different. Also ask for designs to be made to look like the shape of some object in the room.

RECOGNIZING INCONGRUITIES

1. Give the child practice in selecting the correct body parts of specific animals (i.e., the tail of a bear would not be right for an elephant). More difficult experiences of this same idea would be distinguishing among bird beaks or animal teeth (as to whether the animal is carniverous or herbiverous, etc.).

2. Play social studies games to match plants and animals, occupations, modes of travel, etc., to specific places on the earth—the equator, the ocean, the arctic, the desert, an island, etc.

3. Teach likeness and difference: *How are horses, mules, oxen, trucks and tractors alike? How are they different?*

4. Ask the child to find the object in a picture or paragraph which is not related and does not belong; or to separate a single picture from a group of pictures in which it would not belong.

5. Use jigsaw puzzles, making some of the pieces the correct shape but not the correct picture to fit the subject.

G
R
A 4
D
E   CLASSIFYING PICTURES

Ask the child to find the one picture that does not belong with the other three.

1. Three foods that are customarily served hot, such as soup, corn-on-the-cob, baked potato, and one food served cold, such as watermelon.

2. Pictures of team sports, such as football, basketball, and soccer, and for contrast, a picture of a skier.

3. Pictures of sports involving physical exertion and one involving mental exertion, as chess.

SORTING PICTURES INTO CATEGORIES

Select categories such as use, shape, size, color, etc., for these exercises.

1. Pictures of many kinds of buildings could be sorted by *size* (one-story, two-story, skyscraper) *use* (homes, apartment buildings, factories, hospitals, army barracks, office buildings), and even by *color.*

2. Arrange pictures of about twenty objects in a circle on a mimeographed sheet, leaving the center blank. These objects should include such things as a needle, sewing machine, thread, scissors, bricks, cement, planks, hammer and saw, flour, milk, yeast, an oven. In one-third of your stenciled sheets, draw a picture of a loaf of bread, and have the youngsters choose the things necessary to make it by circling the pictures that apply. On the center of the second group, draw a picture of a building and have

the children circle the things that would be used in making it; on the last, a picture of a shirt, with the same instructions. This could be made harder by including objects that pertain to none of the central figures; or all operations could be done on the same sheet by using red for marking the things that go with the loaf of bread, blue for the building, and green for the shirt.

3.   If you have access to large numbers of book jackets, let the children sort them into categories, such as cowboy stories, fairy tales, adventure stories, science fiction, animals, real people, etc. Then use the sorted jackets as bulletin board displays.

4.   Ask the children to sort pictures of landscapes into geographical regions—deserts, farmlands, forests, mountains, swamps, etc. Pictures could also be sorted into those that pertain to history, geography, science, arithmetic, and so on.

PANTOMIMING AND SEQUENCING

1.   Have the child pantomime a story just read. The story will need to be short with definite action.

2.   A child acts out a charade. The other children guess what story he is acting out. (This can be done as a group or singly.)

3.   Draw a picture with cliff-hanging action: a boy fishing and a skunk sitting behind him; a boy running toward home plate with the catcher just ready to catch the ball; or something similar. Ask the children to draw a picture showing what happened.

4.   A game could be set up by handing out letters on tagboard cards. When each child has received a card, the teacher either calls out or holds up a card with a word printed on it. The children who have the letters that spell that word then arrange themselves in front of the room so that the cards they hold in front of themselves correctly spell the word.

5.   On index cards, write simple three- or four-step sets of directions: (1) Walk to the front of the room; (2) pick up a piece of chalk in your right hand and an eraser in your left hand; (3) skip to the left rear corner of the room; and (4) change hands with the chalk and eraser and leave them on the table. The child reads this once, lays the card down and does the action in the proper sequence. This could be made harder by adding further steps in the directions as the children get good at doing three and four things.

6.   Pictures can be sorted into the proper sequence by the children. Some examples could be: a boy going to school, clean, hair parted, clothes pressed; some part of his school day, recess

or seated at his desk; going home with his shirt-tail out, face dirty, shoe laces untied and dragging in the dust.

7.   Another example could be a series of pictures of the same child being measured against the wall, to be arranged to show his growth over a period of time.

8.   Sequence can be used in arranging dominoes in order, or one could even use the commercial card games.

9.   Pictures of objects could be sequenced by size. The objects themselves could be sequenced by *graduated* size (marbles, balls).

10.   Pictures of the same Boy Scout with an increasing number of merit badges on his sash would be good for sequence.

INCONGRUITIES

The list of possible pictures showing incongruities (something wrong or missing) is endless. Below are some suggestions. These pictures should be on sheets of paper so that the child can finish the picture or mark what is wrong.

1.   A hand with four fingernails.
2.   A boat with the wake extending from the front instead of the back.
3.   A clock numbered backward.
4.   A checker game with all the checkers the same color.
5.   A picture of a western shoot-out in which one combatant has striped candy canes in his holsters instead of six-shooters.
6.   A cowboy on a kangaroo.
7.   Pictures of incongruous animals, as a rabbit with horns, a frog with a long tail, a cow with a horse's mane, etc.
8.   Misplaced marks of punctuation, as an exclamation point at the end of a question, or a question mark at the end of a statement.
9.   Pictures of simple arithmetic problems, one of which has the wrong answer; or perhaps all have wrong answers.
10.   A bicycle with missing spokes in the wheel, or a pedal off, or perhaps a swim fin in the place of one pedal.
11.   A face without eyebrows.
12.   A shirt with no buttons visible.

There are many excellent commercially prepared games and pictures, magic cards, etc., available if the teacher does not care to or have time to assemble her own materials.

TRAINING THE   G
                                R
                                A   5
ABILITY TO CLASSIFY   D
                                E

1.   Matching pictures of objects: Ask the child to pair pictures of familiar objects as quickly as he can. Use a stop watch to effect a challenge if needed.

2.   Ask the child to cut out two each of different shapes from stiff paper. After this is done, mix them up and ask him to match them as quickly as he can.

SORTING OBJECTS

1.   Give the child a box containing many items, all in two or three categories, and have him sort and categorize them according to use, size, shapes, or color. (Examples: nuts, bolts, and washers; or buttons, poker chips, and steel washers.)

2.   The child can also sort such items as groceries—or knives, forks, and spoons into the proper trays—when he helps his mother in the kitchen (McCarthy, 1967).

3.   Slot boxes: Teach the child to sort spools by shape and size into slots in a box; or, to string the spools onto a string according to size, shape, and color.

SIMILARITIES

1.   Through the use of two overhead projectors and two screens (or white walls), project two scenes similar in nature. Ask the children to point out similarities and differences.

2.   Using a projector place transparencies with pictures of items arranged to include categories with one picture isolated from the others. For example:

Palomino	Clydesdale	Morgan	Palomino Horse
Horse	Horse	Horse	in different
			pose

Ask a child to note differences and name the horses. You should search through the proper journals for pictures of interest to fifth graders. These pictures may be placed in order on a sheet of paper, and transparencies may be made from the arrangement. Suggestions for categories are: farm equipment and animals, sports, household items, model planes, trucks, or cars.

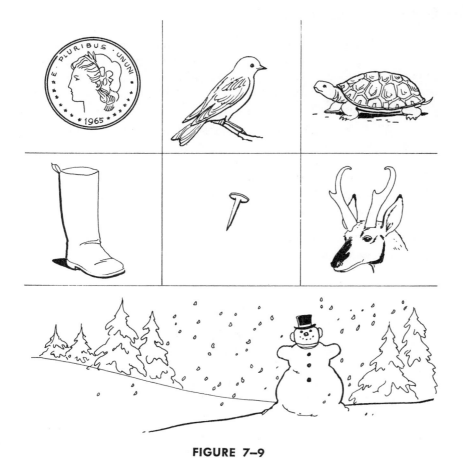

FIGURE 7–9

3. Pass out groups of pictures, such as those shown in Fig. 7.9, and ask the children to identify the picture that completes each of the following statements:

    a. The boy moves with the grace of an *antelope*.
    b. The girl has the voice of a *canary*.
    c. The dress is white as *snow*.
    d. The pace was as slow as a *turtle*.
    e. The new car shines like a *silver dollar*.
    f. The meat was as tough as a *boot*.
    g. The student is sharp as a *tack*.

4. Making designs: Show the child a design on a block or card and have him construct the designs using shapes which have been cut out prior to the training session. Then ask him to try to make the same designs on the blackboard with chalk, or at his desk with pencil or crayon.

RECOGNIZING THE INCONGRUOUS

1.   Tell the child stories with incongruities, and help him to recognize what is wrong by using picture cards that show the incongruous element. Or, have the child match the incongruities so they make sense (e.g., a dog riding a bicycle matched with a boy barking at a cat).

2.   Write sentences like the ones suggested below, and have the child spot the errors, cross them out, and fill in the correct form.
   a.   The man *eight* his lunch.

   b.   That boy can run like a *dear*.

   c.   I will *except* the honor.

3.   Use visual-motor coordination exercises, where the child will add to a picture that which has been left out or is not complete.

THE ABILITY TO CLASSIFY   G R A D E 6

1.   Show the pupils pictures of farm animals, such as cows, horses, pigs, sheep, goats, ducks, chickens. Talk about the pictures in relationship to the concept of domesticated animals.

2.   Show pictures of wild animals such as lions, elephants, zebras, hippopotamuses, giraffes, tigers, crocodiles. Help pupils to understand the difference between wild animals and domesticated animals.

3.   Bring in pictures of various pets such as cats, dogs, goldfish, parakeets. Help pupils to understand the meaning of this "pet" classification of animals.

4.   Assemble pictures of various machines and tools for different industries. A good starting place might be tools related to yard work: lawn mower, rake, hoe, shovel, lawn edger, digging fork. Help pupils to understand how these tools are related.

SORTING

The ability to sort objects, pictures, and symbols by use, shape, size, or color can be developed by exercises such as these:

1. Which group does not belong with the others?

   a.   bbbbb   bbbdb   bbbbb   bbbbb

   b.   pppqp   ppppp   ppppp   ppppp

   c.   ppppp   qqqqq   qqqqq   qqqqq

   d.   ddddd   ddddd   ddddd   dddbd

2. Which numeral does not belong in each line?

   a.   2, 4, 5, 6, 8, 10, 12

   b.   1, 3, 5, 7, 9, 10, 11

   c.   5, 10, 15, 13, 25, 30

   d.   3, 6, 9, 12, 16, 18, 21

   e.   1, 3, 9, 18, 27

   f.   2, 4, 8, 16, 20, 32, 64

3. Which word does not belong in each line?

a.	duck	chicken	pig	goose
b.	bear	deer	canary	fox
c.	sheep	goat	horse	zebra
d.	cat	dog	whale	snake
e.	canoe	gunboat	steamshovel	raft

Give pupils practice sorting objects that go together on the basis of color. Beads, poker chips, or marbles may be used for this—virtually all classrooms will have one of these. Impromptu exercises can be arranged as needs arise.

Cut out triangles, circles, squares, pentagons, and hexagons from construction paper. Give pupils practice associating these shapes. For example, hand the pupil a circle and ask him to pick one like it from a group of geometric shapes. Hand him a square and repeat the process.

SEQUENCING

1. Prior to the class period, record a story using the tape recorder. After the student listens to the story, instruct him to arrange the events in sequential order. Write the events on strips of paper ahead of time, so that the student can manipulate them without having to copy them first.

2. The technique used above can be used with other stories to train pupils to learn what comes first, what comes next, etc. Tape recording the stories is a good idea.

3.   Clip out comic strips (of the four-panel type to begin with) and cut them into individual panels. Let the pupils practice arranging these in the right sequence. Particularly good comic strips which you wish to keep may be pasted on cardboard to make them more durable.

RECOGNIZING THE INCONGRUOUS

1.   Duplicate the pictures of Fig. 7.10. Ask the pupils to find what is missing in each picture.

2.   Duplicate the pictures of Fig. 7.11. Have your pupils find the distortion in each picture.

3.   Secure from magazines some pictures which you will cut into four parts and arrange in a different order from the way the picture appeared originally. Have the pupils arrange the picture in the correct way. Colored pictures are more readily enjoyed by the pupils, and variety in size will also add to this enjoyment.

TRAINING THE

ABILITY TO CLASSIFY   G R A D E S **7 & 8**

1.   Collect a large number of pictures, photographs, drawings, and sketches. Ask each student to select from the group those that relate to a given subject. (Examples of such categories: football, baseball, basketball, golf, fishing, hunting, automobiles, spacecraft, astronauts, cooking, sewing, clothing, homes, school buildings, churches, cowboys, animals, farming, lakes, guns, rivers, boats, Indians, and others.)

2.   Give the student some word cards, asking him to sort them (big-bigger-biggest; short-shorter-shortest). In this exercise the student would select the cards with the appropriate characteristics, but the sequencing of the cards would come at a later time.

3.   Give the student a group of cards including number cards, word cards, picture cards, and others, and ask him to group them properly. (Example: The student might be given three cards with numbers, three with pictures, three cards, each with a single word, and three cards with a paragraph of writing. The student then would arrange the cards in four groups as listed above.)

Find what is missing in each picture.

FIGURE 7–10

Find the distortion in each picture.

FIGURE 7–11

4. Play games similar to the TV programs of *Password*, *Match Game*, and others.

SORTING

1. Provide a number of hand tools from which each student selects those that would be used in a given trade or activity, such as carpentry, mechanics, gardening, sewing, cooking, hunting, fishing, writing and drawing.

2. Give the student some craft work, such as simple plaiting, weaving, or braiding, in which a simple pattern is repeated. This is an activity that develops color sense.

3. Use play coins in various ways. For instance, the student could arrange the coins by size, value, or engraving (heads or tails).

4. Have the student perform tasks of measuring—a student could measure three other students to determine their height. Or, students could measure the room, a desk, or a car to see the relative size of each object. If the room were thirty feet long, five or six boys could lie down to get a better understanding of the size.

5. Use jigsaw puzzles. Perhaps the first could be one of the United States. This would help the students in understanding the relative location and size of the different states. The students could plot imaginary trips between two cities, such as their home town and the nation's capital. This will aid them in understanding direction, distance, location, and geographic features.

SEQUENCING

1. Give the student a stack of books and ask him to sort them. He could arrange them from shortest to tallest, from thinnest to thickest, from dullest to brightest, and by subject matter.

2. Use card games to teach sequence. (Examples: *Old Maid*, *Books*, *Rummy*, *Solitaire*, and other commercial card games.)

3. Give the student word cards to be arranged in the proper sequence (big-bigger-biggest, hot-hotter-hottest, slow-slower-slowest).

4. Use historical events and occasions. Have cards with such wording as *Revolutionary War, 1776; Civil War, 1861; First World War, 1917;* let the student place the events in proper sequence.

5.   Use number cards, and let the student place them in even and odd order.

6.   Use Crossword puzzles, criss-crosses, and other puzzles.

RECOGNIZING THE INCONGRUOUS

Give the student a group of word cards in which a series pertains to a given subject and one is incongruous. The student will then select those that properly relate to each other. Some possible categories are states, cities, verbs, nouns, adjectives, and objects. Or, use picture cards instead of word cards.

CB ACTIVITIES

Exercise 1

Draw a design on paper showing two lanes on a highway and designate the directions.
Ask the following questions:
1.   Why would Driver #1 call Driver #2 an *East Bounder?*
2.   Why would Driver #1 say that he was a *West Bounder?*
3.   Which direction would Driver #1 be asking about if he said, "What's it like over your shoulder?"
4.   Why would Car #1 be called a *four-wheeler?*
5.   Why would Car #2 be called an *eighteen-wheeler?* (Any large truck is called an *eighteen-wheeler.*)

Exercise 2

Match the following:
1.   double nickel (c)   a. 10-20
2.   mile marker (d)   b. 10-04
3.   ten-four (b)   c. 55
4.   ten-twenty (a)   d. roadside number every mile
5.   location (a)   e. yes
6.   negatory (g)   f. Breaker
7.   affirmative (e)   g. no
8.   CBer asking for channel (f)

Visual Closure

Visual closure ability is the ability to make perceptual interpretation of any visual object when only a part of it is shown. Studies on visual closure have been made by the earlier Gestalt psychologists and the term is a part of their principles of organization. Relative to the closure process, most studies have involved the visual modality.

If a child shows a deficiency in the visual closure process, follow these guidelines while teaching her in a group situation:

1. Permit her to first trace correct copies.
2. Allow ample time for processing the visual stimulus.
3. Provide adequate light with no reflections.
4. Use auditory cues when possible.

VISUAL CLOSURE ᴳᴿᴬᴰᴱ **K**

1. Show the child incomplete representations of familiar objects—shadows or silhouettes—and ask him to identify them. (See Fig. 8.1.) Point out areas that are clues to identification and

NAME THE PICTURES

FIGURE 8–1

discuss them. Gradually introduce representations that are less distinct and therefore more complicated. For instance, ink blots or clouds with definite forms may be used.

2.   Pictures with forms such as witches or squirrels hidden in them are to be found in some children's magazines. The child identifies these hidden forms. Figure 8-2 presents an abstract design which contains a hidden picture.

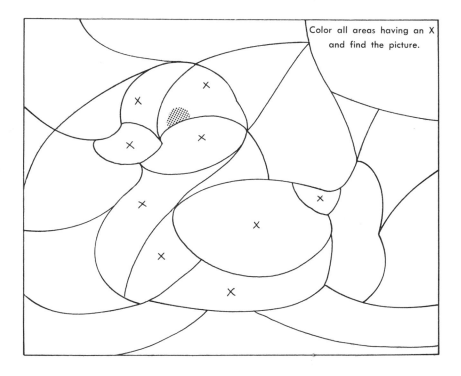

Color all areas having an X and find the picture.

FIGURE 8–2

3.   The child can complete forms, such as designs, by noting discrepancies between the model and the nearly identical, but incomplete, form. A similar activity requires him to connect a set of dots, or numbers. He must identify the form, if possible, before it is completed. Forms may be numbers, letters or pictures, as in Fig. 8.3.

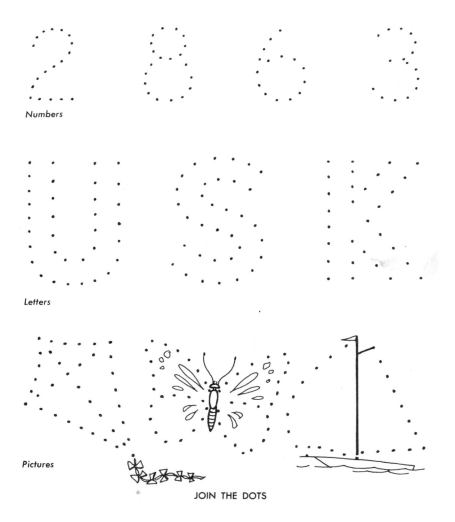

Numbers

Letters

Pictures

JOIN THE DOTS

FIGURE 8–3

4. Variations of Completion of Shapes.*
    a. Materials needed are overhead transparencies with partial shapes drawn on them. Flash partially completed shape on the board and let a child draw in the missing part. Perhaps two students could work on the board at once.
    b. Materials needed are poster board with partially drawn figures. Have children draw in the missing parts.

---

* By Wilma Jo Bush.

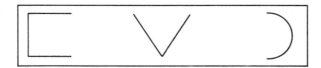

FIGURE 8–4

5. Guessing Game.* Materials needed are transparencies of objects. Flash a part of the picture on the board and see if children can identify it. Keep clearing more of the picture until it can be named. These pictures may be cut out of catalogs and pasted on typing paper for display in the game.

6. Find the Missing Part.* Materials needed are simple pictures of things the children know. Cut the pictures apart. Put one part in one place and the other part in another place. Pieces can be on a table, or standing in the chalk tray. Ask the children to match the parts. If sandpaper is on the back of the parts, the pictures could be put on the flannel board; or they could be pasted together on a large piece of paper. To make this activity more difficult, use pictures that are more complex and cut them into more pieces.

7. Completion I* Show a picture of an incomplete human figure to a child and ask him to complete the picture. Use figures of boys, girls, women, and men from catalogs and cut off one part of the body before showing the figure to the child.

8. Completion II* Cut out pictures of furniture, cars, trucks, or any common object from catalogs. Cut off one part and ask child to complete the picture.

9. Use five different stuffed animals and a 12″ x 12″ or 30 cm x 30 cm cardboard sheet. Have the children close their eyes. Cover the back portion of an animal with cardboard and ask what is missing. Do this activity in various ways with all the stuffed toys until the children become very skilled at this game.

10. Use flash cards with pictures of animals similar to the stuffed animals used previously. Cover half of the picture and ask what is missing. Play this game with many variations until the skill of memory is developed.

11. Arrange all stuffed animals behind chairs, boxes, tables, etc., leaving some parts showing to the class. Ask the children to describe what they are seeing; then ask them to name the animals.

* Visual Closure activities beginning with #9 (with the exception of the CB activities) are provided by Marian Giles.

12. Hold up a flash card picture partially covered and ask the children to identify the stuffed animal which matches the picture.

13. Make an overhead transparency of animal pictures leaving out parts of the animal bodies. Have the children move their fingers over the paper to indicate the missing parts of the bodies.

14. Make a ditto sheet from the previous drawing and ask the children to outline the animals and color them completely.

15. Using objects found in the home, such as a telephone, a broom, pots and pans, wastebaskets, and dishes, vary the learning activities as shown in items 9–14 previous.

16. Make ditto sheets showing strips of boxes containing the household objects drawn incompletely.

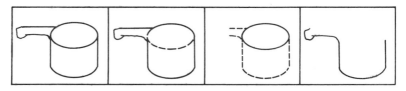

FIGURE 8–5

17. Show a picture of a boy or girl partially covered with a square of cardboard. Ask what part is missing. Check to see if all the children know all parts of the body.

18. Using stick-on material, let children find the missing parts of the boy and girl and stick them back on. The *Peabody Language Development Kit* kindergarten level has the complete materials for this activity.

19. Make up similar games with pictures of trucks, houses, furniture, buildings, farm animals, trees, and toys.

20. Vary these games by moving from concrete objects to pictures to individual worksheets.

21. Using pictures of five different subjects, as in number 19, supply paste and construction paper to the children and allow them to choose a picture and paste immediately on the colored paper. If the pictures are cut into parts, the game is more interesting. Let children hang their pictures in the classroom when completed.

22. You design 10 pictures of partially hidden animals. Ask children:

    a. How many animals do you see in each picture?
    b. What is this (pointing) animal?
    c. Is it a zoo animal or a farm animal?

  d. What parts are missing?

  e. Name the animals you see.

  23. Hide the pictures completely and ask what animals were in pictures #1, #2, etc.

  24. Have children close their eyes and revisualize the animals on the cards.

  25. Ask the children to draw their favorite animals that were on the pictures. Draw the whole animal. (Leave pictures out where children can see when necessary.)

GRADE 1

  1. *The Frostig Visual Perception Program* has hundreds of activities which help to develop visual closure abilities in young children. These activities are grouped under the title of *Figure-Ground Exercises*. There are also many exercises in *Pictures and Patterns* which Marianne Frostig and others at the Marianne Frostig Center for Educational Therapy developed. Directions for using these exercises are available in the excellent guides which accompany the programs. Frostig has stressed continuously that these activities are to be closely integrated with the child's regular reading and language curriculum. *They are not to be used in isolated drill sessions.* When one specific exercise is taught within the regular reading lesson, correlated with oral language, role playing, written activities such as spelling, and even math, the training transfers easily to skills necessary for reading and spelling. Teachers should use much variation and rich, creative ideas when correlating perceptual training with grade level content and subject matter.

  Many of the following suggestions for using the Frostig materials in training visual closure abilities in young children were contributed by Gad Alon, an educational therapist who taught at the Frostig Center for 6 years.

  For the first grade level, start with the easiest exercises and move rapidly on to more difficult activities. This technique is called *pacing* and is a critical technique for slow-learning children. The smoother the pace, the better comprehension develops. Remember to keep the child as relaxed as possible so that he is free to retain what he is learning.

  2. Using a figure-ground activity from the *Frostig Program*, the following variations can be presented.

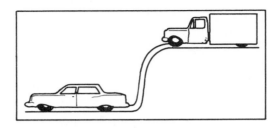

FIGURE 8–6

a. Ask what is shown in the picture.
b. Generalize to daily living. "Where have you seen one of these before?"
c. Categorize—trucks, cars, bus, train.
d. Discuss uses of each type of vehicle.
e. "Why do we carry people in cars and goods in trucks?"
f. Show pictures of trucks in a busy street and ask child to point out all of them, putting a ☐ on the one by the blue building, a △ on the one which is parked by the telephone pole, and an ◯ on the one by the red light, etc.
g. Ask the child to color the picture following directions, such as, color the truck yellow, color the road brown, color the car red.
h. Make up math problems, such as "How many trucks do we have? If we took away 3 of them, how many would be left?"

3.   Construct a dot-to-dot picture by having child place tracing paper over a simple drawing. With a pencil, make dots along the outline of the picture showing through the tracing paper. Remove the top paper and let the child complete the drawing, going from dot to dot.

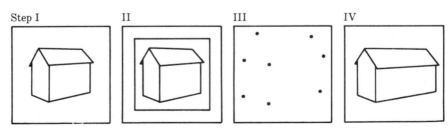

FIGURE 8–7

4.   Give the children a worksheet with six human figures partially completed.

FIGURE 8–8

The children are to complete each figure, making sure it has:

a. head (eyes, nose, mouth, ears, hair)   e. legs, feet
b. neck   f. chest
c. shoulders   g. trunk
d. arms, hands   h. clothing

After completing the drawings, the children may color them, cut them out, and paste them on construction paper in creative ways.

G
R
A 2
D
E

1. Train visual closure skills while learning to read and spell basic sight words which are difficult to spell phonetically. The Dolch sight words are excellent for this activity.

Example: A	B	C
1. then	1. then	1. t_e_
2. once	2. once	2. _nc_
3. there	3. there	3. __e_e
4. said	4. said	4. s__d
5. here	5. here	5. _er_

Have the children trace the *A* Column carefully. Next, have them close their eyes and write the words in the air. Then let them outline the words in dots in Column *B*. Fill in the missing letters in the same words written in Column *C* while verbalizing the words.

2.   Viewing objects through mirrors helps to train visual closure skills.

   a.   Put several objects on the table (for example, keys, book, pencil, vase).
   b.   Arrange them in a certain order you will remember.
   c.   Allow the student to look at the arrangement for 5 seconds.
   d.   Turn the student's back to the table and quietly rearrange the objects.
   e.   Have student look at the table through his hand mirror. Give verbal directions to put the objects back into the original order.

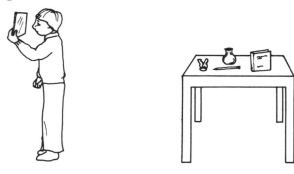

FIGURE 8–9

3.   Using jigsaw puzzles, have the child construct the puzzle while verbally describing the shapes needed one after the other. It sometimes gives better results to turn the puzzle facedown so that the child will have fewer clues for aid in construction.

Now and then, withhold pieces of the puzzle and let the child work around it, finally describing verbally the specific piece he needs for completion.

4.   Cut large pictures into odd pieces. Give the child one piece and let him try to describe the rest of the picture. This activity strengthens visual imagery and closure skills.

GRADE 3

1.   Using content from the basic social studies curriculum, have the students locate and outline with their index fingers specific places on a map in their textbooks.

2.   On a new piece of tracing paper, make dots over the outline of the map at ½ inch or 2.5 cm intervals. Remove the paper and complete the dot-to-dot drawing freehand.

3.   Color the map, cut it out, and paste it where it goes on a larger map of the specific area used by the whole class. For example, if each student is completing a different state, the whole U.S. map can be completed very quickly and accurately.

4.   Have students draw maps of the neighborhood where their school is located. Cut the map into pieces with boundaries made by streets/blocks. Place familiar markings on the blocks. Ask the pupils to put these pieces back in their correct places.

5.   Construct graphs and discuss what they mean to the reader. Why do graphs help you get a whole picture of what the story is about? Which do we remember better—a long paragraph, or a simple graph which tells the same information? Correlate this activity with the grade level content used in math, science, and social studies.

6.   Look at pictures in textbooks of regular subjects and ask questions which require close attention to details in the foreground, background or key figure of the picture. Use pictures of increasing difficulty until their visual closure ability is fully developed. After students become skilled at this task using two-dimensional pictures, have them look out the window and do the same thing with their own three-dimensional depth perception.

7.   Art activities are a great help in training visual closure skills. Have the child fold colored paper many times, each time unfolding it and counting the squares. Cutting the paper at designated places creates original designs. Verbalize as you work.

Note: Care must be taken at upper grade levels to correlate activities with the regular curriculum consistently. Never use isolated drill sessions which take valuable time for these exercises. Students at the pre-adolescent periods resent being removed from the grade level content even when they know they are falling behind their classmates. These ideas should be changed to fit the daily course content and sequence used in the particular grade level.

1.   Use a list of essential words which must be recognized immediately by sight. Note: if a student is riding his bike and

comes quickly upon a big box marked *Explosives*, he won't have the time to "sound it out"; he must recognize it by sight.

When teaching essential words (included here), use tracing techniques, visualizing with eyes closed, writing in the air or on one's other arm, connecting dots or a partial outline of the word, filling in missing letters, and rainbow writing on the board with colored chalk.

    a. Teacher writes the word on the board with large and relaxed movements.

    b. Student traces the word with index finger floating over the surface.

    c. With yellow chalk, student traces over the word.

    d. With green, blue, red, etc., student traces over the word until the rhythm and ease of writing flows through the arm and hand.

2. The following exercise will aid in the development of perceptual speed which is an integral part of visual closure.

    a. Use a tachistoscopic presentation of words and pictures. Have the child underline the same word on his worksheet which flashed on the screen through the tachistoscope. Gradually decrease the exposure times until the student reaches his limit for clear visualization.

    b. Develop rapid recognition of letters, words, short sentences, and pictures by using the tachistoscope regularly. Make up exercises using the vocabulary from the student's grade-level material. Science words make interesting games which also increase the motivation for practice.

3. Use graphs and charts found in social studies, math, and science textbooks to strengthen visual closure skills. Let students work in pairs, measuring each others' height with a measuring tape. Teach bar graphs with the measured heights of the class. Design questions to be answered from the information on the graph:

    a. Who are the three tallest boys in class?

    b. How many students are above the 4 foot mark; below 4 feet?

    c. How many students are exactly 4′2″?

    d. How many inches (centimeters) taller is Steve than Betty?

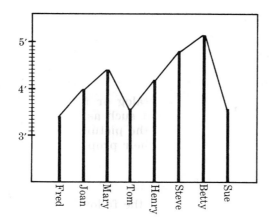

FIGURE 8–10

4. Students in the upper grades are usually very interested in space and astronomy. Use an astronomical map and divide the blocks into 5-inch squares. Have each student measure a 10-inch square on his paper. Teach the proportion of 2:1. Each student should then take one square and double its size. The stars and constellations should be two times bigger than the original. Display the students' work after they label their constellations.

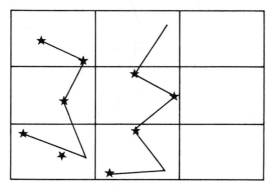

FIGURE 8–11

5. An excellent commercial game which aids in the development of visual closure abilities is *Star Chips* (Hughes, 1974). The game involves matching colors, number of dots, and the geometrical shapes of the chips. This motivating game for adolescents has countless patterns which can be made. The game may be purchased from Robert A. Hughes, Colorado Game Products, P. O. Box 475, Fort Morgan, Colo. 80701.

CB ACTIVITIES*

Exercise 1

Cut out pictures from a catalog or from CB brochures. Cut out parts of the CB equipment such as the speaker, knob, or a wire. Place these pieces from the picture in a row. Ask the student to place them back into their proper places very quickly.

Exercise 2

Ask the student to complete the following letters to make full words.

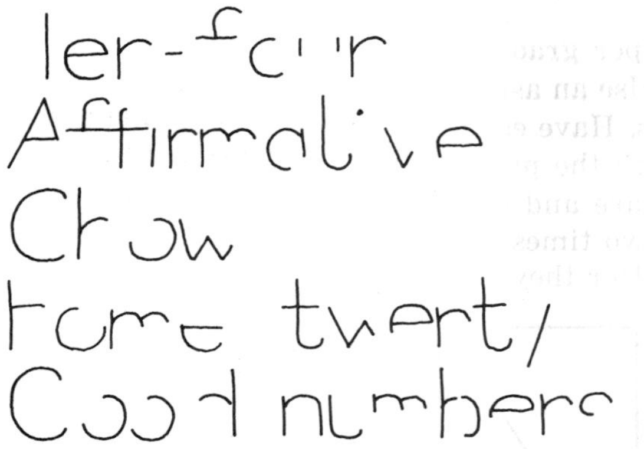

(Ten-four)
(Affirmative)
(Chow)
(Home-twenty)
(Good numbers)

Make up several series of words and place them on a stencil for duplicating. Practice daily with one series until the student is able to complete the assignment quickly.

---

* By Wilma Jo Bush.

⑨

Visual Memory

Visual memory refers to the ability to remember objects, events, or words seen. Some children may not remember these graphic symbols because of the distortions caused by visual form perception, visual figure-ground and visual-spatial problems. Others have difficulty remembering because content varies according to meaning; and for unknown reasons, some content is meaningless to some students. The teacher should include the following as a means of aiding the process of visual memory:

1. Use many auditory cues.
2. Write words that have been seen.

3. Organize information to include parsing, or divisions, e.g., as in telephone numbers, 352-4842.

4. Teach to overachievement.

5. Review daily the information that will be required on assessments.

G
R
A
D
E K

HOUSES

Watch for different kinds of houses that may be seen on the way home. Notice what materials they are made of. Ask, "What kind of house do you live in? Materials? Color? Size, such as apartment house? Brick? White? Two floors? One floor?"

SEQUENCING

Materials needed are cardboards with arrangement of designs on them.

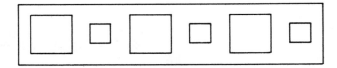

Have children reproduce the designs by pasting like figures on a piece of paper. For more advanced children, show the picture and then place it facedown and have them reproduce the arrangement by memory. Should a child need to see the master copy again, let her go look at the card. Some children could cut out the shapes and arrange them. Some children could draw the pattern.

WHO'S MISSING

Direct one child to turn her back to the group and to cover her eyes. Point to another child to leave the room. The remaining children quietly switch their positions. When "it" turns around and faces the group she must try to guess who is missing before the other children count to five slowly. The game is repeated with a new "it."

"I SEE"

Take a walk around the immediate neighborhood. Tell the children before you leave that they are going to try to see and *remember* as many things as they can. Choose one child at a time to point out all the things she sees and name them. You should provide an example: "I see a tall tree. I see the sidewalk. I see the lightpost. I see the grass." Encourage the children to see increasingly smaller or less conspicuous objects on subsequent trips—the cracks in the sidewalk, a paper cup in the gutter, clouds in the sky, house numbers.

THINK

Ask questions as follows: "What will we see if we go to a farm?" "What will we see if we go to the supermarket?" Other suggested places for imaginary trips are the park, the neighborhood, a shopping center, a pet store.

"TELL ME WHERE . . ."

You buy shoe laces? . . . You hang your coat? . . . You get your hair cut? . . . You sleep at night? . . . You got your pet? . . . Your grandparents live? . . . Your father works? . . . You play when you go home from school? . . . Most birds go in the wintertime? . . . Some animals sleep in the wintertime?"

ARRANGING STORIES

Have a child arrange a series of pictures to make a story. At first, three pictures represent a maximum. When the pictures are arranged, the child tells the story. Examples: A boy preparing dog food, a dog eating; mother preparing food, a family eating; a snowy scene, a man shoveling snow. A simple comic strip like "Peanuts" may be used after it has been cut apart, mounted on lightweight cardboard, and laminated.

TRACING

Material needed is transparency of figure to be flashed on chalkboard, or large sheet of paper and chalk, crayons, or felt-tip pen. Flash the picture on the chalkboard. Let the child trace it. Before the picture is complete, turn the machine off and let the child tell you what is needed to complete the picture. Turn the projector on again, and let the child complete the picture.

BODY TOUCH

Touch parts of the body in a lengthening sequence: head, knee, foot, ear. There are a number of children's songs which can be used for this type of activity and which introduce auditory vocal aspects. The children may play this game standing in a line; each child adds a new body part to touch. You may act as a leader. After you have performed the entire sequence (four or five touches, to begin with), the children perform the complete sequence.

TOUCH

You say, "I am going to point to one of you. That person will jump up, go across the room, and touch something—maybe the piano, maybe the table, a book, or anything in this room. Then she will sit down and I will point to some one else. That person will go touch the same thing the first person touched, and then touch one more thing before sitting down. The third person will have to remember both things that were touched before, touch them, and then think of something new to touch before sitting down. Now watch closely. Are you ready?" Point to the first child and repeat directions as necessary until the children can remember the game sequence. Help by asking, "What did Joe touch? What did Gary touch?"

You can play a more complicated form of this game by touching the children who set the touch pattern. For example, Mary touches the table. John touches Mary and the table, and then the pencil sharpener. Jane touches Mary, the table, John, the pencil sharpener, and then the floor. Harry touches Mary, the table, John, the pencil sharpener, Jane, the floor, and then a chair. (This game sounds more difficult than it actually is.)

DO AS THE SIGN SAYS

Make cards with signs on them.

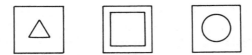

Give directions that include when the △ is shown, the children clap their hands. When the ☐ is shown they are to tap their toes. When the ○ is shown they are to do both at the same time. Activity could be changed from time to time.

STUFFED ANIMALS

Introduce one stuffed toy animal at a time. Read a story about it, if you have one at hand. Discuss: "What do they eat? Where do they live? Would they make a good pet? Draw a picture or write a few sentences telling or showing what you would do with the animal shown." After several stuffed animals have been introduced, arrange them in the order of the students' choice. Push them in a pile and ask a child to arrange them just like they had been. Arrange them in order, hide them, and remove one. Ask a child to name the one that was taken away.

I SPY—COLOR GAME

Hide five colored balls made of construction paper or bean bags around the room where the children can find them. Choose five children to hide their eyes. When the signal "ready" is spoken, these children walk to find the balls. When a ball is found, the player would say, "I spy a red ball," etc., and bring the ball to the circle. When all balls have been found, those who found them hide them again.

WHAT IS MISSING?

Use cards with outlined figures which have something missing. Have children identify the missing part. Discuss the use of object and experiences a child might have had with it. "Where would it be found?"

COMPLETION OF SHAPES

Materials needed are overhead projector; transparencies of plain outline of simple picture; chalk, chalkboard, or large sheet of butcher paper or newsprint. Flash picture on the chalkboard or paper. Identify the picture. Have the child trace the figure. Before it is complete, cut off the projector and let the child tell you what it lacks for completion. Turn light back on and let her complete it.

MY SHADOW

Materials required are child-size pieces of wrapping paper and black felt-tipped markers. Place a piece of wrapping paper on the floor. Direct a child to lie down on the paper. Trace her outline with the felt marker. Take care to include details like five fingers, shoelaces, and special identifying outlines such as pigtails. Hang the outline picture on the wall at floor level so that the child may closely compare herself with her outline. Later the child may add with crayons her features and her clothing. The items of clothing should be made to correspond in color with the clothing the child is wearing that day.

ACTION-MEMORY GAMES   G R A D E 1

Remedial exercises with first graders could begin with action games.

1. You will demonstrate patterns by using your hands and arms in a variety of ways. The children are to repeat these patterns from memory after each presentation. Examples:

    a. Place hands together with palms pressing.
        Place hands apart.
        Place hands together (as in first position).
    b. Right arm up.
        Right arm down.
        Right arm outstretched.

All activities are silent ones. The children must try to remember what they have seen.

2. A Game: Three children arrange themselves in a row. Another child looks at them, then covers his eyes as the three children "scramble" or take their seats. The child then goes to each of the three, takes him by the hand, and arranges him in

the original order. (More children can become involved as competence in the game increases.)

USE OF HANDS

As the child develops in motor control, hand exercises involving sequencing can be introduced. This should aid in the transition from large-muscle activities to the use of pencil and crayon.

Hand Signals

Signals should be worked out, understood, and practiced individually before introduction of sequence. (Some signals which could be used: one finger held up, two fingers, and so on; a circle made with index finger and thumb; crossed fingers.) When the child can make these signals, the teacher patterns two or three and the child copies them in order. As the child is able to use a crayon or pencil with success, these signals could be written instead of, or in addition to, begin copied by the hand. (1, 11, 111, X, O, etc.)

Arranging Objects

Various objects are arranged in a sequence by the teacher. They are then removed and the child rearranges them in correct order. Begin with two or three. Some objects which might be used: wooden geometric blocks, buttons, toys (different toys at first—later, toys alike except for color, a missing part, or other subtle difference), beads, sea shells. This activity might be initiated by having two identical sets of objects and letting the child copy the arrangement made by the teacher. It might also be varied by taking one object out of the pattern and letting the child find the missing object from a selection of other objects and replace it in the pattern.

Arranging Pictures

A child looks at an arrangement of pictures selected without any particular association. After they are removed and shuffled, the child arranges them in the original order. Pictures with associations may also be used, i.e., pictures of trees depicting the seasons, pictures of animals in stages of growth, etc.

Pictures which illustrate a very simple and familiar story or nursery rhyme may be arranged in order as the story is told; then they can be shuffled and rearranged by the child. These pictures should be mounted on cardboard or tag board and pre-pared for use both on the flannelboard and a table or desk, so that the child can have practice with several planes (horizontal and vertical).

USE OF PENCIL AND CRAYON

When the child is able to use pencil or crayon with success, present the following activities.

1. Copying patterns: The child can trace simple patterns and designs at first, then follow dots which form a pattern. Simple patterns and designs may be mimeographed with an area left on the paper for the child to copy them. Later, very simple designs can be copied from memory. The teacher might have a supply of these designs made on cardboard or tag, and they could be colored.

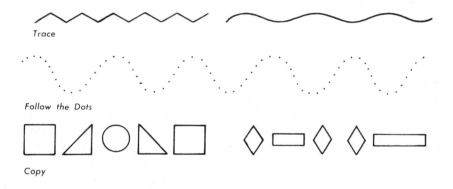

Trace

Follow the Dots

Copy

USE OF LETTERS AND NUMBERS

When a child has become familiar with numbers and letters (not necessarily complete knowledge), these activities can be used.

1. Writing Name: With letters cut from felt, wood, or sand-paper, write the child's first name. Let him copy it until he can do it from memory. If he has a long first name, you might be able to shorten it with a nickname, or help him learn it by spacing two or three letters at a time. Later, write the name on paper with the same letter style, and let the child copy it with the cut-out letters.

2. Spelling: Paste words of sandpaper or felt on tag-board cards and add a picture of the word. For instance:

Cat

Let the child trace the letters with his finger, then copy the word with identical letters on the flannelboard or on his desk. Remove the card after he has had some practice, and let the child assemble the word from memory; give him back the card and let him check his word and correct it, if necessary. Be free with help and praise.

3. Numbers: The sequence of numbers can be learned with numbers cut of felt, sandpaper, or other materials. (They can even be made with pipe cleaners.) Wooden blocks with numbers painted on them or wooden cut-out numbers may also be used. At first, let the child arrange numbers in order, using some form from which to copy. Then let him arrange from memory, using only two or three at a time, until he can arrange up to nine or ten.

When number order is thoroughly learned, let the child use the same method to: (1) arrange numbers not in order, (2) arrange and copy pairs of numbers, (3) find a missing number from numbers in order, having several sets of numbers from which to pick. Or, allow the child to look at a short series of numbers not in order, then remove one as the child hides his eyes, and ask him to find the missing number from a selection of several numbers.

G
R
A
D
E

VISUAL MOTOR ACTIVITIES

1. Plan a game, such as **Fruit Basket Turn-over**, where children change seats. Then ask a child to see if he can direct the children back to their original seats. This could be changed and elaborated upon by scrambling numbered cards, or different colored cards, or alphabet cards. Each time, the child establishes the correct sequential order, thus strengthening his sequential memory.

2. Place pictures of activities which tell a story on a flannel-board. Then ask the child to group the pictures in a sequence

that makes a story he can tell. Pictures might be of a boy, bicycle, ball, house, park.

3. Divide a story—*The Three Little Pigs*, for instance—into three parts. Arrange a simple playlet with four characters. A wolf and the three pigs could act out the story. (Make simple masks from paper.) Put three or four sentences on the board and ask the children to write them in the order in which they happened.

4. Have a child look at a page in a picture dictionary or catalogue and then try to recall the pictures. No particular order or sequence of response should be emphasized initially, but sequencing is the ultimate goal.

5. *Nicky* (first grade), and *Uncle Funny Bunny* (second grade), (Young *et al.*, 1961), have good exercises in sequencing.

6. Place objects or geometric cut-outs on a tray or on stiff cardboard. After showing these to the children, rearrange them; then ask a child to place them back in the original order. Change the design; add to or take from the number as progress is made.

7. Have the child trace dot-to-dot pictures using numbers or the alphabet. Books of these may be purchased at any variety store or you can create your own. Begin with 1-1 and work toward 1-20 as progress is made. Use only eight or ten letters to begin with and write the sequence at the top of the paper.

8. Place several objects before the child for him to name. Then have him turn around or close his eyes while you remove one of the objects. Ask him to recall which is missing. Gradually this can be expanded to removing two or more items. The items could be a car, truck, gun, airplane, book, eraser, glass, ball, or other things found in the classroom.

9. Continental Press publishes a group of stories designed for exercise in sequencing. They are read to the child, who lists the events of the stories in the order in which they occurred.

10. The child carefully observes a row of pictures and, after the pictures are removed, names the pictures in their proper order. Pictures would be those of animals, toys and people.

11. Write consecutive numbers from 1 to 15 on the chalkboard in three columns, spaced vertically about six inches apart and horizontally about twelve inches apart. The following short simple words could be used also:

cat   toy   dog
hat   go   on
tin   pet   fun

Have each child stand about five feet from the board and read aloud the words in each line. After reading the last word of one line, he should, without moving his head, shift his eyes very quickly to the next line and see how rapidly he can follow the word just read with the first word of the new line.

12. Put several objects on the reading table. Talk about them and let all the children view them. Ask one child to leave the room and, while he is gone, remove one object from the table. When the child returns, ask him to tell what was removed. Limit the number of guesses according to ability of the group. The more objects on the table, the more difficult the game.

13. When the child is learning to write his name, give him a piece of heavy tagboard with the name written on it, and allow him to trace it.

14. Children with a problem in visual-motor sequencing feel more successful when they are allowed to trace. It gives them an opportunity to be pleased with what they have produced. An ice cream lid saved from lunch in the cafeteria can be used by the child to develop and reproduce many designs and pictures.

15. To teach the child to write numerals or letters, show him "in the air" with large muscle movements before attempting to do it at the board or on paper.

16. Draw the following forms in black ink on 6 x 6 white cards or on tagboard:

Expose one of the forms for five seconds. Then have the child reproduce the figure on the chalkboard. This activity may be gradually increased in difficulty by exposing two figures at a time, then three, and so on. If individual flannelboards and shapes are available, use them. Put one of the shapes on your flannelboard and ask the child to put the same one on his. At first you will need to leave yours in place until the child has done his. Later, you can remove the pattern before the child starts to reproduce it. Make the shapes from flannel and felt scraps or colored construction paper if necessary.

17. There are many mazes that can be made, and many that can be bought commercially. Dot-to-dot pictures with numerals or alphabet letters can also be used. (These are often found in the Sunday "funnies.") Most teachers are familiar with these things, but one activity that might be new to some is the "Chalk Talk." First, show the child the completed picture, and then proceed to do it with him.

18. Let a child go to the window, look out, and return to his seat. See how many things he can name in the order he saw them through the window.

19. Picture pages of old workbooks or textbooks may be pasted on tag board and cut to be placed in correct order.

20. Finding hidden objects in a large picture (an activity often to be found in *Highlights For Children*, *Humpty Dumpty*, and *Children's Digest* magazines) can be done in an order specified by the teacher.

21. Paste a picture that children would like on heavy cardboard and cut up into squares like a jigsaw puzzle. Have the child assemble it.

22. Have the child arrange in sequence pictures illustrating the steps of a task. Comic strips would be good for this.

23. Have the child observe numerical patterns of red and black checkers. Then mix the order and ask him to recall the original pattern.

24. Have the student read numbers from the telephone book, particularly his own number and his friends' numbers. Have him repeat a number until he can remember it, then dial the number using a toy telephone.

25. Use an overhead projector to show various groupings of numbers, pictures or letters. Let the child look, then cover one picture and have him guess which one you have covered.

26. Make pictures of the rainbow out of scrap construction paper. Take a color away and let the child guess which color it was.

27. Make a pattern of wooden beads, old beads, or various buttons. Let the child look for a few seconds, then see if he can repeat the pattern.

28. Sand and paint variously-shaped scrap blocks from the lumber yard. Arrange them in a sequence, then remove one and let the child guess which one was removed.

G
R
A
D
E
3

MOTOR ACTIVITIES

1. Using a small group of children, give each child a letter-card. The teacher (or another child) holds up a word-card for about five seconds, then takes it down. The children with the letter-cards then arrange themselves in correct order to spell the word.

2. A variation of the preceding activity: After the children with letter-cards form themselves in correct order to spell a word, ask another child to study the word for about five seconds. Then have the children with letter-cards scramble, and ask the other child to rearrange them so as to spell the word correctly.

3. The same activity may be varied for use with only two people. A child is given several letter-cards. After he has observed a word for a few seconds, he attempts to arrange his letter-cards so as to spell the word correctly. This could be used with the spelling words for the week.

4. Use "Scissorettes" shapes, such as those in Fig. 9.1, cut from stiff paper or cardboard. Glue small magnets on the backs of the shapes. On a magnetic board make a design or simple picture from the shapes. After the child has viewed the design or picture for a few seconds, remove the shapes and ask him to rearrange them in the same design. (*Note:* If you do not have a magnetic board, a metal stove protector, found in most variety stores, is a good substitute. It can be used on an easel, chalk tray, or laying flat on table or desk.)

5. Scissorettes shapes may also be cut from felt or flannel and used on a flannelboard.

6. Draw any kind of figure or design on stiff paper or cardboard. Have the child lay colored string or yarn on the design, following the lines carefully.

7. Give the child three or four, or more, sheets of paper and have him place them side by side. Tell him to number the sheets

BASIC SCISSORETTES SHAPES

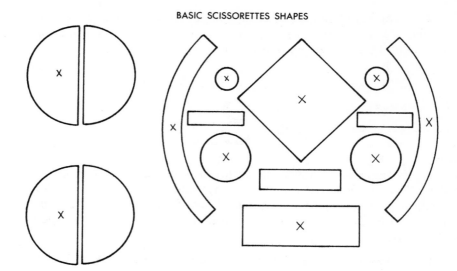

(Note: The figures which have X's on them may
be cut from black, or other colored paper.)

FIGURES

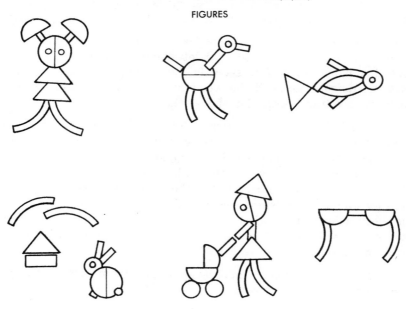

FIGURE 9–1

(Scissorettes shapes reproduced by permission of *Highlights For
Children*)

from left to right. On sheet number one, have him draw a worm; on sheet number two, a chick with his beak close to the ground; on sheet number three, a chick with a worm in his mouth. Scramble the sheets, and let the child rearrange them in sequential order. He may or may not tell a story to go with the drawings.

Other sequences which might be used are:

a. Number one, a mouse hole in a wall; number two, a mouse; number three, a cat looking around a corner; number four, a cat licking his chops (or, to have the mouse "triumph," the cat could have a mousetrap on his tail or nose).

b. Number one, an open bird cage; number two, a bird flying through the air; number three, a cat with a feather in his mouth; number four, several feathers in the air.

As the child rearranges these in sequential order, he may or may not want to tell his own story about what happened in them.

8. In the preceding activity, the teacher might draw the pictures herself, then let the child rearrange them in sequential order.

9. Write on the board a simple word, perhaps one which has already been introduced to the child. Let him look through magazines for samples of the letters that form the word. When he has found the letters, let him paste them on a sheet of paper and draw a picture that represents the word.

10. Draw story figures on pasteboard or cardboard; make them as large as the child, but not too bulky for him to handle. Leave holes for the child's face to be the face of the figure and

for his hands to hold it (see figure). As you read or tell a story, have the children arrange themselves as the characters are introduced. After the story, the "characters" scramble and another child puts them back in the right order.

11. Here are some of the things which may be arranged in a sequence for the child to view, scramble, and rearrange.

a. Library books: Choose several books which are simple to read, yet within the child's interest level. This may also be a means of interesting the child in reading one or more of the books for himself.

b. Geometrical designs, some of which may be found in Fig. 9.2.

GEOMETRIC DESIGNS

FIGURE 9–2

c. Cookies of various shapes: If these are wrapped in transparent paper, the children may enjoy eating them after a successful (or even unsuccessful) try at arranging them in sequence.

d. Indian designs.

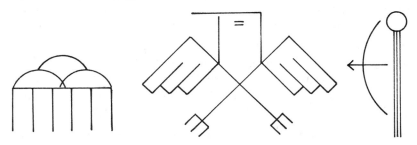

e. Seasonal symbols: You can concentrate on one season of the year (witch, jack-o-lantern, ghost, goblin, black cat for Halloween), or mix symbols of various holidays throughout the year. The latter could be sequenced in the order of occurrence through the year. (Examples: January—snowman, snowflake, or a large 1 on a card; February—picture or silhouette of Lincoln, Washington, or a valentine; March—shamrock; April—Easter egg, bunny; May—basket of flowers, Maypole; June—flag for Flag Day; July—firecracker, liberty bell; August—bright sun, autumn leaf; September—school house, autumn leaf; October—mentioned above; November—turkey, pumpkin, shock of hay; December—Christmas tree, gift, star.)

f. Stars of graduated sizes; or any other shape of various sizes.

g. Flowers of all kinds.

h. Letters of the alphabet: These may be various letters, or the same letter in varying sizes or several types of manuscript.

i. Animals: Several sizes of the same animal or various animals.

j. Fruits and/or vegetables.

k. Alphabet blocks with different letters turned up, or wooden blocks which are various shapes.

l. Hats of all kinds.

m. Musical instruments.

n. Coins: in descending or ascending order of value.

o. Words.

12. Help a child type his name or a sentence or his spelling words. Using a primary typewriter, show him the position of the letters contained in one word at a time (or portions of longer words). Then let him type the word, remembering where the letters are on the typewriter keyboard.

13. On a tray or table arrange various articles, such as a book, pencil, spool of thread, vase, box, leaf, doll, and paper of pins. Have the child observe what is on the tray. Then mix these articles with a few others and let him pick out the original ones, replacing them on the tray in their original pattern.

14. Dot-to-dot pictures may be used for the child to trace. Dots are sequenced either by numerals or letters. (See Fig. 9.3.)

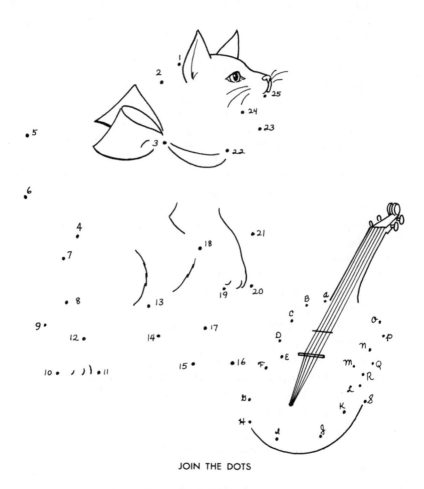

JOIN THE DOTS

FIGURE 9–3

G
R
A 4
D
E

SUGGESTED ACTIVITIES

1.　Cartoons have both motivational and sequential value. Use a series of picture cards showing a story sequence. The pictures (with no words) may be taken from comic strips, or found in readiness books. The child is to arrange them into the most meaningful sequence. Comic strips that might be useful include *Henry* and *Peanuts*.

Later, use comic strips with some words (which would help the child to arrange the pictures in sequence). This activity leads to future auditory-motor sequence exercises.

2.　This activity is to encourage careful observation of details in a picture. Three cards show the three basic meals of the day. Instruct the child to note the details of the pictures and to arrange them in relation to his own eating experiences.

3.　Another similar activity uses a series of cards showing such items as a lunch sack, a milk carton, napkin, sandwich, candy bar, and a trash can (see figure). Have the child arrange them in the sequence he would use them if he were going to picnic in a nearby park. First he would probably open the sack, take out the napkin, open the milk, eat the sandwich, eat the candy bar, and then place the sack and wrappers in the nearby trash can.

4. A series of beads having various shapes and colors is used for this activity. Briefly show the child a drawing of the arrangement of beads, then cover it. From memory, he strings or arranges the beads in the same sequence.

5. To move into geometric shapes from the above activity would be beneficial. Show the child a drawing of squares, rectangles, triangles, and circles, and have him try to remember how the shapes were arranged. These shapes could be arranged in various ways, starting with only a few and continuing into more and various shapes.

6. Following geometric shapes, this activity gives meaningful practice in both reasoning and motor sequencing. Five cards show a series of lines and range from one line to a figure with a five-line combination. The child is to sequence them from the simplest to the most complex. The card series could be extended so that the figures would contain more lines.

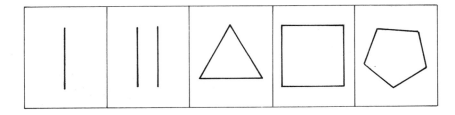

7. Show a drawing of blocks to the child and have him arrange his own blocks to match the drawing. This activity should follow the previous ones because of its complex nature. The drawing offers more of a challenge than an actual setup of the blocks. However, it may be necessary to use the actual setup of the blocks at first.

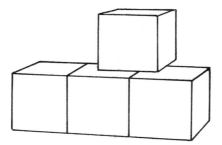

8.   These same procedures could be used with words. Start with one-syllable words, and use either or both of these methods. On a card, write the word for the child while he watches, or have the word already written for him. The child looks at the word, noticing configuration and letter sequence. Turning the card over, he writes the word and then checks it with the original to see if it is correct. These cards may be filed alphabetically in a box for future use.

From this activity, advanced children could even go into foreign words. This ties in with auditory-motor sequence, and would be good for the later grades and for children who are interested in beginning a foreign language.

9.   This activity is beneficial for visual-motor sequencing and provides drill in telling time. Any number of cards can be used. The cards show clock faces with the hands in different positions. Tell the child to arrange them from the earliest in the morning to noon. He might explain what he would be doing at each of the times marked on the cards (sleeping, eating, getting to school, recess, math, etc.). From this, he could even draw a series of pictures depicting the above activities of his daily life and arrange them in sequential order.

10.   This activity would be fitting with social-studies and science discussions. A group of pictures could show a series of steps that a certain product must go through to get to us. This drawing shows cotton from the tiny plant, the mature plant, cotton picking, ginning, cloth, and finally the final shirt or product. Other products such as wheat or paper could be used in the same manner.

11.   Pictures could be arranged by the students to make compound words. Later the child could use three cards combining endings with pictures to make new words (horseshoe, houseboat; carpenter, grasshopper).

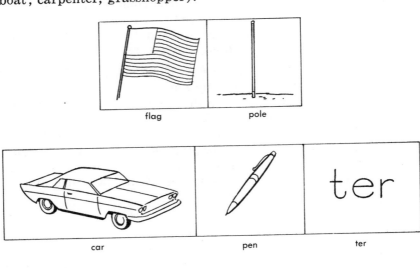

flag   pole

car   pen   ter

FINE MOTOR MOVEMENTS   G R A D E 5

1.   Select colorful, meaningful pictures from magazines. Cut them into pieces like a jig-saw puzzle. Tell the child what the picture represents and ask him if he can put it together so that the story is made into a picture. (*Note:* It is very important to choose pictures of interest to a fifth grade child. The tutor will

need to become familiar with the interests of an individual child.)

2. The Sunday Supplements have interesting sequencing games which vary by the week. Cut these out and keep a supply on hand. The Join-the-Dots game is one of the common ones which all ages appear to enjoy.

3. Using flannel, cut out designs of various shapes. Place them on a flannelboard according to difficulty. Let the child view them for five to ten seconds. Then have him reproduce the order of designs from memory.

4. From any printed source, cut out words that are a part of a child's vocabulary. Have the child arrange these in meaningful sentences. Encourage him to talk as he works, to see if it will help him think sequentially. Be sure there are enough words to make the sentences.

5. Choose cards containing the reading and spelling words for one week. Flash these before the child quickly, three at a time. Have him repeat the three in correct order. The number can be increased according to the child's ability.

6. Visit hobby shops and select unique commercial puzzles. If individual tutoring is done, let the child help select the puzzles. Encourage the child to explain his choice of each puzzle piece as he puts the puzzle together. This last step is a very essential part of a sequencing activity. The feedback is an aid to remembering in most instances.

7. Cut pictures of houses having different shapes. Lay them out in a pattern and have the student observe them. Mix them, then ask him to reassemble them in the original order. The number of items will be determined by the needs of the student.

8. Use the Fernald method of employing visual and kinesthetic stimuli simultaneously with new words (Fernald, 1943). Have the child say the word, letter by letter, as he traces over the pattern with his finger. He may also trace the letters in the air. After ample practice, he should be able to write the word from memory.

9. Buy books which contain mazes from hobby shops. Have the child complete one of the mazes at each tutoring session. Progress from the very simple to mazes which are more difficult.

SEQUENCING SITUATIONS

How to Make a Bed

Type each instruction on a separate strip of paper for the child to rearrange, or write them in the wrong order on the board.

1. Tuck the sheet under the mattress.
2. Put the pillow case on the pillows.
3. Put the mattress cover on securely.
4. Get the clean sheets from the shelf.
5. Put the top spread on and smooth out neatly.
6. Place the top sheet on and tuck in at the end of the bed.

Raking Leaves

Use the same technique as in bed-making.

1. Get large bushel basket.
2. Put on work clothes.
3. Pull the rake across the grass.
4. Empty basket in the containers in the alley.
5. Fill the bushel basket.
6. Put on work gloves.

SEQUENCING DIRECTIONS

1. Write on the board directions from one main point—whether it be the movie theater, shopping section, or some nearby store—to the school. The directions should be out of sequence. Let a child go over the directions as they are and place them in correct order by numbers or in some other way. The sequencing may begin at the school and progress to a nearby point, or it may begin at the nearby point and end at the school. Example:

1. Begin at   *(store name)*   .
2. Turn to your   *(left on street name)*   .
3. Turn to your   *(right on street name)*   .
4. Straight ahead to   *(school name)*   .

The same activity can be applied to directions coming to or going away from the home room (to the principal's office, for instance).

2. Variations of the above may include sentences with directions in correct order as to right or left, but the street names may be left out. The child should fill in the blank spaces. Example:

1. Start at _____.
2. Go one block on _____.
3. Turn to the left on _____.

4. Turn to the right on _____.

5. Go straight ahead to the _____.

In all of the three situations above the child, of course, must be familiar with the directions, the streets named or the halls and rooms in the building.

SEQUENCING SENTENCES TO MAKE STORY

1. Ask the child to tell you a story about anything of interest to him. Write the story on the board as he tells it. The sentences are then scrambled and placed on the board out of order. Another child, or the same one, may then rearrange them correctly.

2. Use some fairy story or well-known current event. Place sentences out of order and follow the previous procedure. Examples of situations:

a. Football game
b. Halloween Carnival
c. Summer vacations (with only five or six main points)
d. Home experiences
e. Christmas events
f. Household duties
g. Schoolroom duties

OTHER SEQUENCING

Pictures

Find pictures of the first six Presidents of the U.S.: Washington, Adams, Jefferson, Madison, Monroe, Adams. Train the child to repeat these automatically and to identify each one correctly by sight. Scramble them and ask child to place them back in the correct order. This may be varied by selecting pictures of movie stars, football players, or any other well-known people.

Memory for States

Make up a series of 8 x 11 (20 cm x 30 cm) cards. On each card, group several shapes of states and under each, label the state by its name. After showing one card for 5 seconds, ask, "Which ones of the states are in the eastern United States?" Show another card and ask which ones are in the western United States. Vary this idea by cutting out the shapes and asking students to place them in correct juxtaposition with each other. This task should be done after the students have been shown a map of the entire United States for 15 seconds.

Words

Choose the spelling words of the week for this game. Teach the children to say them in a certain order. They must also learn to read each spelling word. Then the words are printed, cut out, and scrambled. The children arrange them in the original order.

COMMERCIAL MATERIALS

1.   **Anagrams.** The classic word-building game requiring the construction of words of three or more letters. (Halsam Products Co. About $2.00.)

2.   **Basic Sight Vocabulary Cards.** For children eight years of age or older. (The Garrard Press. About 82¢.)

3.   **Judy See Quees.** Sequence storyboards utilizing the comic-strip technique of separate episodes in well-known stories or familiar experiences. (The Judy Co. Series of four, about $4.50 per set; to series of twelve, about $20.00 per set.)

4.   **The Autokinetic Handwriting Program.** A kinesthetic approach to teaching handwriting, both manuscript and cursive. (Autokinetic, Inc., Box 2010, Amarillo, Texas.)

5.   **Link Letters.** For building words and sentences. (Milton Bradley Co. About 60¢.)

SUGGESTED ACTIVITIES   G R A D E **6**

Memory Sequencing

This activity consists in allowing the child to look at a number of things in a certain order or pattern, then asking him to re-create the order without looking at it. The list indicates the great variety that can be achieved with this exercise.

1.   Letters of a word.
2.   Words of a sentence.

   3. Pictures in a series.
   4. Children in a line.
   5. Persons in a family.
   6. Colored blocks in a row.
   7. Articles of clothing (top to bottom).
   8. Pictures of cars (largest to smallest).
   9. Pictures of airplanes (largest to smallest).
  10. Paper folding (to fit an envelope).
  11. Countries (use the index of book; put countries in order according to size, both in area and in population).
  12. Any objects (omit one; the child replaces the objects and decides which one is missing).
  13. Instructions in order.
  14. Numbered shapes that form a figure.
  15. Numbers in a stack (odd and even).
  16. Places on a map.
  17. Telephone numbers.

Typing

Let the child see a word, find the letters on the typewriter, and punch the proper keys to type the word. Begin with his name, and then go on to other words.

Mazes

Make up a maze, and let the child find his way from one place to another—maybe from home to school.

Cartoons and Stories

Cut pictures from a cartoon strip. Let the child view these in sequence; then mix them and let him put in order again. You could begin with *Peanuts* and progress to a more difficult strip.

Let the child put the happenings in the story in a sequence by the use of pictures.

Homonyms

Show the child pairs of homonyms: *brake—break; pair—pear; see—sea; maid—made; pier—peer; blue—blew.* Separate the words and let him put as many pairs together as he can.

Join-the-Dots

Use comic strips as patterns for join-the-dots puzzles. Sequencing could be by numbers or letters.

Categories

Write a subject (geography) on the board. Under this, place pictures or words to match the subject (mountains, rivers, lakes). Do this with several subjects. Then remove the words or pictures and see if the child can place them with the right subject.

Word Syllables

Divide a word into syllables. Let the child view the word, then erase it and see if he can divide it correctly (mos-qui-to, ge-og-ra-phy).

Prefixes and Suffixes

Let the child view words and their prefixes or suffixes; then take the prefixes and suffixes away and see if he can replace them on the proper words. Use simple words at first; then work up to more difficult ones.

SUGGESTED ACTIVITIES   G R A D E S **7 & 8**

1. Arrange measuring cups in ascending (or descending) order. Mix them, then have the child place them in order. Repeat with measuring spoons, mixing bowls, open-end wrenches, socket wrenches, bits, or pliers. (The sequence might be varied: place biggest next to smallest; let those in center be almost the same size.) Use plates or bottles or glasses for variations.

2. Vowel sequence: Using simple words, omit *a* in first word, *e* in second, *i* in third, *o* in fourth, and *u* in fifth. (Examples: r*a*te, r*e*ad, r*i*de, r*o*ad, r*o*ute.) Have the child discover what is missing.

3. Use chips of wood (anagrams) to arrange sequences of words or short sentences. Anagrams is a form of sequencing. Children might play it individually, working for longer and longer words or making simple sentences; or they could play competitively.

4. Show a rainbow. Then give scraps of material or strips of colored paper to the children for them to arrange in the sequence of colors in the rainbow (red, orange, yellow, green, blue, indigo, violet).

5. Have the children tell which words have been omitted from this story.

Our Town's First Automobile*

In the year of 1910 in a small town in Texas, two businessmen, Mr. Ed West and Mr. Lee West, purchased their first car. It rumbled along over the unpaved _____ about ten miles _____ _____. This was the first car in this town and the _____ were all excited and interested to observe it as it was _____ up and down the streets. The owners knew very little about the car's _____ and they were very careful to try to follow the written _____. On one occasion Mr. Lee West decided to back the car out of the _____ which had been built in the back yard. He forgot his instructions and _____ directly through the end of the garage. Thereafter, the brothers decided it would be safer not to depend on remembering how to back the car. When they repaired the end of the garage, they built in another _____ and drove the car in the _____ and out the _____.

If the children have trouble filling in the blanks, suggest these words: *instructions, streets, front, operations, garage, an hour, driven, drove, door.*

6. Have the child write the twenty-six letters of the alphabet in proper order, then number the letters 1 to 26. Then have him figure out what this says:

(8-1-22-5)　(1)　(8-1-16-16-25)　(8-15-12-9-4-1-25)
H a v e　a　h a p p y　h o l i d a y

Suggest that the child write a message with numerals.

7. Fernald's suggestions for remedial techniques include tracing with the hand any missed words. Encourage the child to find his own method of learning a new word, perhaps scanning a paragraph to see if there are words he doesn't know, underlining them lightly, writing each word and tracing it. In spelling, Fernald suggests a contest written at the blackboard. (The team with the fewest errors wins.) Let the child have

---

* By Wilma Jo Bush.

time enough to look at the words and fix the forms in his mind. Use only words in the vocabulary of the child. In written work, obliterate incorrect words entirely and write in the correct spelling. (Fernald, 1943)

8.   First Day in School. Tell the students, *This is the schedule given to Tom Jones when he enrolled in Junior High School. Classes are 50 minutes each.*

8:30	Math 7a	Room 112
9:30	English 7a	Room 102
10:30	P.E. 7a	Basement
11:30	Study Hall	Auditorium
12:00	Lunch	Cafeteria
1:30	History 7a	Room 204
2:30	Homeroom	Room 108
3:30	Science 7a	Room 114

Study the floor plan (see Fig. 9.4) *and, with a colored pencil, move from class to class as quickly as you can. (Note:* Reproduce a floor plan in large quantities on ditto.) Arrange different schedules for other students. Time them with a stop watch and, when working with a student alone, let him try to beat his own time.

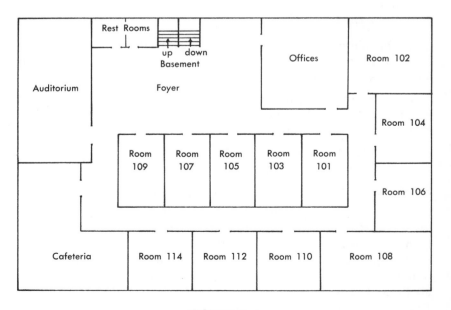

FIGURE 9–4

CB ACTIVITIES

Exercise 1

Make a series of cards with the 10-code written on one side and the meaning on the reverse side. Make a series of cards, in addition, with a single word from the stated meanings of the 10-codes (words that can be read out of context). These cards are to be used, if needed, for specific reading problems.

1. Flash the card with the 10-code and ask the student to provide the meaning.
2. Flash the meaning and ask for its 10-code equivalent.

Exercise 2

1. Place the 10-code cards in a series, for example, 10-04, 10-20, 10-08; cover the cards and ask student to repeat the order as presented.

2. Place the 10-code cards in a series as previous example. Cover the cards and ask student to *give the meanings of the 10-codes in order* rather than repeating the numbers.

Exercise 3

From the vocabulary of a CB manual choose any definitions. Present complete sentences, typed or written, as follows. Ask the student to read each sentence and then, without looking, repeat the sentence from memory. Choose some of the least used expressions on CB, as well as the more commonly used ones.

1. threes (best wishes)

2. bread or lettuce (money)

3. catching Z's (talking a nap)

4. What are you pushing? (How many watts is your radio?)

5. two-wheeler (motorcycle)

6. a truck "goodied" up (a fancy truck)

7. bubble trouble (tire problems)

8. walking on (someone else talking on channel already in use, or interfering with talk already in progress)

9. fatload (overload)

10. green stamps (police summons)

Part IV

Expression

Wilma Jo Bush
and
Claud "R" Zevely

Expression of verbal meaning and communication is a process dealing with two different modes, manual expression and verbal expression. In the former, meaning is conveyed by the face and/or hands; in the latter, meaning is shown by spoken sounds. In either case, the two individual processes may be examined from different aspects.

The process of producing spoken sounds may be examined as mechanical speech and as language with meaning. Vygotsky (1971) discriminates between the two by using the terms *speech* and *thought*. Luria (1973) differentiates speech components by beginning with the most elementary form, *repetitive speech*, then adding the *naming of objects*. From these two he moves to another dimension by considering the aspect of cerebral organization of *expressive speech activity as a whole*.

The process of manual expression may be examined from the aspect of motor action and the aspect of meaningful communication. Motor action may be considered to be the mechanical aspect of manual expression, which is dependent upon the musculature, neurological organization, and chemical aspects of the body. The second aspect of manual expression (not in hierarchical order) deals with ideational fluency of movement, i.e., making the proper movements necessary to express specific thoughts. The activities in this section of the text deal with the kind of training that will aid in the *development or the remediation* of meaningful language communication with both linguistic and manual symbols, i.e., the ideational fluency expressed vocally and manually.

Children typically develop the skill of communication during infancy and in the childhood years prior to entry in the public

249

schools. There are some children, however, who are not so fortunate. Among many homes there is experiential deprivation. Other children may lag in maturation or have brain injuries. Whatever the cause, the need for special training is evident when children have not learned to communicate properly. This inability is generally classified as an *expressive language disorder*. Children hear what is said to them and theoretically (without information to the contrary) it can be assumed that they understand and are auditorally processing what they are hearing. If the problem deals with input dificiencies and the children are *not understanding* what is being heard, then another category, *reception*, rather than *expression*, is involved.

Wallace and McLoughlin (1975) point out some examples common to children who have difficulty formulating words and sentences. They state that these children tend to use very simple sentences, and they may string together isolated words and phrases. Grammatical errors most frequently cited involve the use of plurals, verb tenses, and prepositions; for example, "She were running," or "Me go with you go." We have noted that some talkative children, when confronted with a question about some item, seem to go blank, and do not respond, except to nod their heads slightly. Other children may speak in single words or short phrases and are not recognized as having language disorders (Lerner, 1976).

Johnson and Myklebust (1967) relate motor movement to speech movement and cite inability to move various parts of the body (when the motor system per se is not deficient) to be a state of *apraxia*. They also state that although the children *can* actually remember, they have poor interaction between the memory and motor systems. Thus, the Johnson and Myklebust position is that some learning disability children with language difficulties are unable to execute particular motor patterns to produce various speech sounds. The problems involved in such expressive deficits are numerous: difficulty in expressing phonetic sounds, difficulty in syntactical arrangement of words in a sentence, and difficulty in remembering a series of words or phrases. According to Luria (1973) some children may have repetitive speech and may be able to name objects yet will have no narrative speech. He suggests that they have no intention or plan which must be recoded into the verbal form to be molded into a speech expression. Thus, when no plan is actively formed because of a deficit, there will be no spontaneous active speech.

The importance of experiences to aid expression cannot be underemphasized. De Hirsch, Jansky, and Langford* (1966)

---

* Jansky and de Hirsch (1974) have reported another account of their project, *Preventing Reading Failure.*

found in their research project on predicting reading failure that the test *Number of Words Used in a Story* proved to be by far the best predictor of reading failure than any other expressive language measure used. They relate that "richness of verbal output, whether related to environmental stimulation or to inherent linguistic endowment or to both, is apparently an excellent sign" (p. 37). They state further that the test *Organization of a Story* showed a statistically significant association with end-of-second grade achievement. Responses to this test require the ability to integrate details into a meaningful whole. This ability can also be considered to be a part of expressive speech.

Relative to *manual expressive problems*, de Hirsch et al. found that graphomotor ability showed a fairly high correlation with the students' reading and writing 2½ years later. This nonverbal motor problem (manual expression) involves the purposeful movements necessary for cutting, opening, jumping, climbing, riding, and hammering. The meaning of the gesture or movement may be understood, but execution of the gesture/movement may not be possible. Individuals experiencing such difficulties may also have difficulty with time concepts and mathematics (Johnson & Myklebust, 1967).

It can be summarized that expressing speech sounds, executing the linear scheme of a sentence, and remembering words for the purpose of speaking are major aspects of verbal expression. Other nomenclature are related or synonymous to the term *expressive problem: aphasia/dysphasia, dysnomia, aspontaneity of speech*, and *adynamia*. The major aspect of expression through manual movement is the function of executing proper movements to communicate ideas. A related term for manual expression is *nonverbal apraxias* (Johnson & Myklebust, 1967).

Proper attention to the communication of ideas should be noted and proper experiences for speaking and expressing manually should be provided when training children developmentally. For remediation purposes, children should be provided ample opportunity and time to process their thoughts before verbal or manual responses are made. If they have not learned to express themselves effectively from the ordinary experiences occurring during their home life, one must try a variety of techniques and methods to facilitate the acquisition of these skills. This section of the book provides many activities to aid in both the development and remediation of expression. Among these activities is the Zevely (1973) collection of jump rope jingles and two lists of good poetry (also selected by Zevely) to use with elementary school children* and with secondary school youth. Since the

---

* Sister Mary Consilia (1970) has found that poetry is beneficial in the development and remediation of expression problems.

jingles and lists are not classified by grade, they are located before graded activities for verbal and manual expression. The
lists may be used to help both verbal and manual expression.

JUMP ROPE SONGS AND CHANTS*

Lady, lady at the gate
Eating cherries from a plate.
1, 2, 3 (etc.)
(The child's name may be substituted for "Lady, lady.")

*   *   *

I asked my father for fifteen cents
To see the monkey jump the fence.
She jumped so high she reached the
    sky
And didn't come back till the last of
    July.

*   *   *

Ice cream soda
Ginger ale pop
Tell me the initial
of my own sweetheart
A, B, C, D (etc.)

*   *   *

One, two, button your shoe.
Three, four, shut the door.
Five, six, pick up sticks.
Seven, eight, shut the gate.
Nine, ten, big fat hen.

Down by the river, down by the sea,
Johnny broke a milk bottle and
    blamed it on me.
I tole Ma, Ma tole Pa,
Johnny got a licking, so ha, ha, ha.
How many lickings did he get?
1, 2, 3, 4, 5 (etc.)

*   *   *

My Mother, your Mother, lives across
    the way.
Every night they have a fight,
And this is what they say.
"Icka tacka soda cracker
Icka tacka boo
Icka backa soda cracker
Out goes you."

*   *   *

Chickity, chickity, chop
How many times before I stop?
1, 2, 3, 4 (etc.)

*   *   *

Rhymes Involving Change in Speed

Mother, Mother, I am able
To stand on a chair and set the
    table,
Daughter, Daughter, don't forget
Salt, vinegar, mustard, pepper,
Cedar, cider, red hot pepper.

*   *   *

__(name)__ , __(name)__
with a curl,
Will you jump as my best girl?
Slow at first, now thats' the way,
On we go to the break of day.

*   *   *

Mable, Mable,
Set the table
Don't forget
The red hot pepper.

*   *   *

"Fire, Fire!" says Mr. McGuire.
"Where, Where?" says Mr. O'Dare.
"At the barn," say Mr. Karn,
And it burns hotter, hotter,
    hotter, etc.)

*   *   *

_____
* Collected by Claud "R" Zevely, West Texas State University.

Rhymes Involving a Stunt or More Than One Jumper

Teddy bear, teddy bear, turn around.
Teddy bear, teddy bear, touch the ground.
Teddy bear, teddy bear, show your shoe,
Teddy bear, teddy bear, that will do.
Teddy bear, teddy bear, go upstairs.
Teddy bear, teddy bear, turn out th light.
Teddy bear, teddy bear, say "Good Night."

*   *   *

I love coffee, I love tea.
I want _____ to jump with me.

*   *   *

(Tune: "Tramp, Tramp, Tramp")
Vote, vote, vote for ___(1)___
Here comes ___(2)___ in the door
___(2)___ is a lady that we really
   ought to know.
So we don't need ___(1)___ any more.

*   *   *

One and one are two.
Two and two are four.
Four and four are eight.
Now it's time for spelling.

*   *   *

(Rope is swung from side to side on the
first two lines. It is turned overhead
on the last 10 lines.)

Mother, Mother, I am ill.
Send for the doctor over the hill.
In comes the doctor, in comes the nurse,
In comes the lady with the alligator purse.
"Measles!" says the doctor. "Measles!"
   says the nurse.
"Measles!" says the lady with the alligator
   purse.
Out goes the doctor, out goes the nurse,
Out goes the lady with the alligator purse.

House for rent
Inquire within,
When I move out
Let _____ move in.

*   *   *

Mama, Mama, I am sick
Send for the doctor quick, quick,
   quick.
Mama, Mama, turn around.
Mama, Mama, touch the ground.
Mama, Mama, are you game?
Mama, Mama, spell your name.

*   *   *

Blue bells, cockle shells,
Easy, easy over,
Here comes the teacher with a big,
   bad stick,
Now it's time for arithmetic.

*   *   *

C-A-T spells *cat*,
D-O-G spells *dog*.
O-U-T spells *out*,
And out goes you.

*   *   *

Onery, twoery, tickery, seven,
Allibuy, crackibuy, ten and eleven,
Wire, bridy, limber lock,
Three geese in a flock,
One flew east and one flew west,
And one flew over the cuckoo's nest
O-U-T spells *out* for
   you, and you, and you.

*   *   *

Cinderella, dressed in yellow
Went upstairs to kiss her fellow
How many kisses did she get?
1, 2, 3, 4 (etc.)

*   *   *

Down in the valley where the green grass grows,
there sat (a child's name) as sweet as a rose.
She sang, she sang, she sang so sweet,
Along came a fellow and kissed her on the cheek.
 (name) , (name) , aren't you ashamed,
to have such a friend without any name.
How much money does he give you a week?
1, 2, 3, 4 (etc.)

*   *   *

Teddy Bear, Teddy Bear
Turn around.
(child makes complete turn maintaining jumping rate)

Teddy Bear, Teddy Bear
Touch the ground.
(child stoops and touches ground)

Teddy Bear, Teddy Bear
Tie your shoes.
(attempts to tie shoe)

Teddy Bear, Teddy Bear
Be excused.
(Child runs from rope without stopping the rhythm of the rope)

ABC Jump Rope Song

A for ant who works all day,
B for boy who wants to play.
C for cat who caught the rat,
D for dog who chased the cat.
E for eggs found in the nest,
F for frog who jumps the best.
G for goat who eats all day,
H for horse who runs away.
I for ink: red, black, and blue,
J for Jane and Joseph, too.
K for king and kite and key,
L for limb and apple tree.
M for mill with water wheel,
N for nuts, the squirrels' meal.

O for ox, works like a horse,
P for pudding, good of course.
Q for queen with flower crown,
R for raindrops falling down.
S for snowman growing thin,
T for top that likes to spin.
U for us who learn to write,
V for vine with blossoms bright.
W for wing of bird,
X for X ray you have heard.
Y for year, for yacht, for you,
Z for zebra at the zoo.
Now you've heard my A B C's:
Tell me what you think of me.

(Seven beats per line, for *W* say *double U.*)

Spanish Jump Rope Songs

Uno, dos, tres, cuatro, cinco
Cogi' a (name) de un brinco
seis, siete, ocho, nueve, diez
Se me ha escapado otra vez.

One, two, three, four, five
I caught (name) with one jump
Six, seven, eight, nine, ten
He has escaped once again.

On count of five, jumper points to a person who jumps in
for counts of six, seven, eight, nine, and out on ten.

*   *   *

Uno, dos, tres
aplaudamos a la vez.
Cuatro, cinco, seis
toquemos nuestros pies.
Siete, ocho, nueve
Nadie se mueve.

One, two, three
let's clap once.
Four, five, six
let's touch our feet.
Seven, eight, nine
Nobody moves.

Y diez	And ten
saltemos todos a la vez.	let's jump at the same time.

Several children jump together with one calling count and action.

*   *   *

Brilla, brilla, estrellita,	Loose translation of
Díme lo que eres tú	Twinkle, Twinkle Little Star
Luz que tiemblas en el mar,	
Brilla, brilla, sin cesar.	

One child jumps, last line is "Shine, shine without stopping or do not stop."
Then jumper continues jumping and counting jumps until he misses.

*   *   *

Da me un beso, por favor.	Give me a kiss, please.
Cuantos besos quieres tú?	How many kisses do you want?
Quiero, uno, dos, etc. . .	I want one, two - - -

Jumper counts the number of kisses he wants until he misses.

*   *   *

POETRY

Elementary Level

Aldis, D. "Feet," *Sung Under the Silver Umbrella*. Edited by Literature Committee of the Association for Childhood Education. N.Y.: Macmillan, 1956.

Asquith, H., ed. "The Hairy Dog," *Every Child's Book of Verse*. New York: Franklin Watts, 1968.

"Before Me Came Up from Below," *Whirlwind Is A Ghost Dancing*. Edited by N. Belting. New York: E. P. Dutton 1974.

Behn, H., ed. "Crickets," *The Golden Hive*. New York: Harcourt, Brace, Jovanovich, 1966, p. 47.

Blake, W. "The Lamb," *The Looking Glass of Verse*. Edited by J. A. Smith. N.Y.: Random House ,1959.

Ciardi, J., ed. "About the Teeth of Sharks," *Peas and Honey*. New York: L. W. Singer, 1967.

Ciardi, J., ed. "Summer Song," *The Man Who Sang Sillies*. New York: J. B. Lippincott, 1961.

Coatsworth, E., ed. "My Soul Remembers," *Poems*. New York: MacMillan, 1957.

"Eagle Speaks, The," *The Trees Stand Shining: Poetry Of The North American Indians*. Edited by H. Jones. New York: Dial, 1971.

Edey, M., & Grider, D. "So Many Monkeys," *Time for Poetry*. Edited by M. H. Arbuthnot. Chicago: Scott Foresman, 1952.

Ferrie, T. H. "Swallows," *Reflections On A Gift of Watermelon Pickle*. Edited by S. Dunning, E. Leuder's, & H. Smith. New York: Lothrop, Lee and Shepard, 1967, p. 27.

Field, E. "The Duel," *The Moon Is Shining Bright as Day*. Edited by O. Nash. New York: J. B. Lippincott, 1953, p. 116.

Field, R., ed. "My Inside Self," *Poems*. New York: MacMillan, 1929, p. 115.

Field, R. "Something Told the Wild Geese," *Wings from the Wind*. Edited by T. Tudor. New York: J. B. Lippincott, 1964.

Field, R., ed. "Vegetables," *Taxis and Toadstools*. Garden City, N.J.: Doubleday, 1926.

Frost, R., ed. "A Peck of Gold," *You Come Too*. New York: Holt, Rinehart & Winston, 1959, p. 55.

Frost, R., ed. "Come In," *You Come Too*. New York: Holt, Rinehart & Winston, 1959, p. 55.

Frost, R., ed. "Looking For A Sunset Bird In Winter," *You Come Too*. New York: Holt, Rinehart & Winston, 1959, p. 18.

Frost, R., ed. "The Birthplace," *You Come Too*. New York: Holt, Rinehart & Winston, 1959, p. 58.

Frost, R., ed. "The Pasture," *You Come Too*. New York: Holt, Rinehart & Winston, 1959, p. 14.

Holman, F. "I Hear You Smiling," *At The Top Of My Voice; And Other Poems*. Edited by F. Holman. New York: W. W. Norton, 1970, p. 9.

Hughes, L., ed. "April Rain Song," *The Dream Keeper*. New York: Alfred A. Knopf, 1960.

Hughes, L. "Mother to Son," *Weary Blues*. Edited by L. Hughes. New York: Alfred E. Knopf, 1967.

"In Praise of Their Sultan," *Watkins' Anthology Of American Negro Literature*. New York: Random House, 1944, p. 128.

Irving, P., ed. "Legend," *The Whispering Wind: Poetry By Young American Indians*. Garden City, N.J.: Doubleday, 1972, p. 79.

Irving, P., ed. "Why," *The Whispering Wind: Poetry By Young American Indians*. Garden City, N.J.: Doubleday, 1972, p. 81.

Jarrell, R. "The Bird of Night," *To See the World Afresh*. Edited by L. Moore and J. Thurman. New York: Atheneum, 1974.

Keils, P. "Ten Billion, Ten Million, Ten Thousand and Ten," *Sounds Freedom Ring*. Edited by B. Martin, Jr. in collaboration with P. Brogan. New York: Holt, Rinehart & Winston, 1973.

Kilmer, J. "The House With Nobody In It," *Silver Pennies.* Edited by Blanche J. Thompson. New York: Mac-Millan, 1929, p. 115.

Lear, E. "Calico Pie," *Golden Treasury of Poetry.* Edited by L. Untermeyer. New York: Golden Press, 1959.

Le Gallienne, R. "I Meant to Do My Work Today," *Children's Literature.* New York: Holt, Rinehart, and Winston, 1972.

Livingston, M., ed. "Lamplighter Barn," *Wide Awake and Other Poems.* New York: Harcourt, Brace, Jovanovich, 1959.

Milne, A. A., ed. "Furry Bear," *Now We Are Six.* New York: E. P. Dutton, 1955, p. 93.

Milne, A. A., ed. "Wind On The Hill," *Now We Are Six.* New York: E. P. Dutton, 1955, p. 93.

Moffitt, J. "To Look At Anything," *Reflections On A Gift Of Watermelon Pickle.* Edited by S. Dunning, E. Leuders, & H. Smith. New York: Lothrop, Lee & Shepard, 1967, p. 21.

Nash, O., ed. "An Introduction to Dogs," *Golden Treasury of Poetry.* New York: Golden Press, 1959.

Nash, O., ed. "The Tale of Custard the Dragon," *Golden Treasury of Poetry.* New York: Golden Press, 1959.

Nemerov, H. "At the Airport," *Wonders and Surprises.* Edited by P. McGinley. New York: J. B. Lippincott, 1968.

"Old Men Say, The," *Bury My Heart At Wounded Knee.* New York: Holt, Rinehart & Winston, 1971, p. 420.

"Poor Old Lady," *Golden Treasury of Poetry.* Edited by L. Untermeyer. New York: Golden Press, 1959.

Richards, L. "Eletelephony," *Worlds of People.* Edited by M. Bailey and L. W. Leavill. New York: American Book Co.

Riley, J. W. "Little Orphan Annie," *Children's Literature.* Edited by M. A. Nelson. New York: Holt, Rinehart & Winston, 1972.

Roberts, E. M. "Mr. Wells," *Under The Tree.* Edited by M. Roberts. New York: Viking, 1950.

Sandburg, C. "Buffalo Dusk," *The Sandburg Treasury.* Edited by P. Sandburg. New York: Harcourt, Brace, Jovanovich, 1970, p. 176.

Sandburg, C. "Fog," *Silver Pennies*. Edited by B. T. Thompson. New York: MacMillan, 1929, p. 48.

Service, R. W. "Cremation of Sam McGee," *Adventures for Readers*. Book II. New York: Harcourt, Brace, Jovanovich, 1953.

Thayer, P. "Casey at the Bat," *Casey at the Bat*. Edited by E. L. Thayer. Englewood Cliffs, N.J.: Prentice-Hall, 1964.

Updike, J. "Sonic Boom," *Sounds Freedom Ring*. Edited by B. Martin, Jr. in collaboration with P. Brogan. New York: Holt, Rinehart & Winston, 1973.

"When The Day Is Cloudy," *The Trees Stand Shining: Poetry Of The North American Indians*. Edited by H. Jones. New York: Dial, 1971.

Whitman, W. "I Hear America Singing," *Golden Treasury of Poetry*. Edited by L. Untermeyer. New York: Golden Press, 1959.

Wynne, A. "A Wish Is Quite A Tiny Thing," *Silver Pennies*. Edited by B. J. Thompson. New York: MacMillan, 1929, p. 63.

Junior High and Senior High Level

Barnefield, R. "The Nightingale," *An Anthology of World Poetry*. Edited by M. Van Doran. New York: Harcourt, Brace, Jovanovich, 1936, p. 1073.

"Before Me Came Up from Below," *Whirlwind Is A Ghost Dancing*. Edited by N. Belting. New York: C. P. Dutton, 1974.

Behn, H., ed. "Crickets," *The Golden Hive*. New York: Harcourt, Brace, Jovanovich, 1966, p. 47.

Blake, W. "The Piper," *An Anthology of World Poetry*. Edited by M. Van Doran. New York: Harcourt, Brace, Jovanovich, 1936, p. 1148-9.

Browning, R. "Home-thoughts, from abroad," *An Anthology of World Poetry*. Edited by M. Van Doran. New York: Harcourt, Brace, Jovanovich, 1936, p. 1214-5.

Byron, G. G. Lord "She Walks in Beauty," *An Anthology of World Poetry*. Edited by M. Van Doran. New York: Harcourt, Brace, Jovanovich, 1936, p. 1184.

Coleridge, S. T. "Kubla Khan," *An Anthology of World Poetry*. Edited by M. Van Doran. New York: Harcourt, Brace, Jovanovich, 1936, p. 1179-80.

De La Mare, W. "Tired Tim," *Worlds Of People*. Edited by M. Bailey & V. W. Leavill. New York: American Book, 1961.

Dickinson, E. "I'm Nobody," *Poetry Festival*. New York: Dell, 1966.

"Eagle Speaks, The," *The Trees Stand Shining: Poetry Of The North American Indians*. Edited by H. Jones. New York: Dial, 1971.

Field, E., ed. "The Duel," *The Moon Is Shining Bright as Day*. New York: J. B. Lippincott, 1953, p. 116.

Field, R., ed. "My Inside Self," *Poems*. New York: Mac-Millan, 1929, p. 115.

Frost, R., ed. "After Apple-picking," *Selected Poems*. New York: Henry Holt, 1929, p. 79.

Frost, R., ed. "A Peck of Gold," *You Come Too*. New York: Holt, Rinehart, & Winston, 1959, p. 55.

Frost, R., ed. "Birches," *Selected Poems*. New York: Henry Holt, 1929, p. 81-3.

Frost, R., ed. "Blueberries," *Selected Poems*. New York: Henry Holt, 1929, p. 193-9.

Frost, R., ed. "Come In," *You Come Too*. New York: Holt, Rinehart & Winston, 1959, p. 25.

Frost, R., ed. "Flower-gathering," *Selected Poems*. New York: Henry Holt, 1929, p. 210.

Frost, R., ed. "Looking For A Sunset Bird In Winter," *You Come Too*. New York: Holt, Rinehart, & Winston, 1959, p. 18.

Frost, R., ed. "Mending Wall," *Selected Poems*. New York: Henry Holt, 1929, p. 96–8.

Frost, R., ed. "Nothing Gold Can Stay," *Selected Poems*. New York: Henry Holt, 1929, p. 11.

Frost, R., ed. "October," *Selected Poems*. New York: Henry Holt, 1929, p. 171.

Frost, R., ed. "The Pasture," *Selected Poems*. New York: Henry Holt, 1929, p. 3.

Frost, R., ed. "The Road Not Taken," *Selected Poems*. New York: Henry Holt, 1929, p. 163.

Frost, R., ed. "The Sound of the Trees," *Selected Poems.* New York: Henry Holt, 1929, p. 166.

Frost, R., ed. "Stopping By Woods on a Snowy Evening," *Selected Poems.* New York: Henry Holt, 1929, p. 12.

Frost, R., ed. "The Tuft of Flowers," *Selected Poems.* New York: Henry Holt, 1929, p. 93–5.

Gibran, K., ed. "The Cortege," *Secrets of the Heart.* New York: New American Library, 1965, p. 147–58.

Hafiz. "A Persian Song of Hafiz," *An Anthology of World Poetry.* Edited by M. Van Doran. New York: Harcourt, Brace, Jovanovich, 1936, p. 148–50.

"He Is Like the Lotus," *An Anthology of World Poetry.* Edited by M. Van Doran. New York: Harcourt, Brace, Jovanovich, 1936, p. 247.

Holman, F., ed. "I Hear You Smiling," *At The Top Of My Voice; And Other Poems.* New York: W. W. Norton, 1970, p. 9.

Hughes, L., ed. "April Rain Song," *The Dream Keeper.* New York: Alfred A. Knopf, 1960.

Hughes, L. "Kids in the Park," *Windows, Walls, Bridges.* Edited by U.S. President's Special Action Office for Drug Abuse Prevention. Washington: U.S. Government Printing Office, 1975, p. 27.

Hughes, L., ed. "Mother to Son," *The Weary Blues.* New York: Alfred Knopf, 1967.

Ignatow, D. "Two Friends," *Windows, Walls, Bridges.* Edited by U.S. President's Special Action Office for Drug Abuse Prevention. Washington: U.S. Government Printing Office, 1975, p. 32.

"In Praise of Their Sultan," *Watkins' Anthology Of American Negro Literature.* New York: Random House, 1944, p. 128.

Irving, P., ed. "Legend," *The Whispering Wind: Poetry By Young American Indians.* Garden City, N.J.: Doubleday, 1972, p. 79.

Irving, P., ed. "Why," *The Whispering Wind: Poetry By Young American Indians.* Garden City, N.J.: Doubleday, 1972, p. 81.

Jansky, J., & de Hirsch, K. *Preventing reading failure: Prediction, diagnosis, intervention.* New York: Harper & Row, 1972.

Kilmer, J. "The House With Nobody In It," *Silver Pennies.* Edited by B. J. Thompson. New York: MacMillan, 1929, p. 115.

Kipling, R., ed. "The Choice," *Rudyard Kipling's Verse Definitive Edition.* Garden City, N.J.: Doubleday, 1940, p. 185.

Kipling, R., ed. "Christmas in India," *Rudyard Kipling's Verse Definitive Edition.* Garden City, N.J.: Doubleday, 1940, p. 53.

Kipling, R., ed. "England's Answer," *Rudyard Kipling's Verse Definitive Edition.* Garden City, N.J.: Doubleday, 1940, p. 177.

Kipling, R., ed. "Gunga Din," *Rudyard Kipling's Verse Definitive Edition.* Garden City, N.J.: Doubleday, 1940, p. 404–6.

Kipling, R., ed. "If," *Rudyard Kipling's Verse Definitive Edition.* Garden City, N.J.: Doubleday, 1940, p. 578.

Kipling, R., ed. "The Juggler's Song," *Rudyard Kipling's Verse Definitive Edition.* Garden City, N.J.: Doubleday, 1940, p. 668.

Kipling, R., ed. "The Native-Born," *Rudyard Kipling's Verse Definitive Edition.* Garden City, N.J.: Doubelday, 1940, p. 191–4.

Merivale, J. "The Storm," *An Anthology of World Poetry.* Edited by M. Van Doran. New York: Harcourt, Brace, Jovanovich, 1936, p. 256.

Moffitt, J. "To Look At Anything," *Reflections On A Gift Of Watermelon Pickle.* Edited by S. Dunning, E. Leuders, & H. Smith. New York: Lothrop, Lee & Shepard, 1967, p. 21.

O'John, C. "This Day Is Over," *The Whispering Wind: Poetry By Young American Indians.* Edited by P. Irving. Garden City, N.J.: Doubleday, 1972, p. 67.

"Old Men Say, The," *Bury My Heart At Wounded Knee.* New York: Holt, Rinehart & Winston, 1971, p. 420.

Poe, E. A. "Annabel-Lee," *An Anthology of World Literature.* Edited by M. Van Doran. New York: Harcourt, Brace, Jovanovich, 1936, p. 1343–4.

Roberts, E. M., ed. "Mr. Wells," *Under the Tree.* New York: Viking, 1950.

Sandburg, C. "Buffalo Dusk," *The Sandburg Treasury.* Edited by P. Sandburg. New York: Harcourt, Brace, Jovanovich, 1970, p. 176.

Sandburg, C. "Fog," *Silver Pennies.* Edited by B. J. Thompson. New York: MacMillan, 1929, p. 48.

Sandburg, C. "Grass," *An Anthology of World Poetry.* Edited by M. Van Doran. New York: Harcourt, Brace, Jovanovich, 1936, p. 1387.

Simon, P. "The Dangling Conversation," *Windows, Walls, Bridges.* Edited by U.S. President's Special Action Office for Drug Abuse Prevention. Washington: U.S. Government Printing Office, 1975, p. 40–1.

Stanley, T. trans. "Old I Am," *An Anthology of World Poetry.* Edited by M. Van Doran. New York: Harcourt, Brace, Jovanovich, 1936, p. 271.

Thayer, P. "Casey at the Bat," *Casey At The Bat.* Edited by E. L. Thayer. Englewood Cliffs, N.J.: Prentice-Hall, 1964.

Theognis. "Poverty," *An Anthology of World Poetry.* Edited by M. Van Doran. New York: Harcourt, Brace, Jovanovich, 1936, p. 262–3.

Thompson, F. "Arab Love-Song," *An Anthology of World Poetry.* Edited by M. Van Doran. New York: Harcourt, Brace, Jovanovich, 1936, p. 1258–9.

"When The Day Is Cloudy," *The Trees Stand Shining: Poetry Of The North American Indians.* Edited by H. Jones. New York: Dial, 1971.

Whitman, W. "You, Whoever You Are," *All Around America through Literature.* Edited by E. Daniels. Chicago: Scott, Foresman, 1963.

Wordsworth, W. "I traveled among unknown men," *An Anthology of World Poetry.* Edited by M. Van Doran. New York: Harcourt, Brace, Jovanovich, 1936, p. 1166–7.

REFERENCES

Consilia, Sister Mary. Meeting total needs of learning disabled children: A forward look. *Proceedings of the*

Seventh Annual Conference of the ACLD, Philadelphia, Feb. 12–14, 1970. Originally published in S. A. Kirk & J. M. McCarthy, *Learning Disabilities.* Boston: Houghton-Mifflin, 1975.

de Hirsch, K., Jansky, J. J., & Langford, W. S. *Predicting reading failure.* New York: Harper and Row, 1966.

Johnson, D., & Myklebust, H. R. *Learning disabilities.* New York: Grune and Stratton, 1967.

Lerner, J. W. *Children with learning disabilities.* Boston: Houghton-Mifflin, 1976.

Luria, A. R., *The working brain.* New York: Basic Books, 1973.

Vygotsky, L. S. *Thought and language.* Cambridge, Mass.: M.I.T., 1962.

Wallace, G., & McLoughlin, J. A. *Learning disabilities.* Columbus, Ohio: Charles E. Merrill, 1975.

Zevely, Claud "R." Jump Rope Jingles. Canyon, Tex.: West Texas State University, 1973.

10

Verbal Expression

Verbal expression, or *vocal encoding,* refers to the ability of a child/youth to express ideas in spoken language. If a student cannot describe simple objects, or if the student seems to have no reservoir of information about things in general, then this student may have an ideational fluency problem. Training should provide opportunity and time for all oral responses. Moral support and verbal cues also should be given when the difficulty in searching for words is noted.

Verbal expression deficits, especially severe ones, may be due to lack of central control of speech mechanism, but they may also be due to misunderstanding what has been heard or seen (visual and auditory reception). In addition, they may be due to vocabulary deficits, to deficits in retrieving words, or to the inability to associate ideas satisfactorily for expression.

Kirk and Kirk (1971) suggest that remediation should include (1) practice in imitating sounds, choral reading, and singing games; (2) vocabulary training; (3) provision of aids in completion of words and sentences; (4) use of the telephone; and (5) the telling stories and recording messages on tape. It is particularly important that you provide ample time for the child to complete his sentences and that you assist him with words in a natural way. You should also practice telling stories to a child before he or she is expected to talk about them.

G
R
A
D
E
K

TELL ABOUT FRUIT

Let the child select and describe from real or toy foods his favorite, relating the shape, size, color, and taste. Then let him tell a story about it; for example, how and where it grew, how his family prepares it, and how and when it is served and eaten.

"I SEE"

Say, "I see a _____," and point to the object. The children provide the name of the object. Soon they may be able to say the name of the object, its color, or what it is made of. "I see a pink chair"; "I see a wooden pencil." This game can include where the objects are used, how they are shaped, and many other concepts.

FIELD TRIPS ·

Slides taken of the children during field trips or while they are participating in ordinary school routines can be used later for specific discussion because they stimulate verbal responses and recall.

LOOK AND TELL

Put a collection of everyday objects in the center of the table. Provide a question clue and ask the children to pick the right object. Examples:

aluminum foil plate	"What's round and shiny?"
knitting needle	"What's long and sharp?"
toothpick	"What's short and sharp?"
piece of fur	"What's fuzzy?"
bottle opener	"What do you open pop with?"
chalk	"What do you write on the board with?"
pencil	"What do you write on paper with?"
ring	"What do you wear on your finger?"
necklace	"What do you wear around your neck?"

The children are requested to answer with a complete sentence. Example: "An aluminum foil plate is round and shiny."

I SPY

"I Spy" is an easy game for many children. A child says, "I spy something yellow (or any other color)." He adds one clue at a time until someone guesses the right object. "It is round. It will bounce." "A ball," answers a child, who then spies something another color. Vary this game by allowing one child to name a color and then allowing a limited number of children to move to some object of that color named. Each child must describe the object he has touched.

WALK INTO A PICTURE

This game can be played by showing a large painting or photograph or by projecting a scene from a filmstrip. In turn the children say the color of something they see while "walking along" in the scene. "I see a brown road," says the first one. The next child repeats what was said: "Joe saw a brown road," and then adds, "and I see green leaves." The next one says, "Joe saw a brown road. Jimmy saw green leaves," and adds, "and I see yellow flowers." This game continues as long as children can find new things to add or until every child has had a turn.

COMPLETE THE STORY

Begin a simple action story on a familiar theme. Ask for and utilize suggestions: "What do you think happened next?" Continue the story as long as it moves without too much difficulty. *The Sequencing Boards* from the Bank Street Early Childhood Discovery Materials of Macmillan provide an excellent opportunity for additional practice in completing a story. The *Turn the Page Books* and the *Name and Know Book* from the same series is another good source.

PETS

Discuss pets and the possibility of having some pets in the room. Plan to set up an aquarium. Have all the equipment ready the next day, and let the students decide what should go in first, second, etc.

PRETEND

"Would you all like to pretend to be the teacher for a little while? You will have to tell us how to do something, such as coloring circles, putting on a coat, making steps with the short and tall blocks, or making a design with the colored blocks. What would you like to teach?" Offer suggestions if the children need help at first.

GUESS WHO?

"Let's pretend to be animals in a zoo, but don't tell anyone your name! We will only tell something about ourselves as animals and see if anyone can guess our names. Like this: 'I am a large animal with four legs. I have a very pretty coat with black and white stripes. Can you guess my name?'" If no one guesses "zebra," continue. "I look a lot like a horse. Yes, I am a zebra. Now it is your turn to describe the animal you are going to pretend to be."

GETTING ACQUAINTED WITH LEARNING CENTERS

This game is an excellent way to involve the children with the classroom environment by familiarizing them with the facilities, as well as allowing for an informal time to discuss and set up classroom rules for behavior.

You and an aide may walk to each center and ask such questions as: "How many children could work here?" Let the children decide the number. "How are the blocks arranged in this center? After we have worked in this center, how could we put the blocks away again? How do we act in the Library Center?" (Quiet.) "What would make our room look better? Think about it and tell us tomorrow. Look about the room and see if we are good housekeepers." Let children give their reasons and answers. As new equipment is brought out, discuss its use and care.

This activity could be repeated each time a new learning center was added to the classroom.

MY NAME IS _____.

This simple game would be especially appropriate for the first day of school. You, your aide and the children wear name tags. Teacher: "I am Ms. _____. I am your teacher." Touch name tag and say: "This is a name tag and this says my name. We pinned a name tag on you and it tells us your name. We are going to play a game with this ball. I will say, 'My name is _____', and roll the ball to _____. He will say, 'My name is _____ ___', and roll the ball to one of you. After you tell your name, you may roll the ball to another friend until everyone has had a turn." You will probably need to say the sentence for children who are reluctant to talk at the beginning of school.

SHARING TIME

A child brings an object from home to share with the group. Let him talk freely, but prompt him with such questions as: "What color is your rock? Where did you find it? How does it feel? I wonder what makes it sparkle? Do you have a lot (collection) of rocks at home? Where do you keep them?"

Prompt the child until he has told as many things about the object as he can. The class can be encouraged to bring things which pertain to a unit of study if you keep parents informed of what the children are studying at any given time during the school year.

TALK ABOUT THINGS

Animal, bird, or insect cards may be used. A child draws a card from a selection which is facedown on the table. "Tell me one (two or three) things about the card you have drawn." Responses could be: "It has four legs. It has a long neck. It has spots. It lives in a zoo (or the jungle.)"

PICK A PICTURE

Collect simple action pictures and allow each child to select one. "Pick out a picture that makes you think of something. Tell us what it makes you think of. Make up a little story about those people (or animals)." Help the child with questions and suggestions.

PICTURE DICTIONARIES

The Little Golden Dictionary (plus many others) are suitable to use in motivating vocal responses. (If two dictionaries are bought, the pictures can be cut apart, pasted on colored poster board, and laminated so that each child can hold an individual card.) The child picks a picture to tell about. His description is supplemented by your reading of what the dictionary has to say about that particular entry.

SURPRISE BOX

You bring a box of surprises to the class. "Guess what I found when I went for a walk yesterday?" After discussion, show leaves, nuts, shells, etc. "Shall we bring what we find tomorrow and share it with the class?" Discuss place for things that we find and bring to class (table).

The Surprise Box could be used throughout the year to elicit interesting classroom discussions. This activity lends itself very well to emphasizing a theme or unit of study.

G
R
A   1
D
E

Activity 1: Shadow Show

Use for background a large piece of butcher paper extended between two poles or chains with light behind it. The story of *The Three Billy Goats Gruff* is easy to use for a shadow show. The characters should be made of heavy tagboard and large enough for the child to manipulate with ease. Patterns for the characters can be obtained from color books or flannelboard cutouts. A long slender stick is glued to back of each character for the child to hold. A narrator will read or tell the story. When the narrator comes to a quotation, the child behind the screen talks for his character. Since the child is hidden from his audience, he seems to forget himself and talks with ease; he feels that he *is* the character he is playing. He may also give the sound effects for the story.

Activity 2: Play Acting

Children love to dress in costume and become other people. They tend to forget themselves and are not aware that it is their own voices that they hear. Costumes can be cut from cardboard, with just the child's face showing through. Such characters as Goldilocks and the three bears can be made as large as the child and painted with tempera. These can also be purchased from school-supply companies. The child holds the costume up to him as he acts out his part.

Activity 3: Child's Own Story

The most important word in the world for a child is his own name. When a child's name becomes a part of his first reading experience, he quickly identifies with sentences and vocabulary. Let the child dictate short sentences about himself. The teacher writes the sentences on a chart tablet with felt pen. A photograph of the child or a picture he has drawn of himself may be posted on his story. The child likes to tell or read his story to others even though he may not know all the words in isolation.

Activity 4: Taste-Smell-Feel

Three shoe boxes may be used and labeled *Taste*, *Smell*, and *Feel*. Place in the boxes such things as small pieces of candy, grapes, nuts, salt, and sugar for tasting. Flowers, onions, perfume, fruit, coffee, tea, and many other things can be used for smelling. Fur, silk, glass, cotton, iron, rocks, feathers, and things of different shapes may be used for feeling. The child will be allowed to taste or smell or feel these objects and tell something about them.

Activity 5: Show and Tell

Children delight in sharing things they have found or been given. A child who is very shy may be encouraged to show something to the small groups at tables, but will later be able to go to the front of the classroom and talk to all the children about something he is holding in his hand. If a child brings something that is unfamiliar to the others, he will be encouraged through other children's questions to use several sentences to discuss the article.

Activity 6: Clay Modeling

Shy children may be given modeling clay to make something. After completing it, they can tell someone about what they have created.

Activity 7: Guessing Game

The teacher will place on a table a number of familiar things, such as a round red ball, pink glass bottle, green toy truck, or any other things which can be described easily by the child. After the child has seen all the things, the teacher will cover them and let the child reach under the cover and get one article. The child must identify the article by using a complete sentence before he can bring it out to show other children. This game could also be played by putting each thing in a separate bag and letting the child insert his hand into the bag.

Activity 8: Choral Reading

Children enjoy choral reading and it is a good way to help the child with a vocal encoding disability. For first graders the poems should be short; nursery rhymes are especially good.

Activity 9: Giving Directions

Help the child to listen and tell others how to carry out directions for fire drills, simple organized games, work activities, and rules of procedures in the classroom and school.

Activity 10: Self-Concept Building

You explain that each child in the room is unique. Each one is capable of doing something of value. If any single child does not respond with the recognition of his own capability, you must point out something the child can do (walk straight, sit upright, smile, look peaceful, or some activity out of the school of which you are aware).

After you have given the request for each person to respond, the children are to share one thing that they can do. Following this sharing session, emphasize that each child is worthwhile. Reinforcement with positive remarks should be given periodically to all the children.

Activity 11: Picture Reading

For practice in literal picture reading, ask *What do you see in the picture?* Have the children enumerate all the objects seen in the picture, then recognize and name simple actions portrayed. To stimulate interpretive picture reading, ask: *What is happening in the picture? What are they doing in the picture? Can you tell me the story of the picture?*

Activity 12: Describing Objects

Teach the children the game **Heavy, Heavy Hangs over Your Head.** Let one child leave the room and then collect several items to be guessed. The child comes back and the students take turns holding one of the objects over the child's head and describing it so that he can guess what it is.

Let the students play the game **Little Lost Child.** One child leaves the room and the teacher chooses another child to be the "little lost child." This child hides under the teacher's desk; then all the other children change desks. The child outside the room is called in and he chooses someone to describe the lost child to him. If he cannot guess who it is from that description, he goes on to another child and asks them to describe the little lost child.

Let one student look out the window and describe some object he sees, such as a bird, a school bus, a tree, or a dog. The children in the room try to guess what he sees.

TAPE RECORDERS

A tape recorder can be a useful instrument in working with students who have a vocal encoding disability. At first the novelty of the recorder and hearing their own voices will be motivation enough, but in order to keep this motivation active, a teacher must soon have well-planned activities. Here are six activities, and as a teacher becomes accustomed to using the tape recorder, she will be able to think of many more.

1.   Record for your records a personal interview with the student. This will be useful in planning future activities that are of special interest to him. Ask leading questions such as: *If you could have any animal in the world, what one would you choose? Why? If I had the money to buy you a new dress (or shirt), what color would you choose? Why? Count these beans for me. If we could go to the grocery store, what would you buy? What game would you like to play with your father (or mother)? Bark like a dog. What sound does a cat make? A cow? A horse?* Etc. Be sure to let the student hear his interview.

2.   Record a very short story on the tape. Explain to the child he can hear the story as many times as he wishes; then let him record the same story in his own words. Let him listen to his story.

3.   Bring a radio, a record player and children's records to class. Let the student listen to programs on the radio, then choose the type of program he wants to do. It can be the news, weather, a disc jockey, etc. If the student wants to, play the radio show for the class.

4.   Show a short fairy-tale filmstrip to the child; then ask him to tell you about the story and record it. The instructor can evaluate the student's progress by comparing this recording to the one made earlier on storytelling.

5.   Read a story such as *Jack and the Beanstalk* to the children. Let the children choose the character they would like to be in the story and do a radio show acting out the parts. Tape the show and then let them listen to it.

6.   Take the class on a field trip to the fire house and record their impressions while they are there. Play the tape back to them the next day in class.

LANGUAGE EXPERIENCES

1.   Give the child tempera paint, a brush, and a large sheet of paper, and let him paint a picture. For vocal encoding, ask the child to tell about his picture.

2.   Play a game using five pictures of various objects. Let the students choose sides. One student picks up a card and describes the object on the picture without calling it by name. His side has three chances to guess the object; if they don't get it, the other side gets three chances. The side that gets the correct answer scores a point.

3. Play a game with the children on giving and following directions. Give such directions as: *Get under your desk; stand on the left side of your chair.* Play the game a few times with the teacher giving the directions; then the students will be able to give the directions by themselves.

4. Let the children play school. Set aside a corner with reading charts, word cards, pencil and paper, and any other items they might choose to use. Keep the groups to two children and let them take turns being teacher. Then watch out—you'll see what kind of a teacher you are!

5. A good way to help the child in vocal encoding and motor development is to use a jumping rope and teach them the rhymes that children use while jumping rope. An example would be:

> *Teddy Bear, Teddy Bear, turn around.*
> *Teddy Bear, Teddy Bear, touch the ground.*
> *Teddy Bear, Teddy Bear, touch your knee.*
> *Teddy Bear, Teddy Bear, run out for me.*

If jumping the rope is too difficult for the child, just lay the rope on the floor and let the child jump over it while he says the rhyme.

GRADE 2   DESCRIBING OBJECTS OR PICTURES

1. Display familiar objects or pictures. Let the child choose which he wishes to describe and tell everything he can about it. You may use fruit, toys, magnets, simple tools, pictures of airplanes, boats, animals, birds, etc.

2. Let the children bring from home some unusual object or picture of particular interest and have them tell about it.

3. Fill a bag with familiar objects, such as mentioned above, and call it *Our Surprise Bag.* Let a child place his hand into the bag and select an object by feeling. Let him display the object and tell all he can about it.

PRACTICING SPEAKING IN SENTENCES

1. Ask questions such as: *What is your name? What is your favorite color?* or *What is your address?* If he does not reply with

a complete sentence, help him structure his response into a sentence.

2. Ask the children to use spelling words in sentences.

3. Give incomplete sentences and let the child begin with what you gave and complete the sentence. Eventually, he may be able to add other sentences to the first.

    1. If I could be any animal I want to be, I would be a . . . (Some may be able to tell why.)

    2. When I grow up, I want to be a . . .

GIVING DIRECTIONS

1. Give children an opportunity to tell how to go home from school, how to go to the store, how to go to Mary's, etc.

2. One child may give directions for another child to carry out in the classroom. For example: *Go to the chalk board and draw a circle and a square.*

3. Children may give directions on how to play a new game which they have learned at a party, at Sunday School, etc.

CHILD TEACHING OTHER CHILDREN

Most children will enjoy teaching their own skills to the others.

    1. Tell how to fold paper and cut out a snowflake.

    2. Explain how to perform a newly-learned athletic feat.

    3. Tell others how to make a jack o'lantern.

    4. Explain how to play jacks, marbles, etc.

    5. Explain how to play a new game.

TELLING STORIES

Giving children an *opportunity* and *providing a time* for storytelling may help overcome vocal encoding disabilities.

Before actually telling stories, it would be well to have discussions and let the children tell what kind of stories they like, why they like them, what characters they like best, etc.

Children's first storytelling experiences should be in telling a story they have heard or had told to them many times. Expect only a few sentences at first. Praise them often for their efforts. They may, a little later, read very short and easy stories and tell the story to the class.

Still later, some may enjoy making up and telling stories of their own. Often they can get ideas from interesting familiar words (elf, green shoes, pointed hat, magic). You may suggest topics for a story, such as: *Tell us a story about a kangaroo (a monkey, a clown, etc.).* Some children enjoy adding an ending to a story you begin.

RIDDLES

Children love riddles. Encourage them to make simple riddles. (Example: *I have a long tail and I like to eat bananas. My name begins with an m. What am I?*)

TELLING HOW AND WHY

Children are often inclined to forget their shyness and vocal encoding problems if given an opportunity to talk about something they are proficient at doing, or something familiar.

1.   How I feed my pet turtle.
2.   How I fly a kite.
3.   How I pop corn.
4.   Why I like to be a Cub Scout.
5.   Why I like my music lessons.

DISCUSSIONS

Science and social studies classes offer ideal situations for discussions. Children may tell about a trip to the bakery, a community helper, a science experiment, etc.

DRAMATIC PLAYS

Children may dramatize a story from their basal reader, a story from a library book, or a story one of the members of the class has made up. They may make "pretend" telephone calls to thank someone for a gift, to invite a friend to a party, etc.

GAMES

Games offer good opportunities for children to practice vocal encoding.

For practice in beginning consonants, blends, vowel sounds— and vocal encoding—you might try variations of the following:

1. Going Places One child begins by saying *I am going on a picnic and I am taking some milk.* Next one may say *I am going with you and I am going to take some money.* Each must take something with the same beginning sound. Long or short vowel sounds, blends, etc., may be substituted in this game.

2. My Rocket Ride One child may begin a game by saying *I rode a rocket to the moon and I took a dog with me.* Next one could say *When I ride a rocket to the moon, I am going to take a duck* (or he might say *a dog and a duck*).

3. The Zoo Game The teacher may ask such questions as *Who can hop like a rabbit? Who can walk like an elephant?* or *Who can walk like a duck?* The child who gets to perform the act must first answer in a complete sentence: *I can hop like a rabbit. I can walk like an elephant. I can walk like a duck.*

4. Rhyming Game One child begins by saying *I have a hat.* Next may say *I have a hat and a cat.* The third child may say *I have a hat, a cat, and a bat.*

5. What Happened Game A child begins the game by making statements such as: *I went to the store to buy some bread. I forgot my money. What do you think happened?* Or *When I went to the fair, I got lost. What do you think happened?* Other children answer with their own ideas as to what happened. The teacher may have to think of the original ideas until the children have had much practice.

G
R
A
D
E

3

TECHNIQUES

Incomplete Stories

Set up a situation which could happen to the child and let him supply the likely ending. Example for a boy of this age: *This morning your mother could find only one pair of trousers for you to wear. These pants were slightly too small, but you and your mother decided you would have to wear them anyway. After your arrival at school, you began a football game with the other boys. Just as you bent over to hike the ball* . . . Allow him to finish the sentence with the likely answer about a rip; then ask him to tell what he would do about this accident.

Set up similar situations, adapting your story to the individual child's sex, age and interests. Make them situations to which he will know a likely ending, and all he has to do is put it into words.

Descriptions

Keep available several collections of small objects. Suggested for boys of this age are small replicas of cars, planes, boats, etc.; suggested for girls, clothing items for a small doll such as Barbie. Provide the collection and let the child select an item, describe it, and answer your questions regarding its uses and functions.

Looking Up Facts

You give an assignment that requires the child to look up some fact in a book such as the *Golden Dictionary* or any book of facts in the school library. Each child is allowed to go to the library with a small group to find the requested information. The facts are shared verbally with the group upon return to the room.

Telephone Situations

Devise a number of telephone subjects to use with these children—such as the following: Tell the child to pretend Mother has called from the grocery store and asked him to read the grocery list to her, since she left it lying on the desk. Allow time for thought; then let him complete the make-believe conversation.

Framing Pictures

Make a frame from heavy tag. The child takes it to the window and holds it away from him to pick out "his picture" from the overall scene. He then describes "his picture." Use this device while out on the playground as an informal activity.

Experience Stories

Give these children frequent opportunities to relate their very own stories to you. These could be fact or fantasy and, for best results, type the stories for them.

Comic Strips

Find comic strips which are appropriate for use with children and run them off without the words in the balloons. Let the child study the pictures, then tell you what he thinks the characters are saying.

Filmstrips

The following filmstrips are especially valuable in getting the the child to think of labels: *Name the Right Word, Synonyms, Homonyms,* and *Find Another Word* all can be purchased from Eye Gate House, Inc.

Use the following strips with the child for vocal encoding in regard to meaning: *Read and Tell* is a set of nine strips including such titles as "Jack and the Beanstalk" and "Hansel and Gretel." The second half of these strips repeats the previous pictures but without the captions. The child retells the events depicted. *See and Tell* is a set of nine strips designed to improve observation and oral expression. These also come from Eye Gate House, Inc.

Language Master

Prepare a set of blank cards with action pictures and no words. The student may record alone and a busy teacher may come back later to listen to his tapes. An example would be a picture which brings forth the response *The girl is catching the ball.*

Practice in Asking Questions

This is an activity for two children. One child secretly decides to be something (elephant, submarine). The other directs questions in an effort to guess his partner's identity.

Highlights Handbook

The Highlights Handbook, *Creative Thinking Activities* (Myers, 1965), contains many useful questions for use in vocal encoding. Examples:

1. Why do more people wish for rain in summer than in winter?
2. How could a blind person know when food on the stove is burning?
3. Why may it be easier to make a dress shorter than to make it longer?

4. Why can't a puppy pick up a penny like you can?

5. How are a turtle and a fish alike? How are they different?

6. What is the difference between a bookmark and a mark in a book?

7. "Here, Tippy. Here, Tippy," Walt called. He walked down to Third Street, circled the block, and headed toward home. When he arrived, he asked his mother to take him out in the car. What had happened?

8. One morning, about ten minutes after Patsy arrived at school, her puppy also arrived. The puppy did not follow Patsy closely enough to see her. How did the puppy find its way?

9. What would you do if the barber cut your hair shorter than you wanted him to cut it?

Tape Recorder

Tape the sound sequence of an activity and let the child tell you what is happening. (Example: On the tape is heard the sound of steps, a door opening, the door closing, steps again, a car door opening, car door closing, roar of a car motor, and finally the sound of the car going into the distance).

G
R
A   4
D
E   SUGGESTED ACTIVITIES

1. Use large mounted pictures for display. One child is chosen to be *It*. He mentally selects a picture, turns his back to the display, and describes the picture. The first child to guess which picture is being described is next to be *It*. Pictures drawn by the children may be used, or pictures related to units of study, seasons, or events may be selected.

2. Children may write plays and use peers for characters. Oral participation, whether spontaneous or rote, is important. When a story has been read, the group may extemporaneously act it out.

3. Eye Gate Films* produces a series of children's stories consisting of a series of colored pictures with the story written below the pictures. The first twenty pictures and sentences tell

---

* Eye Gate House, Inc.

the story. The last twenty pictures are the same as the first, except they have no written message. It is the child's task to retell the story in proper sequence by looking at the pictures.

4.   The teacher gives a definition for a word. The children listen carefully. If a child says the definition is not correct, he must define it properly. (Example: *A turnip is a flower in our yard.* Correction: *A turnip is a vegetable in our garden,* or *A tulip is a flower in our yard.*)

5.   Children select a character from stories read to them. They make up a riddle about one of the characters and other members of the class try to guess who the character is. For example, a child may say *I am a very brave boy. I am also very wise. My brothers went up into the mountains with me to visit a very old man. The man captured my shadow. Who am I?* The first child to guess the right answer is the new *It.*

6.   The children are divided into two groups. You alternate asking questions to individuals in each group. When the questions are answered correctly, a point is given to the group. At the end of a designated time, the students add their points to determine which group has won.
In this game, you ask questions which must be answered with a complete sentence explaining use of an object. First the child must guess what you have in mind. You say, "I am thinking of something in this room and it begins with a *T*. What do you do with this object?" The child must answer with a statement which shows that she understands what you are thinking. An example of an answer could be, "You are thinking of something in this room that has books on it. We can use this object to sit at and study." Then the child may either add that it is a *table,* or an alternative play would be to give two points if another in that group can add that it is a table.

7.   Give the children simple sentences. They are to make the sentences more descriptive or colorful by adding words. You may say *Jane has a dress.* The first child may say *Jane has a new dress.* The second child may say *Jane has a new blue dress.* When the sentence becomes depleted, a new one may be supplied by the children or the leader.

8.   A variation of Activity 5 is for the children to describe a place where an event in one of their stories happened. The other members of the class are to identfy the place. An event in a story may be described. The children tell when it happened. An event

may be described from a familiar story and the members of the class tell why it happened.

9. A leader may say *I am thinking of a word that sounds like mop.* The children try to guess the word without saying the word. They may ask, *Is it a toy?* and the leader may answer, *Yes, it is a top.* Or the leader may say, *No, it is not a top.* The children will then try again.

10. A variation of the above activity is to let a child begin the game. He tells the class that he is thinking about something they have learned in a previous story. He then gives one statement telling a specific thing about that which he is thinking. For instance he might say, *The bird I am thinking about lives in the far north.* The other members of the class try to read his mind. If they do not succeed, he gives them another clue. The one who guesses the name of the bird becomes the leader.

11. The teacher supplies several short paragraphs, each written on a separate sheet of paper. Each child reads his paragraph and supplies an oral conclusion. He may also be asked to supply reasons why this may be incorrect. Examples for such paragraphs follow:

a. Jack drove the car into the garage. The right front fender was crumpled.

b. The timid horse stood near the gate. She was skinny and her coat had lost its shine.

12. The class is divided into two teams. The leader gives three words, such as hatch, fly, and gallop. Then the leader calls on a player to give three sentences, using one of the words in each of the sentences. Each sentence must be a complete and understandable thought. The players take turns. Each correct sentence receives a point, and the team receiving the most points wins.

13. Children may be asked to give directions for performing a skill, playing a game, or arriving at a given place. They may also give directions for activities. For example, they may ask another child to perform a series of tasks like: *Pick up my pencil, put it on your desk, and bring me your book.* If it seems that children are not following through, it may be well to get them to repeat the directions before attempting to do the activity.

14. Have the child think of words—any words—and say them as rapidly as he can. Count the words the child says in one minute. If the child can say between 25 and 30 words per minute,

he has no problem. If less than ten, he needs to play the game often.

15. Use a picture and get the child to tell you a story (make-believe) which is stimulated by ideas gained from the picture. The story may be typed for re-reading later.

16. The tape recorder is very useful to stimulate and motivate speech. It can be used with storytelling or oral reading.

17. The Language Master is especially good for teaching new words, phonemes, proper pronunciation, sentence structure and syllabication.

18. Field trips may be taken, and when the group returns, the children are asked to relate new experiences to the teacher. They may also relate these experiences to previous ones. The stories they relate may be typed for them to read aloud or take home.

19. A child may tell of unique experiences which he would like to share with others. Children from varying ethic backgrounds have much to offer in cultural enrichment.

20. The teacher may begin a story and ask the child to finish it, or each child in the group may add to it until the story is finished. Discuss different types of stories and encourage children to supply surprises, excitement, disappointment or satisfaction to the ending. New words and understanding grow out of such experiences. Often this type of storytelling suggests to the children true experiences they enjoy relating.

21. Making poems is a wonderful method of vocal encoding. Children love repeating rhythmic sounds, especially if they are products of their own imagination.

22. Tongue-twisters such as *Sea Shore* and *Peter Pinter* are good. Children will bring a wealth of new ones from home and friends.

1. She sells sea shells down by the sea shore.
2. Peter Pinter picked a pint of pickle peppers off the pepper stalk. Where's the pint of pickle peppers Peter Pinter picked?
3. The big black bear had a big black bug on his big black back.

This exercise may not be encoding, but the vocal practice involved should be an aid to a child having vocal encoding difficulties.

23. Puppet play and storytelling with puppets may be used to remediate faulty vocal encoding.

24.   Use the telephone as a means of stimulating conversation; telephone etiquette can also be taught through this experience. You might present imaginary problems and let the child handle the situation as he would if it actually happened to him.

a.   You need a telephone number, and you do not have a directory.

b.   You answer the telephone and the person for whom the call is made is not at home.

25.   Children who find it difficult to communicate in group discussions can often do well if they wear an earphone set and pretend to be an airplane pilot or a radio announcer. They will re-enact the news items of the day or land a plane safely with very few suggestions.

GRADE 5

ACTIVITIES

1.   It's fun for children to use binoculars. Allow the child to look through the teacher's binoculars and describe what he sees. Perhaps he will see a bird and get interested in reading about birds.

2.   It seems that everyone has a favorite season of the year. Have the child tell about his favorite season of the year. The teacher might ask the child to draw a picture showing the season and tell her about the picture also.

3.   Allow the child to bring his hobby to school and tell the class or the teacher about it. If he doesn't have a hobby, let him talk about what would make a good hobby for him.

4.   Finger paint to music and make up a song while painting. If the child is hesitant to sing, perhaps he would like to compose a verse or story about the picture while the record is playing.

5.   Have the child look at a picture and tell a story about it. It's a good idea to have several pictures from which the child may choose.

6.   As the child or the class finishes a project, ask the child to tell how it was done. The child might want to take the project to another room and tell that class how it was done.

7.   All children like to hear and read tall tales. Allow the child to tell a tall tale or to read one and then tell it to the teacher or the class.

8.   Boys like to help their fathers work. Ask the boy how he helps his father and get him to tell about it. He may know exactly how to do something that the rest of the class would like to hear. (Teacher could probably learn something too!)

9.   The girls will want to tell about things that they can do— cooking, sewing, candlemaking, papier mache, or perhaps even making the baby's formula.

10.   There's always an opportune time for the child to tell about when he had mumps, measles, or some other disease. (The only trouble with this activity is that he wants to tell about all of them!)

11.   It's lots of fun to make puppets. It's even more fun to make them act in a story or play. Have the child use the puppets with a story he already knows. He will probably think it's fun to make up his own story. (If the child is behind something, and only the puppets are showing, he is more likely to do well.)

12.   Have the child explain an arithmetic problem, a science demonstration or project, or any activity that he or the class has done.

13.   Allow the child to be *It* in games, and to give directions for playing them. Examples are **Simon Says, I Spy,** or any other games that require talking.

14.   Children are always interested in special holidays and seasons. Ask the child to tell how to dye Easter eggs. Have him tell how he would decorate a Christmas tree if he had all of the decorations that he wanted to use. Vary these according to the ethnic and religious background of the children.

15.   Have the child tell about things that he would like to invent.

16.   Ask the child what he does over the weekend. Ask him what he would do on Saturday if he could do exactly what he wanted to do.

17.   Have the child draw a floor plan of the school or his house and tell about it.

18.   Use every opportunity to let the child give directions in getting to different places. Map reading is an excellent way to get child responses.

19.   Have the child finish problem stories:

a.   Joe and Frank were digging around in the rocks looking for the entrance to a cave. All of a sudden, Joe felt a pain in his leg. He saw a big snake and knew that he had been bitten ...

b.   Jane and Sam had gone to the fair with their parents. Jane became so interested in watching people shoot at the dart board that she forgot about staying up with the others. She found that she had been left behind and became very frightened ...

c.   Bill's mother left him to watch his two-year-old brother for a few minutes while she went into the post office. Bill got out of the car and tried to catch a colorful butterfly. While he was out of the car, his two-year-old brother slipped out of the car, and when Bill looked around, no one was in the car ...

20.   More ways of saying words: Have the child think of words that mean the same as *said*, or *big*, or *little*, for instance. *What words tell how we might feel? What words tell what kinds of weather or climate we have? What are some color words?* (*smoky, golden, pinkish, pale, ruddy, emerald, amber, ruby, scarlet, crimson, azure, aquamarine, creamy, chocolate*)

21.   Riddles: Have the child look at an object and think of a riddle he could ask someone.

22.   *Here is a list of words. Can you tell a story using all of these words?* The words could be put on cards and a card put aside when the word has been used. (*autumn, fields, harvest, frost, pumpkins, haystacks*)

23.   Interest inventory: Ask the child the questions and write what he tells.

24.   Participation stories: Have a child tell a story and the other children participate in the sound effects (*Brave Little Indian, The Lion Hunt, One Winter Night*). He may want to make up his own story and assign parts to the other children.

25.   Pantomime: The group or teacher makes meaningful gestures and asks the child to describe what they are doing.

26.   Blindfold the child and let him feel objects and tell you what he thinks about them.

27.   Dictionary usage: Ask the child to find a certain word in the dictionary, read the definition silently and then tell what the word means. Perhaps it would be helpful to the child to make a sentence with the word.

STORYTELLING   G
                 R
                 A   **6**
                 D
                 E

Experience Stories

Motivate the children by reading or telling a story about something that relates to their background or experience. The children then tell related experience stories. (snakes, an accident, a storm, a school trip)

Picture Stories

Ask a child to study an interesting and appropriate picture and then tell:

1. What happened in this picture?
2. How does this picture make you feel?
3. Associate and pronounce a *word list* with objects in the picture and then tell a story using some of the words.

Tutor-Speech Stories

1. The child listens to a story on tape or on a record and then tells the story.
2. The child watches and reads a filmstrip, then tells the story.
3. The teacher reads or tells the child a story; then the child tells the story.
4. The child watches television, then tells what he saw and heard.

GIVING DIRECTIONS

1. Ask the children to give directions from school to home.
2. Let the children show and tell how to cover a book properly.
3. Describe how to perform a motor skill such as *Angels in the Snow* or *Jumping Jack*.

CREATIVE POETRY

Select a subject—Thanksgiving Day, for instance. Set the mood by reading several short Thanksgiving poems, then write a few words, such as *turkey*, *Pilgrims*, and *Indians*, on the board. Write other words as the children suggest them. Both teacher and pupils compose the first line, but encourage the pupils to compose three other lines. Aim for a four- to eight-line poem from each child.

GAMES

Baseball Game

This may be played in any of the content areas. Choose sides and designate four bases. Side A asks the first question. Side B must answer in a complete sentence. A child may have one chance to repeat or reinforce; the teacher may supply one important word. The runner must answer four questions to score a "run." After three misses, Side A is out, and Side B is in.

Looking-up Facts

Give an assignment on one day that requires the student to look up a fact in the encyclopedia and to bring the information to class to share on the day following. This activity could be assigned to specific content such as country, season, month, locality, industry, and/or science.

Question-and-Answer Game

Cut as many slips of paper as there are children in the class. Write the word "question" on half of them, along with one other word to suggest a question topic. (For example: *question, president; question, holiday;* etc.) Write the word "answer" on the other papers. Shuffle and let the children draw. Keep this game as realistic as possible. Questions and answers must be in complete sentences.

ORAL BOOK REPORTS

Discuss a book that most of the children have read.

1. Author: What is known about him?
2. Setting: Where and when did this story take place?
3. Characters: What are their actions? What do they feel? Are they good, bad, kind, patient? Do you like and approve of them?
4. Plot: Tell in a few sentences what the story is about.

5. Climax: What was the most exciting or interesting thing that happened? How was the problem solved?

6. Ending: Were you pleased with the ending? Why or why not?

7. Category: What type of story was this?

PROBLEM SOLVING

Pose some problems for the children to resolve.

1. If you had ridden a bus to town and found you had lost your money and no one was at your home, what would you do?

2. If you knew someone had a possession of yours, yet you could not prove this, how would you handle the situation?

3. If you found a dollar out on the playground, what would you do?

TALKS

Formal

Ask each pupil to speak for one minute about a time when he had fun or when he felt happy. The child should go to the front of the room, stand erect, and put hands behind him if he does not know what to do with them.

Suggestions for opening single sentences:

1. My dad is jolly when . . .
2. When my dad is upset . . .
3. Every Sunday afternoon . . .
4. A special time in our family is . . .
5. At the dinner table . . .
6. In my family we always have fun when . . .

Informal

Let the children select their own subjects for short talks.

Discuss the magic that color, sound, and image accomplish in our language.

1. Ask the child to match these words with our five senses.

   a. Sizzling, crackling, pattering
   b. Flavor, savor, watering
   c. Odor, inhale, scent
   d. Scratching, sweaty, pleasure
   e. Magnificent, gorgeous, enormous

2. Blindfold a child and ask him to pick up an object, identify it by touch, name it, and describe it for the class to identify.

3. While the child is blindfolded, ask him to identify an object from its smell, name it, and describe it for the class to identify.

DRAMATIZATION

1. Using a story as the basis, help the children to write a play and act it out.

2. Encourage the children to characterize interesting personalities and animals.

3. The use of puppets will provide humor and relaxation.

GRADES **7 & 8**

TRAINING ACTIVITIES

1. Nonsense rhymes are one remediation technique for faulty vocal expression. Each student is handed a list of rhymes. He selects any one he wishes, then reads it aloud. For example, he chooses the poem, *Elephants*,* and reads:

> . . . but trunks will not,
> even when it is hot,
> hold a big umbrella over their heads . . .

---

* Marian T. Giles.

He may choose a nonsense poem by Ogden Nash, Edward Lear, or Richard Armour. After the selection is read, students will be called upon to explain what has been read.

2. Sentences may be used to show differences in meaning by changing intonation and inflection as one reads. Allow each student an opportunity to say a sentence differently. For example, see how many ways a student can say, *Johnny wrecked my Honda after I'd told him to keep away from it*, or, *Linda hasn't returned my typewriter, and she's had it three weeks.*

3. The Dolch sentence game (Dolch, 1951) using sight phrase cards works well. Twelve cards are kept in use throughout the game. On each card are printed phrases such as: *said quickly, the lady will, to what I say, the dog, say that to me, stop the car, in the brown hat, the officer, to the garage, in the garden, from the house, said loudly.*

Each student in turn will attempt to make a sentence from any three phrases, reading it aloud. He keeps the cards from which he composes the sentence. The teacher, from a stack of phrases she holds in her hand, replenishes cards which are drawn. The game continues until all cards have been drawn, or until a logical sentence is impossible to make. The student who completes the game with the most sentences wins.

4. The student's practice in vocal expression achieves an extra dimension when he works with definitions. Using occupations, ask him to define *teacher, lawyer, doctor, carpenter*, etc.

5. A student might be asked to define, on a simple level, such emotions as love, anger, hatred, jealousy, and happiness.

6. Ask the student to select and read a caption to go under a cartoon.

7. Listen together to Aesop's Fables; then tell what each means. Ask students to relate why certain animals were used to portray certain characters.

8. Students should be able to define certain objects, telling all they can about them. For example: *A ball is to throw; it is round and looks like a circle; we play with it; it has the same shape as the sun.*

9. A student listens to a vocalist singing on the radio or a record, then tells in his own words what the song is about.

10. Small group discussions offer remediation possibilities in dealing with the shy student. A reticent student can sometimes be prompted to vocal expression by relating a news event of which

he is aware. He might describe an astronaut's flight into outer space, giving all the statistical data he can remember.

11. Junior high school age students will also discuss movies or television programs. They are quick to tell how the characters behaved and what events transpired throughout the play.

12. One student begins a story, perhaps about a rescue, and each student in turn adds something to the tale. Students could be placed in imagined situations or predicaments and talk their way out.

13. Tall tales of danger, adventure and intrigue appeal to teenagers. A tall-tale contest could be arranged and a small prize offered for the most exciting tall tale.

14. Students of varying ethnic and religious backgrounds should be encouraged to describe their marriage ceremonies, holidays and other special celebrations. Role-playing with masks and appropriate dialogue may make discussions more spontaneous.

15. Students also use vocal expression in describing motor acts. Girls can demonstrate and talk about such subjects as changing diapers, making a cake, or knitting a sweater. Boys can show and tell how to load a camera, change a flat, build a doghouse or birdhouse, or do a jack-knife off the high diving-board.

16. A more sophisticated level of puppetry could be used in vocal expression. For example, a student could manipulate a puppet policeman directing traffic and could tell what is going through the officer's mind. From behind the puppet stand, the reticent student should be more inclined to "open up."

17. There are numerous ways to utilize vocal expression while the child imitates the tutor's speech. Perhaps one of the best is the repeating by students of short lines of poetry. For example, the teacher might say:

> I sailed the seas,
> the waters so blue,
> to see the world,
> the world so true,
> to learn of the people like me and you.*

The student would repeat the lines, perhaps eventually committing them to memory. Any stanza of a poem would be acceptable, if short enough. The tape recorder, applied here, offers additional feedback. Each student, after hearing the stanza, would repeat it into the recorder, then hear the recording played back.

---

* Marian T. Giles.

18. Letting students take the teacher's role helps them in imitation. For example, the teacher tells a student what to announce to the class, and it's the student's job to give clear instructions to his classmates.

19. Another method of generating vocal response is improvisation. Any teenage-oriented activity is acceptable. For example, a boy asks a girl for a date; a boy asks his dad for the family car; two girl friends discuss the new boy in school.

CB ACTIVITIES

Exercise 1

The student is asked to think of *as many reasons as possible* for the following questions (one reason is sufficient) :

1. Why is a person who is requesting to speak on a channel called a *breaker?*
2. Explain why the West Coast might be called the *Shaky Side.*
3. Why would one CBer say to another, "You might better back 'em down." (should reduce speed)
4. Why would it be said that patrolmen were doing a "flip flop?"
5. Why is the expression, "You got your ears on?" used frequently in CB language?
6. What do you think of CBer is referring to when he says *Bean Store?* Why?
7. Why is a 10-code used in communication over the airways?
8. Why is it wise to specify one channel as an emergency channel?

Exercise 2

Ask the student to think of as many CB handles as he can.

Exercise 3

Ask the student to explain in his own words the need for FCC regulations.

Exercise 4

Ask the student to name as many rules as he can.

11

Manual Expression

Manual expression, or *motor encoding,* refers to the ability to express ideas in meaningful gestures. A child with a manual expression problem will have difficulty demonstrating concrete activities and concepts before others. Since many school activities, such as cutting, opening, and playing, require manual expression skills, the teacher should be cognizant of this disability in some children and be cautious about asking them for demonstrations in the classroom where they may be observed by their peers.

Remediation should involve perceptual-motor training, according to Kephart (1971), as a background to other motor expressions. Kirk and Kirk (1971) suggest that activities dealing with actions, emotions, professions, directions, and gestures should be provided.

Dramatization and pantomiming are standard means of benefiting children having trouble with manual expression. Provide ample time for the movement expression, for it is necessary for children to process the ideas slowly before expressing them. Imitation of movements should be practiced daily.

G
R
A D **K**
E

IMITATION

A basic activity could involve imitation of the body movements of an animal, pet, or baby. After the child can do these movements, let her make the verbal sounds that the subject makes; for example, a rooster flapping his wings and crowing, or a baby crying. Often children do this before they can talk.

MARCHING

Have the children, hand-in-hand, march around to music. They are to make whatever sounds they can.

CHALKBOARD DRAWINGS

Chalkboard drawings using colored chalk is a meaningful manual expression task. Start with simple lines, circles, and stick figures. Later the children can draw crude pictures of animals, pets, and foods.

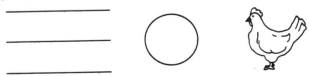

GUESS WHAT IS HAPPENING

Let the child act out a role as "carpenter sawing a plank," "a child with dirty hands," or "a child carrying groceries from the store."

SHOW ME HOW

You ask the students how they brush their teeth, how they get home from school, how their mothers peel potatoes, how should they cross the street, how they put their toys away at home, how they comb their hair, and how they take care of their pets.

THE SIGN SAYS

Make cards with stick figures drawn on them, such as follows:

Show a card and have the children do what the figure shows. As the children progress, the cards can be shown for just a few seconds. Make many figures on individual cards for the children to imitate.

DEMONSTRATION

A child may teach a skill to the other members of the class. For example: bowling. Play bowling sets are inexpensive. Most of the children have seen bowling on TV. If not, help one child and let her show the others.

DRAWING IN THE AIR

Direct the children to draw designs in the air: circles, squares, triangles, numbers, TV screen shapes, boxes, balls.

Vary this game by directing the children to march (in a group) in a circle or in a square. Let one child at a time march after she has been in the group.

ACTIONS

Ask the children to respond to commands as: hide, run, walk, peek, smile, frown, act silly, act happy, cry, bend forward, turn around, move up two steps, move back two steps.

SHOW ME

Ask the children to show what they do when they: brush their teeth; comb their hair; sweep the floor; march in a band; play a musical instrument; drive a car. Add to this list other activities.

GRADES 1 & 2

MOTOR ACTIVITIES

1. This finger play game involves the whole hands:

> Open, shut them. Open, shut them,
> Giving them a clap.
> Open, shut them. Open, shut them.
> Lay them in your lap.
> Creep them, creep them slowly upward
> To your rosy cheeks.
> Open wide your shiny eyes,
> Through your fingers peek.
>
> Open, shut them. Open, shut them.
> To your shoulders fly.
> Let them like the little birdies
> Flutter to the sky.
> Falling, falling, slowly falling,
> Nearly to the ground.
>   (*Bend as near to the floor as possible.*)
> Quickly raising all your fingers,
> Wiggle them around.

2. Charades is a good group activity in which the child acts out a role, such as a carpenter hammering a nail, a doctor using a stethoscope, his favorite television character, or a famous person.

3. **Storm** game: Have the children run about with out-stretched arms (the wind); then have them tiptoe lightly, running fast (the rain). Next have the children jump up and down (the rain falls harder); then jump more vigorously (thunder and lighting). Finally, have the children return to tiptoe activity (light rain) and gradually crouch or lie down (the storm is over). (Frostig, 1964)

4. Give the children practice in hearing the sound *sh* at the beginning of a word: *What do we say when we want someone to be quiet? (Shh!) Sh is the quiet sound.* (Give some examples of words that begin with the quiet sound of *sh;* ask the pupils to give others.) *I am going to read a story with some words that begin with the quiet sound of sh. Put your finger to your lips whenever you hear a word that begins with the sound of sh.* (Read slowly and emphasize the words beginning with the *sh* sound.)

Once upon a time there lived a *sh*ort man who owned a *sh*op. One bright and *sh*iny morning he *sh*ut his *sh*op and sailed away on a *sh*ip. When the *sh*ort man left the *sh*ip, the sun was *sh*ining and no one was about. The *sh*ort man began to *sh*out. Soon he became very hungry. He *sh*ook the branch of a *sh*ade tree and down came an apple. He ate the apple. Then the *sh*ort man sailed on the next *sh*ip for home.

Other activities and stories may be devised for other sounds.

5. **Show-Me** game: The teacher or child may be the leader and ask to have the following pantomimed: Something your mother does at home; something you like to eat; something you like to wear; something a cowboy does, etc. The possibilities here are many.

6. **John Brown Had a Little Indian**: Give each child a number between one and ten. When the children sing the song, each child squats down as his number is sung the first time. When his number is sung the second time, the child stands up.

7. Imagination games: Have the children pretend they are catching a baseball, kicking a football, playing a musical instrument, etc. Many activities lend themselves to this type of imagination game.

8. Children may trace designs that have been cut out—circles, triangles, squares, etc. Then ask them to color one design their favorite color, one design the color of the sky, one design the color of the trees, etc.

9. Use chalk to draw a design as children would for hopscotch. Label the squares *left foot, right foot,* and *both feet.* Then have the children play the game as they would hopscotch.

10. *Put Your Finger in the Air* (Columbia Record J-4-187) is a song using several body movements. It is available in many records shops.

11. The familiar game, **Jack-in-the-Box** (Expression Company, Magnolia, Mass.), is of value in motor expression activities.

12. Songs such as *London Bridge, Here We Go 'Round the Mulberry Bush, Bingo, John Brown's Baby,* and many others, may be used for motor expression activities.

13. Playing the game **Simon Says** is a group activity. An example of this simple level is: *Stand behind your chair. Put your hands up. Hands down.* A more complex level is: *Tap your little finger with your thumb three times using your right hand.*

14. The teacher may begin a story by drawing a stick picture on the blackboard and then letting the child add to the story or finish it.

15. Paste several pictures on a page and show it to the child; then ask him to demonstrate the objects or how they are used. Use pictures of tools, such as a hammer, saw, camera, ax, shovel, and wheelbarrow.

16. The child is directed to show how to:

   a. ride a tricycle (while sitting and while standing)
   b. drive a car
   c. sweep a floor
   d. sing a solo
   e. mow the lawn
   f. swim

In individual training sessions you will help the child make the movements, if he cannot respond voluntarily.

17. Hold up word or picture cards, showing a bird, airplane, dog, elephant, etc. Then ask the child to imitate it.

18. Here is a good singing game for motor expression.

Little Peter Rabbit Had a Fly upon His Nose
(sung to tune of *The Battle Hymn of the Republic*)

Little Peter *Rabbit* had a *fly* upon his *nose,*
Little Peter *Rabbit* had a *fly* upon his *nose,*
Little Peter *Rabbit* had a *fly* upon his *nose,*
And he *flipped* and it *flew* away.

Each time the child says the word *rabbit*, he places his hand over his head to represent rabbit ears. Each time the child says the words *fly* or *flew*, he makes a flying motion with his arms. Each time the child says the word *nose*, he touches his nose with his hand. Each time the child says the word *flipped*, he makes a flipping motion with his hands. When the child can sing the song and do the motions, have him sing the song and leave out the underlined words, but continue to make the motions.

19. Plan a lesson to be read over the public-address system to the class. Preferably it is read by someone else so the teacher can be in the room to see how the students perform. The lesson may include such instructions as: *Johnny, go open the door. Mary, raise your right hand. Tommy, stand on your right foot.* With some groups this activity might be adapted for use on the tape recorder.

20. One child is allowed to show how to perform some task. The children guess what she is doing. Each child is given the opportunity to perform. Simple tasks are appropriate at grades one and two:

eating	climbing
raking leaves	hopping
dancing	picking fruit
swimming	pouring fluids
shoveling	sitting, watching TV

GRADE 3

GAMES

Trades

The players are divided into two groups. A goal line is marked across each end of the play area and one group stands behind each goal. The first group decides upon a "trade." They leave their goal and go to the opposite end of the play area, calling, *Here we come!* The second group asks, *Where from?*

First group: *New Orleans.*
Second group: *What is your trade?*
First group: *Lemonade.*
Second group: *Show us some!*

Then the first group pantomimes their trade while the second group tries to guess the trade. If they guess correctly, they immediately give chase while the others run for their goal. Any players who are tagged before reaching their goal become members of the side tagging them. The game is repeated with the second group choosing a trade.

The group of players who are guessing must maintain contact with their goal line until the chase begins.

Animal Relays

This variation of a relay requires the children to move to a goal line and back while imitating the gait of an animal. Some animal suggestions are: (1) Snail walk—the child puts his hands up and over his shoulders and bends over as he walks; (2) bear walk—walking on all fours with feet going outside of hands; (3) duck walk—walking on two feet in a squatting position; (4) donkey walk—walking on all fours to the goal and imitating the donkey's kick and bray; (5) crab walk—walking on all fours with the face up; (6) lame dog—walking on two hands and one foot.

Charades

The teacher divides the class into two teams, then calls Team One to the front of the room and shows them the word to be acted out. Each child is given the letter he is to represent. By bending their arms, legs, and bodies, the group will form the letters of the word. The opposing team is to guess the word being spelled. If they do this correctly, they receive a point. In the same manner, the second team will form a word for the first team to guess.

Story Plays: Automobiles

The children *pump up the tires*, bending and stretching, working their arms up and down, and making a sound of *sh* as they pump. Then they *crank the automobile*, joining hands in front and make a big circle by swinging their arms. The *engine starts*—they run in place, hands on hips. The "auto" increases speed gradually. A shower approaches, *put up the top* (reaching down, arms extended, and pulling up. The *rain comes down*—they raise arms high, fingers moving to represent raindrops, and go to squatting position. Then they *wipe the rain from the car*—(using up, down and side movements). Finally, they *take a friend for a ride*—One child puts his hands on shoulders of the child in front and they move forward. All stop occasionally for traffic signals.

Story Plays: Indians

The children paddle in canoes to woods (kneeling on left knees, moving arms from front to rear on left side). They walk through the woods with one hand shielding their eyes, look all around among shrubs as if scouting. One of them shoots a bear. (He kneels on one knee, stretches his arms, and aims a bow and arrow. He draws one arm back and makes a soft, hissing noise as the arrow goes through air.) All of them run four or five steps forward to the bear. Several stoop and pick up the bear, throwing it over their shoulders. They walk back to the canoe and paddle home.

Story Plays: Christmas Trees

The children put on coats and hats, run to the barn for sleds and hatchets, then run out to the woods. They chop down trees— with one foot forward, they swing the "hatchets" over the other shoulder. They chop and stoop forward several times to one side and then to the other. Then they place the trees on the sleds and drag them home, hands behind as if holding ropes. They scurry about to secure boards, hammer, nails and saw to make stands for the trees. Then they decorate the trees with presents, orna- ments and candles. The children dance around one Christmas tree, using a game previously learned. Finally, they blow out the candles on the tree.

Countries

1. Have the children make the windmills of Holland by stand- ing in pairs, back-to-back, with right arms stretched diagonally upward, left arms diagonally downward. As they bring their right arms outward and downward, the left arms go up. The movement is continued.

2. They can be Swiss mountain climbers—walking with high steps and using mountain sticks to help.

3. They can try the traditional Oriental walk—With short, quick steps, hands folded. Be sure to tell the children that this is "old-fashioned" now.

4. Or they can be Scotchmen playing bagpipes. They walk around taking deep breaths and playing some tune.

Master and Robot

One child is the *robot*. Another child is his *master* and tells him to walk to the south, to the east, to the north, or to the west.

The master may tell the robot to tap the table in the north part of the room, touch the window which is farthest south, put a book on the east end of a table, or give other orders involving directions. The robot and the master then trade places.

The game may be changed by having the master control several robots; or changing directions to include southwest, northeast, northwest and southeast; or giving commands other than those involving directions.

Automatic Responses

Have the children line up in the group and give simple instruction at a fairly fast pace, about every 4 seconds. First tell them it is their responsibility to stand *free* from others.

Give commands:

hop	touch the floor	touch your	look back
jump up	twist	right ear	squat down
one step	reach up with the	reach up with	stand up
wave	right hand	the left hand	cry
smile	stomp one foot	bend over	wink

Guess Who

Each child acts out his favorite fairy story character. Other children guess which character he has chosen.

Writing Letters in the Air

The teacher writes a spelling word in the air using cursive writing. The children then write the same word on the board or on paper with wide lines.

Do What Chad Did*

For this activity, the children are seated at their desks. The teacher reads the story as the children make the indicated movements.

Chad was a little brown dachshund, a dog with long ears. He belonged to Blake Jordan. He dashed (*swish hands on desk*) about the house and dashed about the house (*repeat movement*). He ran around the room (*make running movements with fingers on the desk*) and he ran (*repeat*) around the room.

---

* By Wilma Jo Bush.

He grabbed (*make grabbing movement*) his bone in his mouth and started to slowly slip (*move fingers slowly across desk*) into the living room where he knew he was not supposed to go. He hid the bone behind the divan (*move hands under desk*). Then he heard someone come walking across the room (*hit knuckles on the desk*).

Betty Jordan said, "Chad what are you doing?" Chad turned his head up to the right (*move head up while turning to the right*). Then he moved his head down to the left (*move head down while turning to the left*). Then he looked up and twitched his nose (*twitch nose*).

Betty knew that he had probably brought his bone in the living room, so she started loo-oooking and loo-ooooking (*turn heard round and back*) and then she saw it!!! Under the divan!!! (*Look under desk*). She said, "Chad—you little dog! WHY DID YOU DO THAT?" (*Children look stern*).

When Betty said this, Chad ran into the other room (*make fast running movements with fingers on desk*). He ran so fast that he bumped into a chair (*hit on desk*). And he bumped into a table leg (*hit on desk*). And, he bumped into a vase on the floor (*hit both hands on desk with palms open*). The vase went CRASH—CRASH (*hit both hands on the desk again and then clap hands together*).

This scared Chad so that he slowly (*move fingers slowly*) walked over to the corner and put his head down, then slowly laid down (*make movements to stopping position with fingers*).

He stayed there until Bill Jordan came in from work and picked him up. He told him to be a good dog—so Chad went to sleep lying in Bill's lap, while Bill stroked his back (*make stroking movements*).

The story should be told with feeling and all movements should be demonstrated. Go through it a second time without demonstrating the movements and see how many of them the children can remember.

Happy, the Bassett Hound*

Emphasize the silence of the movement with this game. Demonstrate all movements until children learn to make the movements without being told.

---

* By Wilma Jo Bush.

The Bassetts had a Bassett hound! He was a big (*hold shoulders high, hands and arms out wide*) BIG dog with long ears (*make movements from the ears down*). He could run (*make running movements in the air with fingers*). And he could walk (*make slower movements in the air with the fingers*). But most of the time, he just poked and poked (*very slow movements in the air*) about the house.

He was happy! (*Make big smiling movements with mouth.*) In fact, Happy was his name! But—he was so POKY! (*Make poky movements again with fingers.*) He was so poky that he would slump down and go to sleep (*let head fall over and close eyes*).

When Kenneth Bassett would come home, Happy would wake up (*eyes open wide*). He would hold Happy until his daughter Martha could start running (*run with fingers in the air*). This was the way Happy would like to play. He would chase her around and around (*make running finger movements around and around*). Martha was always able to get ahead of him and she always won the game—except on one day. While Kenneth held him, Martha started running (*make running movements like a disc turning*). Happy started after her (*start as if to follow in the same direction*). But all of a sudden, he turned (*make movement back the other way*) and headed her off (*put hands together softly*). They both fell on the floor (*drop hands*). They laughed and laughed until Nancy, Martha's mother, came and helped her up.

And Happy poked slowly back over into his corner, because he had used all his energy on that day (*move hands slowly; then drop head as if alseep*).

G
R
A
D
E
4

MOTOR ACTIVITIES

Charades

You can get unlimited ideas from content subjects.

1. Riding a bicycle.
2. Mounting, riding and dismounting a horse.
3. Entering, starting, driving, stopping, getting out of the car.
4. Entering and/or leaving a bus, train or airplane.

5. Television weather reporting.
6. Serving a meal.
7. Grocery shopping or shoe shopping.
8. Preparing to go somewhere (act out putting on coat, hat and gloves).
9. Interviewing someone (hold hand as if a mike is in it).
10. Any good-health or grooming activity (may be incorporated with motor sequencing).

Hand Development

Silhouette an animal on the wall and have the "animal" speak and act out a part of some story just read (class work, or free reading). Hand or finger puppets are used in this way. One hand may react to the other hand, or more than one child may get involved.

Simon Says

The child who is *It* may call out any activity, such as:

1. Fling a finger or fingers.

2. Wiggle any one finger named—left thumb, right index, etc.

3. Wave good-bye—right-handed, left-handed, both, backwards.

4. Neck roll—to the left, to the right.

5. Waist movements, arm movements, leg movements, or any other gross motor function. (Any activity which involves putting arms over head or using shoulders will help in building better body-hand relationship.)

Book Report Time

The child acts out the part he enjoyed most, instead of telling about it. May be very brief or longer, depending on the child and/or the book character.

Action on Mats

The children should be taken to the gym where there are mats available. Have the children line up behind the mat and give directions for each child singly to move across the mat by the directions given. Suggested directions are:

> crawl
> hop
> jump twice, rest, jump twice again
> roll
> crawl and wiggle
> walk fast
> back over on your kees
> walk sideways
> walk with your hands on your hips
> walk and twist as you walk

Clap Hands

Everyone claps in unison (about one per second). Either clap softly or move away from other classrooms. The leader gives a word or clue such as *ham*, the pupil to his right says a rhyming word like *clam* before two handclaps. The one giving an answer in this is the new leader. Prearrangement might specify same vowel, same number of letters, same part of speech, same family, same number of syllables, same beginning letter, synonyms, homonyms, or any other meaningful category.

Walking-Beam Relay

Be sure to keep within each child's ability. A child who could carry a bell in one hand, and a full glass of water in the other while walking on the beam, would probably be demonstrating adequate motor coordination if he did not ring the bell or spill any water.

Forfeit

This may be connected with any content review. To redeem a lost article, the price may be any of the activities needed by that particular student.

Others

Musical Chairs and **Fruit Basket Turnover** give the child practice in moving to a pre-selected command.

Sitting Up

Repeat this exercise two or three times, increasing the speed with each repetition.

> Hands on hips, hands on your knees,
> Put them behind you, if you please.
> Touch your shoulders, touch your toes,
> Touch your ears, touch your nose.
> Raise your hands high in the air,
> At your sides, on your hair.
> Raise your hands as before,
> While you clap one, two, three, four.
>
> My hands upon my head I place,
> On my shoulders, on my face.
> Then I raise them up on high,
> And make my fingers quickly fly.
>
> Then I put them in front of me
> And gently clap them, one, two, three.

Character Imitation

Give directions for the children to act out roles of characters commonly known:

> the Jolly Green Giant
> Mickey Mouse
> Smokey the Bear
> Mickey Mantle
> a cowboy
> a ballet dancer

Fingers Out

This requires no equipment and so may be played any time. Two players engage in it; in a group, players are paired so everyone can play at once. Players count, *One, two, three*. On *three* they put their right hands out simultaneously, either closed or with one or more fingers outstretched. At the same time they should say some number, which they guess will be the number of fingers out on both hands. The player who guesses the correct number of fingers, or the nearest to it, scores a point. Five points constitutes the game.

Do This, Do That

When the leader commands, *Do this*, all the players must imitate him. But if he says, *Do that*, players who imitate him have to drop out of the game. The leader may play a piano or other instrument, dance, skate, kick a ball, or pretend he is sawing a board.

Screw Driver

The children stand with hands on neck and feet apart. They twist their trunks to the right, then all the way to the left. It should be a vigorous twist all the way from one side to the other; emphasize first the right, then the left turn.

STUNTS

Duck Walk

The child does a deep knee bend, hands on knees, and walks forward in this position. He places hands behind his back, palms together, fingers pointing backward to make a duck tail, and walks in this position.

Crab Walk

From squat position, the child reaches backward and puts both hands flat on the floor without sitting down. With head, neck, and body in one straight line, he walks backward on the floor.

Gallop

Have the child do a *follow step*, keeping the left foot in advance, left knee raised high, and back straight. This is done by standing on the right foot with left knee raised high in front. Step forward on left foot and bring up the right to the heel of the left foot. Then raise left knee and repeat. After leading with left foot for some time, lead with the right.

PANTOMIME

Jack-in-the-Box

The feet are slightly apart. Bend the knees deeply on count one. On count two spring high into the air and land on toes. Repeat several times.

Pumping Up Bicycle Tire

This entails vigorous forward, downward bending with decided knee bending and arm stretching downward. Keep good posture position with back flat.

Standing Broad Jump

In preparing to jump, stand on toes with arms above head. Bring arms forward, downward, bending knees and inclining the body forward. Spring from both feet; jump high as well as far, drawing the kneels well up. Swing the arms forward, and upward, as you jump out.

Ball Activity

Bounce a ball with one hand (right, then left). Bounce with both hands. Throw ball to right, center, and left, and from the sides, using right and left hand and then both hands.

Art

Finger painting, using both hands, is valuable here. Have the child make large circles, squares, or any design he chooses that requires large muscular movements.

Tracing

Ask the children to trace large maps, such as those of the United States, their own state, South America, North America, and the Northern and Southern Hemispheres.

EXERCISES

Hopping Exercise

The child hops on right foot when tapped on right shoulder, on left foot when tapped on left shoulder. This exercise helps him to overcome fear of what's behind him. Say *Stop* at any time to see if the child can stop immediately or takes another hop.

Angels in the Snow

The child lies on the floor on his back, with hands to his sides and feet together. At a signal, he raise his hands simultaneously above his head, then down. Then he spreads his legs as far outward as possible. After a few exercises with arms, have him use both arms and legs, increasing speed until he seems to be tired or uncoordinated. This can, of course, be done with a group.

JIGSAW PUZZLES

At first choose puzzles which have large pieces and have shapes imprinted on the background. When a child's coordination develops well enough, choose puzzles with small pieces. Later, choose puzzles without imprinted background, teaching the child to begin at a certain point (margin) or certain parts of the picture.

CHARADES

Have the children act out the following:

1. Fly like a bird.
2. Climb a fence.
3. Lady buying a hat.
4. Teacher instructing a class.
5. Father trying to eat breakfast while reading the newspaper.

G
R
A
D
E

6

CHARADES

The student must pantomime each phrase in order to communicate the idea to the rest of the group.

1. Driving a car
2. Riding a bicycle
3. Playing baseball: pitcher, batter, catcher, fielder, etc.
4. Making a cake
5. Playing a musical instrument: piano, violin, guitar, etc.
6. Imitating:
   a. Doctor examining a patient
   b. Dentist working on a patient's teeth
   c. Mechanic fixing a car

      d.   Cowboy roping a steer
      e.   Teacher or coach
      f.   Beauty operator fixing hair

7. Packing a bag for a trip

8. Loading a car for a trip

9. Catching butterflies

10. Driving a golf ball

11. Putting on makeup, using the hand as make-believe compact

ART

Drawing

Tell the children to illustrate the part of the story they liked best, or the character they liked best. Or, have them draw something they saw on the way to school.

Wiggles

One player draws a short wiggle line. The other player must take this line and make something out of it, using the wiggle line as a starting point. The paper may be turned sideways, upside down, or any way the artist desires. He may draw a house, a bird, an animal, a person, or anything he pleases.

Egghead Sketching

Provide each sketcher with a sheet of paper on which there are egg-shaped ovals. Have them draw faces, using the oval for the head. If desired, crayons could be furnished for coloring the pictures. Animals could also be drawn in this fashion.

Animal Silhouettes

Provide each child with a pair of scissors, a sheet of paper, and a pencil. The leader then calls out the name of some animal—an elephant, for instance. Each child must then cut out an elephant. Three to five minutes may be allowed. The children's names are written on them and they are put on display. Next, a pig, a dog, a cat or any other animal may be silhouetted. If the animals are cut from white paper, pasting them on dark backgrounds will enhance them.

Clay Modeling

Have the children model letters, words, animals, etc. This activity could be coordinated with other lesson content.

Just Like Me

The players may be seated or standing. They may be in rows, in a circle, in a semicircle, or arranged at random. The leader calls, *Just like me.* Every player must be where he can clearly observe the leader for every action of eye, hand, feet, head, or body, and must try to imitate exactly. The leader may sneeze. Everyone sneezes. He may wink his eye, or wag his head, or beat time, or jump up and down, or wave. Whatever he does, everyone must do immediately and together. When he says *at easy* each player must relax with his arms hanging down by his side. The game can end here or a new leader may be chosen.

Pay the Penalty

Ask a person to do something that is very difficult or impossible to do; when he cannot do it he must pay a forfeit which he can redeem by certain activities. Here are some of the tasks which might be used:

1. Put one hand where the other cannot touch it. (hand on the other elbow)

2. Say, *A big black bug met a big black bear,* six times without drawing a breath.

Activities to redeem forfeits:

1. For a boy—imitate a girl. For a girl—imitate a boy.

2. Hop across the room on one foot.

3. Pose as a football player kicking a goal, warding off a blocker, or about to make a forward pass.

4. Stand with back against the wall and try to pick up a handkerchief two feet in front of you on the floor.

Actresses and Actors

Give each player brief instructions for acting:

1. You are an old man (woman) eighty years of age. You lean heavily on your cane. Enter the room and sit down, greeting people in the room as you come in.

2. You are attending a church service. The sermon does not interest you. You get drowsy. You nod. You look about you to see if anyone noticed. You nod. You sleep. You awake with a jump. You pretend to be wide awake.

3. You are at a picture show. Someone wants to get past you to get to a seat. They tramp on your toes. You glare. Someone stands up in front of you and you crane your neck to see. The picture is exciting. At the end, the heroine is saved. You relax. You are pleased.

4. You are buying a hat at the hat shop. The hat you want costs too much. You finally buy another.

5. You hear an explosion nearby and then far away.

6. You hear someone screaming in the next room.

7. You hear a favorite tune or a friend's voice.

8. You see a flash of lighting, a rose, a violet, a horse, a cat, or a dog. Let us tell what you see by the expression on your face and your actions.

Chair Ringer

For equipment, you will need eight loops and a chair turned upside down, legs up and toward the tossing line. Label legs from one to four and play as a rotation game.

Jacks

Equipment consists of five jacks and a rubber ball. Toss the jacks on the ground. Toss the ball in the air; it may bounce once as the player picks up the jacks one at a time, then two at a time, etc. After the ball bounces, the player must catch it with the jacks in his hand before it can bounce again. This can be varied by doing other activities with the jacks before catching the ball, such as "sweeping the floor," or "eggs in the basket" (pick up the jack and put it in the other hand before catching the ball).

Follow Commands

Give commands very quickly to a row of children, about one command per second. Tell them individually or in groups to draw in the air the shape of a square, a rectangle, a circle, a triangle, a diamond, hexagon, an octagon, a baseball, a banana, a human figure.

STORIES WITH GESTURES

These exercises are also suitable for auditory-vocal association.

Funny Bunny

When the word *funny* is heard the children clap their hands. When the word *bunny* is heard, the children slap both hands down on the desk. When both words are repeated together, the children perform both operations—clap hands and slap hands down on the desk.

There was once a funny bunny (*clap hands and slap desk*) who lived in a back yard. He was so funny (*clap hands*) that his owner, Greg Wallis, would sit and laugh at him. Greg said this bunny (*slap desk*) thought that he was a dog. When a real dog would come into the yard, this funny bunny (*clap hands and slap desk*) would chase him in a funny (*clap hands*), hoppy way. The dog would look funny (*clap hands*), look at the bunny (*slap desk*), and then run!

Can you imagine a dog running from a bunny (*slap desk*) rabbit? No one could believe anything so funny (*clap hands*), but it was true.

Every evening the neighbors gathered at the Wallis home and leaned over the backyard fence. They wanted to see the funny bunny (*clap hand and slap desk*) chase a dog!

Continue this game by calling rhyming words to *bunny and funny*. The children must listen carefully and clap hands and slap desk only for the words *bunny* and *funny*.

Say the following words:

sunny	runny	honey	bunny	funny	bunny
funny	sunny	money	sunny	money	runny

These may be repeated over and over for a short time.

Play another variation of this game by making up a story with some names of children in the room. Let the children add events to the story. Have them clap hands when one person's name is called and slap desks when another's name is called. Give each child a chance to have his name called in the game. The times could be designated so that the children could expect to have their names used on certain days.

Hopper

Follow the directions in parentheses for gestures as this story is being told.

Hopper

Little cabin (*with both hands make gesture as though drawing a picture of a house; one hand draws half the house as the other hand draws the other half*) in the woods; little man (*hands to the eyes as though looking through glasses*) by the window stood. Saw a rabbit (*two first fingers sticking up like rabbit ears and make motion as a rabbit hopping*)

hopping by, knocking at my door (*gesture as though knocking on a door*).

"Help me! Help me! Help!" he cried, (*wave hands and arms forward in a distress fashion*) "'fore the hunters shoot me dead." (*With both hands make motions as though shooting a gun.*)

"Little rabbit come inside (*make motions with both hands as though beckoning someone to come*) safely to abide." (*Rock arms as though rocking a baby.*)

GRADES **7 & 8**

DRAMATICS

1.   Divide the class into small groups with three to five students in each group. Give each group a sack filled with objects to be identified (pencil, comb, clothespin, toy gun, whistle, etc.). Try to have one object for each member of the group. Have each group plan and act out a skit in which all of the objects in their sack can be used. Encourage the class to discuss the little drama, and be sure they know each object and its use.

2.   Divide the class into small groups with three to five students in each group. Give each group a different action to portray in pantomime; each action includes a specific object.

1.   Working on a farm—driving a tractor, hoeing cotton, cutting wheat with combine, spraying for insects, etc.

2.   Playing baseball—using a bat, ball, glove.

3.   Working as a secretary—typing on a typewriter, using an adding machine, taking dictation, etc.

4.   Teacher—writing on a blackboard, reading from a book, sharpening a pencil, etc.

Have the groups pantomime their action in front of the class. Let the class guess the activity being performed and the profession being demonstrated.

3.   Assign each child to be a famous person who is associated with an invention or a particular skill. Have each child act out who he is by working with the invention (by pantomime) or demonstrating the skill for which he is noted. Examples:

a.   Alexander Graham Bell (telephone)

b.   The Wright Brothers (airplane)

    c.   Florence Nightingale, nurse (thermometer)

    d.   Mickey Mantle (baseball)

    e.   Arnold Palmer (golf)

    f.   Henry Ford (automobile)

    g.   George Washington Carver, scientist (microscope)

Have the class guess who the person is and what invention or skill is being shown.

For a variation of this game, have the class divide into groups of three to five and themselves choose a person to portray. Again have the class guess who the person is and the action the group is demonstrating.

4.   Use a familiar motion song, such as *My Bonnie Lies Over The Ocean*, to be acted out.

> My (*point to self*) Bonnie (*outline her picture, both hands*) lies (*hands to side of head as if sleeping*) over (*make motions with hands indicating over*) the ocean (*ripple motion with fingers*). (*REPEAT using words of song.*) Oh (*form letter with thumb and forefinger*), bring (*palms up, making motions with fingers toward you*) back (*reach over shoulder, touch own back*) my (*point to self*) Bonnie (*draw her picture again*) to (*hold up two fingers*) me (*to self again*).

Other verses:

> My Bonnie looked into the gas tank
> The height of its contents to see;
> She lighted a match to assist her,
> Oh, bring back my Bonnie to me.

> My Bonnie's complexion is lovely,
> Her face is beauteous to see.
> One day she got caught in a rainstorm,
> Oh, bring back my Bonnie to me.

5.   Some single-situation pantomime ideas for a group include the following:

    a.   Wrap a small jewel box first in gift wrapping and then for mailing.

    b.   Cut a soft lemon pie into six equal sections and serve them to members of the group. (Don't forget the crumbs!)

    c.   Take an excited puppy for a walk on his leash.

    d.   Board a crowded bus with a weekend armload of groceries.

    e.   Watch a parade on a hot day and try to identify a particular person.

    f.   Enter a dark movie theater after a picture has started; find your way to a seat in the middle of the row, at the same time watching the unfolding of a romantic love scene on the screen.

6.   Here are brief stunt and charade ideas.

    a.   Crystal ball gazer—tells fortunes, holds hands, drops ice down back!

    b.   Scene in a toy shop—the toys come alive.

    c.   Small-town telephone operator in action.

    d.   Acting out advertising slogans, jokes, familiar sayings, songs, ballads, familiar titles.

    e.   A night in the police prowl car—*Calling all cars.* (Have several silly things happen, using names of members of group.)

    f.   No Fishing: Three fellows are on park bench. Two are pantomiming fishing; the third is not participating. A policeman asks what they are doing. "Fishing," says third one, "is what they think they're doing." "Why, there's no fishing here!" says policeman. "Okay, then," says third one, and rows away (pantomiming).

CB ACTIVITIES

Exercise 1

Direct the student as follows: "Write the following 10-codes in the air. As you write, think of the meaning of each code."

    10-04 (OK, message received)   10-77 (negative contact)
    10-10 (listening in)   10-27 (change to another channel)
    10-20 (location)   10-08 (standing by)
    10-36 (time)   10-33 (emergency)

Exercise 2

Direct the student as follows: "Write the 10-codes in the sand and then write the meaning."

Exercise 3

Direct the student as follows: "Do not say a word. Be silent and act out the operations necessary to transmit and receive information on the CB."

Part V

Perceptual-Motor Activities

Wilma Jo Bush

In any school program, at any level, the normal academic demands of students require visual-motor and auditory-motor responses. These responses, after long periods of concentration, may deplete energy levels causing some children to respond less skillfully than when they are refreshed or are not experiencing body tensions. Proper spacing of fine-motor activities with gross-motor activities (many of which are dependent upon psycholinguistic functions, as in seeing and responding, listening and responding, and thinking and responding) provides a balance which can help individuals develop better controls for the tension-producing tasks which they must accomplish.

Perceptual-motor activities can directly improve the physical function of the child by stimulating his circulatory and digestive systems and by relaxing his entire body. Indirectly, perceptual-motor activities can increase a child's well-being by satisfying him emotionally.

Since perceptual-motor training can be made an integral part of language training, and since motor activities are beneficial to overall health and skills of children, this section is devoted to activities which deal with these exercises. These games or activities are often described in the fashion of what the child does. The creative teacher may enhance each activity by adding specific directions, commands, or explanations according to the needs of the individual child. You may vary many of the activities by having children express simple number problems (and provide answers) as they are engaging in motor activities; for example, while they are walking straight lines or bending over in calisthenic exercises. Such an added approach can aid in developing attentiveness.

321

The multisensory activities in Chapter 12 are beneficial for children who need training through two or three senses simultaneously before they can learn. It must be kept in mind, however, that the hyperactive child has a tendency to over-react to some stimuli—which is not the case with the calm, sedate, or listless child. Therefore, these activities should be structured to suit the needs of each individual.

12

Multisensory Activities

It has been discovered by many classroom teachers that some children cannot learn through any one sensory channel alone. Introducing stimuli to these children through two or more senses simultaneously has become a popular practice. These techniques use the association of the visual, auditory, kinesthetic, and tactile senses. They have been used to a great advantage by Grace Fernald (1943) and other leaders in the field of learning. The activities included in this section have been added as an enrichment and as a needed supplement for children with a pronounced difficulty in the reading function.

ALL INTEREST LEVELS

BEAN COUNT*

1. Place three groups of 40 or 50 beans approximately 15″ (40 cm) apart on a table.
2. Label three signs (e.g., twos, threes, and fours) and attach in an upright position behind the beans.
3. Divide the class into teams.
4. The first player hops, skips, or jumps to the table.
5. Give the signal to go, and designate the number that the child will count together with the cut-off number, i.e., "Count by twos to 42."
6. If the child counts correctly, his team receives one point.

FERNALD MULTISENSORY TECHNIQUES

The VATK technique (Fernald, 1943) utilizes the association of visual, auditory, kinesthetic, and tactile imagery. Fernald suggests that a teacher begin remediation by telling the child that a new way of learning words will be used to help him. The child should be led to understand that many bright people have had the same difficulty he has and have used this method with success.

Remediation begins by permitting the child to select any word he wants to learn, regardless of length. It is taught by the method described below. The child learns several words by this method and is permitted to spend as much time as necessary on these first few words. Fernald recommends the following procedure:

---

* From *Learning Games for Exceptional Children*, Wedemeyer and Cejka. By permission of Love Publishing Co..

1. The word the child selects is written with crayon on paper in plain chalkboard-size script, or in print. Writing the word on sandpaper is also good.

2. The child traces the word with finger contact, saying each part of the word as he traces it. The finger must be in contact with the paper. If he prefers, the child may trace with two fingers. He repeats this process as often as is necessary for him to write the word without looking at the copy.

3. Words should always be written as a unit. When the word has been written once on a scrap of paper, the student uses it in a story. After the child writes the story, it should be typed and returned to him within twenty-four hours. He then reads it in print.

4. When the story is completed, the child files the word. under the proper letter in his word file box. This gives him practice in identifying the first letter of the word with the same letter in the file. In this way, he learns the alphabet without rote learning and without so much emphasis on letters in words. Also, the practice of using the word file is preparatory training for using the dictionary.

5. It is important that a child know the meanings of all the words he learns and they should always be used in context.

6. After a certain period of tracing, the student will be able to learn new words by looking at them and saying them over to himself.

7. Fernald adds that children with a severe reading problem should not be read to. They must learn to read for themselves rather than to depend on others.

8. Fernald also suggests that, when a child is reading, he be given an opportunity to glance over the paragraph and mark the words he does not know. These are to be written for him as suggested above, and he follows the same procedure in learning each word. These words are also filed in his word file. After this is done, the child may read the paragraph.

KINESTHETIC TECHNIQUES

Textured Flash Cards

Make a set of flash cards designed for individual needs. Stencil a picture to represent the word, and cover the picture with material representing the characteristic feel of the object. For example, a baby chick could be made by using glue covered by "Funny Fur," a fluff found in hobby shops. A ball could be vinyl or plastic adhesive. An egg could be covered with bits of boiled egg shell. (Visit upholstery shops and collect scraps to be used for this purpose.)

1. Give the student an opportunity to hear the word, see the word, feel the object, and write the word in the air (auditory, visual, tactile, and kinesthetic training).

2. The word is pronounced by the teacher and the student finds the flash card (auditory decoding).

3. The teacher reads stories written by students. They listen and retell the story or answer questions about it (auditory decoding).

4. The teacher reads a list of words. Children find cards and arrange them in categories—animals, fruits, etc. (visual-motor association).

5. Students identify pictures and objects from magazines, newspapers, TV, etc. (visual decoding).

6. Children find pictures to match flash cards, cut them out, and place them in the proper categories (visual-motor association).

Games

Games not only interest students but also challenge them.

1. Texas Tour, auditory, visual, kinesthetic training. (*Note:* This is only an example. All other states can be used in this way.) Provide each child with an outline map of the state, a tiny plastic car, and a set of cards having the number words (one, two, three, etc.). On the map trace the main highways and print the names of some of the larger cities. Also, designate a starting place for the tour. Along the highways, near cities, place large numerals, one through ten. (See Fig. 12.1.) Make one set of flash cards having a numeral on one side. Place these face down in a central location convenient for the group.

A leader goes to the center, draws a number, calls it, and students find the word to match the number. Those finding the correct number word may place their cars on that number on the map. The leader chooses another leader and sits down, or the teacher calls on certain ones to be leaders. The numbers will not be drawn in consecutive order so cars may lose mileage, but the game is to see who can get to number ten first.

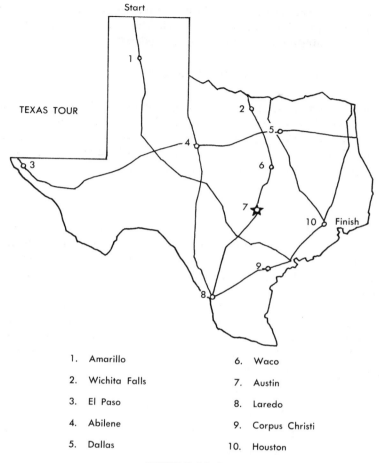

1. Amarillo   6. Waco

2. Wichita Falls   7. Austin

3. El Paso   8. Laredo

4. Abilene   9. Corpus Christi

5. Dallas   10. Houston

FIGURE 12-1

After a leader calls a number and children find the corresponding word, he may ask them to write the word in the air (kinesthetic training).

This game may be varied to teach concepts according to need. For older students it could be changed to social studies. (Examples: *go, stop, curve, caution, slow, exit, enter, minimum speed, maximum speed, detour, north, south, east, west, names of cities,* etc.) The flash cards would necessarily correspond to concepts taught. Outline maps of various states, counties, and cities could be used.

2. Other game possibilities are variations of **Password, Scrabble,** and **Speech-O** (auditory-visual decoding).

3. Draw a large picture on pellon and color it. Place the picture on flannelboard for children to see. Then remove it and

cut it into large rectangles. This makes an interesting picture puzzle. Permit the students to work the puzzle by assembling it on the flannelboard (visual-motor association).

TECHNIQUES UTILIZING BASIC TOOL SUBJECTS

Hopefully the teacher will use all three of these approaches: *see the word, hear the word,* and *feel the word through the tactile or kinesthetic approach.* While we are thinking of multiple-sensory motor exercises for the young child, this would also be helpful for adults having this disability.

Reading

1. **Word Bingo.** Make a very large (at least one yard square) chart identical to the one at the end of this exercise; then make enough small ones—with the same words, but scrambled—for each child in the class. The group of children sits around the large chart, either at a reading table or on a rug or mat on the floor. One child is the leader. He holds up a flash card on which is printed one of the words from the chart. Then he points it out and marks it on the large chart while the others mark their individual ones. This is played as in regular Bingo. The person who "Bingos" first wins a prize.

money	sound	woman	dive	change
weather	sentence	review	finger	angry
science	English	gift	sing	field
verb	child	feel	girl	cotton
window	school	door	study	listen

2. Yarn on cards: Spelled out on white cardboard the common words missed in reading. Write the words lightly with Elmer's glue, over which brightly colored yarn is glued. The children then trace over the words with their fingers. (Children love the feel of the yarn and enjoy tracing by this method.)

3. Command and Reward Box: Find two boxes, such as cigar boxes. In one box place simple commands like *Hop to the board on your right foot.* If the child can read and perform the command correctly, he may draw a reward from the Reward Box. In the Reward Box are such simple sentences as *You may get a piece of candy from my desk.* The commands and rewards could be typed or printed on strips of paper.

4. Allow the child to write a story. He may ask for any word he wishes to use but cannot spell. Each word is written for him and learned by him before it is written in his story. Whatever he writes is typed for him within twenty-four hours, so he may read it while it is fresh on his mind.

5. Say the letters of the alphabet; say and sound out words beginning with each letter.

6. Write a sentence on the board and allow the child to trace it—first with his finger, or two fingers if he chooses. Guide his hand if necessary. Then allow him to trace the sentence with chalk. After this, he should write the sentence without looking at the teacher's copy. The process may be repeated until he is able to do this. He should say the words as he writes them. (The tracing and writing of letters, words, and sentences gives the child the kinesthetic-sensory experiences that supplement the defective visual cues. This method is also helpful for the hard-of-hearing child. He gets the details of the words by tracing them and writing them, so that his reading is benefited by the technique.)

7. The child should do all reading for himself. He should not be read to, either at school or at home. He should not be made to sound out the word when he is reading unless he so desires.

8. Hold a strip of cardboard below a line on a printed page of any reading material so that the left corner indicates the beginning of a group of words. After an exposure of not more than a half second, slip the card over the words. This may be repeated several times, but the duration of exposure should not be lengthened. Always use a phrase, and do not work for more than a quarter- to a half-hour at a time. The child is to pronounce the phrase indicated by the card.

9. When reading, have the child make a light mark under the words he does not know. The words are then pronounced for him, he repeats them, writes them on a piece of scrap paper, and traces them, if it seems necessary.

These words may be put in his Word Box. Use a small file box, such as a recipe file with index cards. The child should use a separate card for each word he does not know. He may print the word in manuscript and write it on the small card. The cards should be filed alphabetically.

Spelling

Write the spelling words "in the air." The children can make this into a game by having one child write the word and choose someone in the class to guess what it is. The teacher could write the word that a child is trying to learn on a strip of paper with a crayon and allow him to trace it until he can write it without looking at the tracing.

Writing

Autokinetic cards may be used (Chronister, 1965). These are cards containing the alphabet and sentences. The child places his paper over the card and traces until he can make the letters without looking at the tracing.

To correct mirror writing, always put the child's hand in a position where he must start on the left side of his paper. This in itself usually corrects the habit.

AUDITORY AND VISUAL MEMORY EXERCISES

Presentation Types

1. **Auditory:** Letters are voiced and a response is sought from the child.

2. **Visual:** Letters are drawn in the sand, on X-ray paper on overhead projector, on clay, etc. The child sees the letters.

3. **Auditory and Visual:** The child sees *and* hears letters through the above methods.

4. **Tactile:** The child has the opportunity to feel raised letters and/or sunken letters.

5. **Tactile and Auditory:** The child has the opportunity to feel and hear the letters; the purpose is to provide a reckoning point.

6. **Tactile and Visual:** The child feels and sees the letters, necessary for developing associations.

7. **Tactile, Auditory and Visual:** The child is given the opportunity to feel, hear and see the letters.

This system is wonderful for its ability to hold the child's attention, and therefore increase his learning ability. Materials useful in developing needed concepts include: arithmetic workbooks—excellent sources for auditory and visual sequential activities; spelling workbooks—useful as a source for auditory-sequential memory, vocal encoding, auditory-vocal automatic, and auditory-vocal sequential activities.

Visual Reception

Visual reception refers to the ability of the child to understand or interpret what he sees. The following are activities used in remediation.

1. Employ the overhead projector to its fullest extent by the use of prepared transparencies. The transparencies can be prepared on X-ray film, using magic markers to draw those items that the teacher feels should be attained by the pupils.

A suggested transparency might be divided into four distinct blocks, the first containing the letter *A*, the second containing a picture of an airplane, the third containing the three forms (printed, written and script) of the letter *A*. The fourth box could be used by the teacher; she should draw or print the letter while the children draw the same in the air or in sand or clay.

The teacher uses her own discretion as to how the different blocks are utilized. She might alternate a picture to suit the boys' interests and then a picture to suit the girls' interests.

Although visual reception is the ability being exercised, other processes would be used as well. The above example demands the use of auditory memory and vocal encoding as well as the visual sense to successfully complete the activity.

Audio-Vocal Association

The auditory-vocal association process refers to the manipulation or mediation of ideas received through the auditory channel and expressed vocally. Some exercises to correct this deficiency are:

1. Using the overhead projector to identify various objects found in stores, factories, zoos, etc.; discuss the objects as the child identifies them.

2. Matching associated objects in pictures, matching similar colors or similar toys while listening to a verbal description of them.

3. Using pictures in which some action is taking place. A verbal description of each picture could be presented to

the child simultaneously, thus stimulating the auditory sense.

4. Developing the understanding of hand signals, motions, or gestures.

5. Telling the story behind a picture while the child examines the picture and decides what is missing.

6. Having the child name as many objects in a picture, or animals found in a zoo or on a farm, as he can. Making a recording of this would greatly enhance the child's interest in the activity.

7. Building the concept of alike and opposite, which tends to encourage the awareness of detail.

8. Problem-solving situations, stories with speculative outcomes, and identifying similar objects are all good.

Visual-Motor Association

This refers to the relating of ideas that are presented visually and are to be expressed motorically.

One type of appropriate activity is to have the child relate the differences and similarities of two pictures. The games of **Wahoo** and **Chinese Checkers** are good exercises in associating figures with a certain form or place.

LANGUAGE DEVELOPMENT ACTIVITIES

Here is a chart which is designed so that the child approaches word recognition through association of sight, sound, and feel.

The first column contains a word for each letter of the alphabet; all of the words suggest sound. These words can be prepared as flash cards with pictures. Compose a sentence and make a story with each word. If the child has limited experience, you may have to fill in the proper sound association for the word and picture.

The second column contains words that appeal to the sense of touch. On these cards, the letters can be made with string glued to the surface. This will give the child a chance to feel and associate the letter with the word and the word with the picture. (The letters may be written, typed, or printed, according to the age and grade level.)

The third column consists of words especially interesting to boys, and the fourth, words interesting to girls, though some appeal to both. Flash cards are prepared and used in the same way. Other words could be added to strengthen the vocabulary.

Word Chart

Letter	1	2	3	4
a	airplane	adhesive tape	automobile	apple
b	bell	balloon	baseball	basketball
c	click	cotton	catch	crown
d	ding	dacron	diving	dancing
e	earthquake	elastic	eating	envelope
f	fiddle	felt	football	formal
g	gong	gingham	gum	goat
h	horn	hemp	helmet	hair
i	iron	insulation	Indian	ice cream
j	jingle	jack-o-lantern	jacket	jewelry
k	knock	knit	kick	kitten
l	lapping	leather	license	lipstick
m	moo	material	milkshake	mirror
n	noise	nylon	nest	necklace
o	organ	orlon	owl	octopus
p	phone	plastic	picnic	party
q	quack	quicksand	quiver	queen
r	roar	rayon	ruler	riding
s	storm	string	saw	swim
t	thunder	taffeta	tackle	telephone
u	ukelele	upholster	uncle	umbrella
v	vroom	velvet	valentine	vacation
w	wham	woolen	world	weaving
x	X-ray	xylophone		
y	yawn	yarn	yesterday	yearbook
z	zing	zenith	zebra	zoology

These words can be written "in the air," on the chalkboard, or on sandpaper. The child may find it useful to trace them with his finger on the desk. If the chart has been prepared as a transparency, the child can write on an overlay, following the pattern on the transparency. As the student is writing, he should be saying the letters to himself.

MULTISENSORY TECHNIQUES

1. A VATK technique which might be used is another version of the popular game of Bingo. Cards similar to Fig. 12.2 may be made from heavy cardboard and used many times. The objects in the squares should be made of textured material such as small circles of felt or small patches of sand glued to the board.

Give each child several beans or other small objects to be placed on the squares. Read numbers from prepared cards drawn from a box. When you say, *Under the N, find the number seven,* a child who has a seven under *N* should say, *I have it.* Then he makes a seven in the air, traces one on sandpaper (each child has a sheet of sandpaper on his desk), and places seven beans

B	I	N	G	O
✳ ✳ ✳ ✳ ✳ ✳ ✳ ✳ ✳ 9 NINE	✳ ✳ ✳ ✳ ✳ ✳ ✳ 7 SEVEN	✳ ✳ ✳ ✳ ✳ 5 FIVE	✳ 1 ONE	✳ ✳ ✳ 3 THREE
✳ ✳ ✳ ✳ ✳ ✳ 6 SIX	✳ ✳ 2 TWO	✳ ✳ ✳ ✳ ✳ ✳ ✳ 7 SEVEN	✳ ✳ ✳ 3 THREE	✳ 1 ONE
✳ 1 ONE	✳ ✳ ✳ ✳ ✳ ✳ 6 SIX	 0 ZERO	✳ ✳ 2 TWO	✳ ✳ ✳ ✳ ✳ 5 FIVE
✳ ✳ ✳ ✳ ✳ 5 FIVE	✳ ✳ ✳ 3 THREE	✳ ✳ ✳ ✳ ✳ ✳ ✳ ✳ ✳ 9 NINE	✳ ✳ ✳ ✳ ✳ ✳ ✳ ✳ 8 EIGHT	✳ ✳ ✳ ✳ 4 FOUR
✳ ✳ ✳ ✳ ✳ ✳ ✳ ✳ 8 EIGHT	✳ ✳ ✳ ✳ 4 FOUR	✳ 1 ONE	✳ ✳ ✳ ✳ ✳ ✳ 6 SIX	✳ ✳ ✳ ✳ ✳ ✳ ✳ 7 SEVEN

FIGURE 12–2

on the proper square. The game continues until one player has filled five squares horizontally, vertically, or diagonally. Remember to caution all players that zero is a free square and may be used as in regular Bingo. Perhaps a reward of some type could be added to increase interest in the game.

2. **Bolts and Nuts** is a VATK technique which has proven very worthwhile as well as entertaining. Materials needed are many bolts and nuts of several different sizes and some muffin pans. Ask the students to put three bolts of the same size in three cups of the pan; put two nuts of the same size in three cups of the pan. Variations of this exercise are unlimited and the children will enjoy following the commands and working with "real" objects.

		A-Airplane	D-Dumbbell
THE MATCHING GAME			
N-Needle	C-Canoe	P-Pipe	J-Jump
W-Whistle	U-Umpire	B-Bat	K-Kite
V-Volley Ball	X-Xylophone	O-Oar	E-Eskimo
S-Ski	R-Rope	L-Lifeguard	G-Glove
I-Indian	H-Hot Rod	T-Tennis Racket	M-Mallet
Z-Zebra	Y-Yo Yo	Q-Quarterback	F-Football

FIGURE 12–3

3. **How Many?**, another number game, is made with stocking boxes, felt, and small miscellaneous objects. On one side of the box, put a numeral 1 made of felt; on the other side, put the word *one*. Glued inside this box will be one object. The object may be a doll clothespin, penny, button, bean, or any object which the child can touch. Prepare boxes for numbers one through ten.

For variety, the teacher may occasionally change the lids to see whether or not the students notice that the numbers do not correspond.

4. **Stand-up Board** requires a wooden board which will stand, four bolts, four washers, four nuts, and four small boards in the shapes of a square, triangle, diamond, and circle.

In the board drill four holes of different sizes. Each hole should fit one bolt, one washer, and one nut. In the smaller boards, drill a hole to fit each of the bolts. The student puts the bolt through the smaller board, then in the proper hole in the Stand-up Board. On the back side he places the right washer and nut on each bolt. This technique is especially helpful for visual-tactile-kinesthetic remediation.

5. **The Matching Game** is a suggestion for matching letters, words, and objects for VATK remediation. One idea is to draw twenty-six squares on a page. Write one letter and one word which begins with that letter underneath the square (see Fig. 12.3). In the square, you could also have pictures of the objects named. The child is given twenty-six felt letters and is to place them in the appropriate squares. (Variation: The squares are left blank and the child is given pictures to place above the letters and words.)

For flannelboard work, the letters, words, and objects may be cut from or backed with pellon which will stick easily to the board. The child is given a few of each and is asked to match them on the flannelboard.

13

Recreation and Motor Activities

ALL LEVELS

Many authorities believe that a child's difficulty with fine motor movement is the outgrowth of a lack of ability in gross motor movements (Kephart, 1971).

Physical growth and motor development progress from the general to the specific, from the gross to refined control. Motor patterns are the foundation for more complex learning because the motor patterns provide the basis for meaningful orientation.

One of the most important generalizations which develops out of the motor pattern is that of laterality. Laterality is an internal process; it is the awareness within the body of the difference between right and left. The awareness of right and left becomes the basis for a person's concept of space. Through combined motor and perceptual exploration, the two are matched so that perceptual information and motor information come to mean the same thing.

It is essential that such matching take place. If it does not, the child lives in two worlds—a motor world and a perceptual world, and he is constantly confused by the two aspects the outside world presents to him.

BARREL RACE*

On a sheet of paper make three circles as shown in the example.

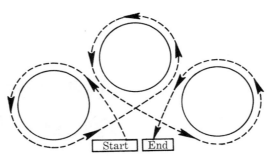

Instruct the children to pretend that they are riding horses and that the circles are barrels. Their responsibility is to ride horses around the barrels by moving their pencils around the circles. The circles should be place in various positions to provide more difficult challenges to the young students.

A variation of this activity could be to place wastebaskets in the room with just enough space for the children to move successfully between. Provide stick horses; give the same instructions and add that they are not to touch the barrels. Two teams may be chosen by you. At the end of a designated period, the team which has moved around the barrels with the least mistakes has won.

---

* From Claud "R" Zevely, West Texas State University, Canyon, Texas.

IMITATION OF MOVEMENT

In evaluating the imitation of movement, one attempts to measure areas of neuromuscular control and the translation of visual clues into motor movements.

The following is a survey designed to detect problems in (1) unilateral movement in which only one arm is required to move, (2) bilateral movements in which both arms move in the same direction, and (3) contralateral movements in which one arm moves downward while the other moves upward. These techniques may be used with all school-age children.

Instructions

The examiner takes a position and the child is to imitate him. The examiner should be sure the child has ample room and is in the proper position before moving to another position. If the child fails to imitate the position taken, he should start again in the previous position. The examiner should rest often or whenever the child wishes.

The examiner is to observe the promptness, preciseness, and definiteness of the child's responses. A child's response may parallel the examiner's movements or it may mirror them. The consistency of his responses is the important thing. If a child sometimes mirrors and sometimes parallels, it is probable that he is weak in basic laterality.

Remedial Techniques

These imitation-of-movement remedial techniques in gross motor patterns are useful for children of all ages.

1. Jumping jacks: Do slowly at first; then increase speed.

2. Hop on right foot; hop on left foot.

3. Step from left to right; reverse right to left.

4. Move legs: left leg forward, left leg backward, left leg to the side, left leg forward, right leg forward, right leg to the side, left leg backward, lift right leg with knee bent, bend left knee with foot extended behind, lift left knee with knee bent, bend right knee with foot extended behind.

5. Passing a ball: Rotate arm in full circle, starting at the side of the body, going back, and releasing the ball in the front at eye level. Be sure the arm is straight at all times. Repeat same with the left hand. Use chest pass with both hands.

6. Marching: Raise right arm and right leg. Alternate left arm and left leg.

7. Lie on back, alternately raising right and left legs.

8. Touch both toes; then raise both hands above the head.

9. Touch right hand to right foot, left hand to left foot.

10. Windmill: Touch right hand to left toe, left hand to right toe.

11. Stand with feet apart and hands over head. Swing hands down between legs, then up as far as they will go, keeping elbows and knees straight.

12. Circle arms: Extend arms and make large circular movements; gradually make circles smaller.

13. Turn in a circle, then halfway to the right and halfway to the left.

14. Combine arm movements with other body movements. (Use the game of **Statue.**)

15. **Follow the Leader:** Walk forward, walk backward, walk to the side, run kick, hop, "bear walk," etc.

REMEDIAL EXERCISES FOR SPECIFIC BODY PARTS

The following list of exercises is set up in a specific program for use in remediation of physical handicaps or deficiencies. The exercises may be used at all levels from the first to the seventh grade and may be made more strenuous by greater repetition or the addition of weights. The exercises should be administered only after proper diagnosis. This may be done by observation on the part of the instructor or by a physical examination by a qualified physician. The exercises are designed to be administered by the untrained person and may be given individually or in small groups. For best results, the exercises should follow the following criteria: They should be (1) simple, (2) localized, (3) have a long base of support, and (4), be on a non-competitive basis. Specific body parts with individual adaptive exercises appear below.

Head Exercises

1. Long sitting position—head circling right and left.

2. Long sitting position—head pushing backward with help.

3. Long sitting with-hands-on-neck position—head turning right and left.

Upper-Back Exercises

1. Lying on the back with knees bent and feet on the floor, elbows bent and arms overhead, a small pillow or folded towel under the mid-dorsal region: Rest in this position.

2. Lying on the back, knees bent and feet on floor, arms out at shoulder level, palms down: (1) Raise chest off floor, (2) relax.

3. Sitting on floor, legs crossed, hands on head: (1) Stretch as tall as possible throughout spine, (2) relax and repeat.

4. Sitting on floor, arms crossed at shoulder level: (1) Slowly move arms sideward as if pushing against imaginary resistance, (2) stretch toward fingertips, (3) return arms to starting position. Keep head still.

5. Lying on the face, arms out at shoulder level: (1) Keeping eyes on floor, raise head, chest and arms from floor, (2) hold, (3) lower.

6. Sitting with legs crossed, arms out at shoulder level: Move arms in small circles forward, upward, downward, and backward, getting most of downward and backward pull between the shoulder blades.

7. Standing, hands behind neck: (1) Bend trunk slowly forward as if against resistance, (2) Return slowly the same way. Keep spine straight.

8. Corner exercise. Facing corner, with arms stretched sideways and hands on adjoining walls at shoulder level: Slowly lean forward, keeping body in good line.

9. Sitting on floor, with trunk erect and legs out straight if possible, hands on shoulders, elbows at shoulder height: Instructor place side of leg against spine, reach over and grasp front of upper arm near elbow, then slowly force arms backward, keeping elbows shoulder high and outward rotated.

10. Sitting on bench, pull wand down back of head and then raise to arms length (with help). Repeat the exercise lying prone on mat, keeping elbows touching mat the entire time.

11. Fling arms sideward from cross to fly (open position with palms out).

Lower-Back Exercises

1. Lying on back, with knees bent and feet on floor:
   a. Bend knees to chest and clasp with hands.
   b. Raise head and try to touch head to knees.
   c. Slowly lower head, trying to touch each vertebra successively to floor.
   d. Slowly replace feet keeping lower back as close to floor as possible.

2. Lying on the back, arms stretched overhead:
   a. Bend both knees upward, and simultaneously, with throwing movement of arms, rise to sitting position, hands clasped around legs.
   b. Stretch tall.
   c. Round back, simultaneously straighten legs, and return to lying position with arms overhead.

3. Lying on the back, arms stretched overhead:
   a. With throwing movement of arms, rise to sitting position and reach toward toes.
   b. With arms forward at shoulder level, stretch throughout spine.
   c. Round back and return to first position.

4. Lying on face, strongly tense gluteal muscles, relax and repeat.

5. Lying on face:
   a. Keep knees straight, tense gluteal muscles and raise right leg off floor.
   b. Lower, repeat to opposite side. Avoid any back movement.

6. Sitting on floor, legs spread, arms out at shoulder level:
   a. Stretch with right hand toward left foot.
   b. Straighten, repeat to opposite side.

7. Standing back against wall, heels out about four inches:
   a. Draw in abdomen and flatten lower back against wall.
   b. Relax—or hollow. Repeat. Keep chest high and shoulders easily back.

8. Lying on back with knees bent, feet flat on floor:
   a. Inhale and draw in entire abdomen.
   b. Exhale and force lower back to the ground. Keep abdomen in and chest up.

9. Lying on back:
   a. Draw knees to chest.
   b. Grasp knees with hands and pull them toward chest.

10. Lying on back:
    a. Draw both knees to chest.
    b. Roll forward and up to a sitting position.

11. Lying on back:
    a. Raise the knees high and well over the chest and head.
    b. Move legs slowly in large circles as in bicycle riding.

12. Sitting, legs spread, toes turned in, arms raised at the side shoulder high:
    a. Swing right hand to left foot, left arm to rear.
    b. Return and swing left hand to the right foot.

13. Sitting, hands at back of neck, chest high, elbows well back:

 a. Slowly twist trunk as far as possible to the right.

 b. Return and twist trunk to the left, keeping the head erect and elbows well back.

14. Stand against wall, heels four inches away, head, shoulders and hips touching. Pull in abdomen and push lower back against wall.

15. Stand four inches away from wall:

 a. Bend body forward at the hips until back is arched.

 b. Slowly straighten up until the lower back, shoulders, and head touch wall.

16. Standing with back against wall: Raise heels, bend knees—knees together and back straight.

17. Passive hanging from top rung of stall bar.

Abdominal Exercises

1. Abdominal breathing. Lying on back, knees extended, arms overhead, chin in, *back flat:* Breathe deeply, raising chest and allowing abdominal muscles to relax. Hold chest up and exhale by drawing abdomen in and up. Inhale without letting chest down; continue in same manner. Keep back flat.

2. Single-leg raising: Lying on back, legs extended on floor, bring right knee to chest, extend and return to floor; bring left to chest, extend, return. Continue with alternate legs, keeping back flat.

3. Bicycle in the air: Lying on the back, bring both knees to chest, flatten back. Make circles in the air with the legs as if riding a bicycle. Keep knees close together and make big circles.

4. Side-lying scissors: Lying on side, abdomen held in, raise both legs a few inches from floor and do scissors kick, legs held straight, movement coming from the hips.

5. Double-leg raising: Lying on back, hands supporting buttocks, raise both legs together, two or three inches from floor. Hold for a short time. Return. Keep back flat. (To be given only after the abdominal muscles have been strengthened.)

6. Standing: raise knees alternately.

7. Abdominal pumping: Lying on back, knees bent, feet flat on floor, begin slow, smooth, rhythmic lowering and raising of abdominal wall by (1) strong, voluntary contraction of abdominal muscles with little or no chest movement to insure action independent of breathing; (2) relaxing and lifting abdominal wall as far as possible without strain (20-40 times daily).

8. Back-lying (alternate knees bending upward and pulling to chest): Lying on back, knees straight, bend first right, then left, knee forcibly upward and pull to chest with hands to avert sudden pressure on abdomen (10-20 times daily).

Lateral-Deviation Exercises

These are exercises for simple left dorsolumbar curve.

1. Side-bending to left. Do sitting first, later standing.

2. Arm bending and stretching, left arm sideways, right arm overhead.

3. Side leg-raise. Lying on right side, head on arm, left hand in front for balance, elbow high, raise left leg, hold, and lower.

4. Leg and arm fling. Standing, fling left leg sideways and right arm sideways-upward.

5. Place left hand on back of neck and right hand on hip. Bend trunk to left.

Neck Exercises

1. Roll head from side to side and in circles. Keep body still.

2. Isometrics: Push with neck forward and backward against dead weight.

Arm-Strengthening Exercises

1. Self-resistant. Stand straight, abdomen pulled tight, shoulders relaxed, arms at sides. Raise the left arm forward to shoulder level, palm down, elbow slightly bent. Place the right hand on the inside of the left wrist. Slowly bend the left elbow, resisting with the right, so that the left arm can just move, until the arm is completely bent. Repeat with right arm. Do exercise three to five times with each arm.

2. **Weight-lifting.** Use a small form of weight, preferably dumbbells. The weight should be sufficient to lift five times, but no more than ten times. Stand straight, abdomen pulled tight, shoulders relaxed, arm to the sides, weights held with palms backward. Slowly lift the weight forward from the fully-extended arm position to the fully-flexed arm position, keeping the upper arms close to the sides. Return slowly. When you can lift this weight ten times, increase the weight to that which you can lift approximately five times.

3. **Partner-Static.** Stand straight with the back against a wall, abdomen pulled tight, shoulders relaxed, arms hanging by the sides, palms facing the wall. Partner grasps both wrists. Try to bend the elbows with the partner preventing movement. Hold six seconds, relax one second, hold six seconds, relax one second.

4. **Push-ups.** Lie on the floor, face down. Curl the toes under. Place the hands directly under, or slightly outside, the shoulders. Push up on the finger tips. Push up to full extension, keeping the body straight. Slowly lower the body to the floor. For people who have difficulty doing the full push-up, use the modified version, which is pushing up from the knees rather than the toes.

Wrist-Strengthening Exercises

1. **Self-Static.** Hold the right arm in front of the body, palm facing up. Bend the wrist backward as far as possible so that the fingers point toward the floor. Place the left palm against the right palm. Push upward with the right, downward with the left. (Tension is felt on front of the forearm and wrist of right hand.) Repeat with left. Hold six seconds, relax one second, hold six seconds, etc. For best results in wrist exercises such as these, place the forearm on a table with the hand extending over the edge.

2. **Sideward Strength (Self-Static).** Hold the arm in front of the body so that the edge of the hand is facing the floor, the thumb toward the ceiling. Cock the wrist downward as far as possible. Place the left hand on the topside of the right hand. Push the right hand upward as hard as possible against the left. (Tension is felt on the thumb side of the right forearm.) Repeat with the left hand. Hold six seconds, relax one second, hold six seconds, etc.

3. **Sideward Strength (Self-Static).** Use same position as above, except bend the wrist toward the ceiling so that the hand

is pointing upward. Place the left hand on the underside of the right hand. Push downward, attempting to push the hand toward the floor. (Tension is felt on the little finger side of the right forearm.) Repeat with left hand. Hold six seconds, relax one second, hold six seconds, etc.

Finger-Strengthening Exercises

1. Close fingers, squeezing hard. Hold six seconds, relax one second, hold six seconds, etc. Alternate hands.

2. Place a rubber ball in the right hand. Squeeze the ball with the fingers in a rhythmic motion until the fingers begin to tire. Place the ball into the left hand and repeat.

Leg-Strengthening Exercises

1. **Back of Legs (Self-Static).** Fold a bath towel several times and lie on the floor, face up. Draw right knee toward chest as far as possible with thigh fully flexed. Lower leg should be parallel with the floor. Place towel around the bottom of the foot. Grasp both ends of towel. Push the leg as hard as possible against the towel, but prevent any movement of the thigh by holding the towel firmly. Hold six seconds, release for one second. Repeat three times. Perform same exercise with left leg.

2. **Front of Legs (Self-Static).** Sit on a table so that legs hang over the edge. Place rolled bath towel under right knee. Grasp forward edge of table with both hands. Cross the feet so that the left ankle is over front of the right ankle. Push upward and forward as hard as possible with right leg until the leg is straight. At the same time, offer enough resistance with the left leg so that right leg can just move. Return to starting position by pushing downward and backward as hard as possible with the left leg while resisting with the right leg. This entire movement should take about twenty seconds. Repeat five times. Then repeat five times with other leg.

3. **Weight-lifting.** For this exercise, use any weight that can be placed on the feet, such as weighted boots (can be secured at any sporting goods store), small sand bags, or other weighted objects. Use weight that you can lift at least three times but less than five times. Sit on table so that legs hang over the edge. Place a rolled towel under right knee. Grasp forward edge of table with both hands. Place the weight on the right foot. Slowly raise right leg until it is straight. Return slowly to starting position. The entire movement should take about twenty seconds. Repeat five to ten times. Then repeat with other leg. (*Note:*

When you can lift weight ten times without rest, add sufficient weight so that you can lift three times but less than five times. Repeat the procedure.)

4. **Partner-Static.** Sit on a bench or table high enough so the feet will swing freely from the floor. Place the leg to be exercised straight out from the table, parallel with the floor. Bend the knee about ten degrees less than full extension. Push up. The partner resists the push by placing his hand on top of the ankle. Do not rise from the table. (Tension is felt right above the knee joint on top of the thigh.) Hold for six seconds. Rest one second. Repeat three times. Perform the exercise with the other leg.

5. **Rope Jumps.** This exercise can be performed individually or in a group. Jump rope on one leg for a number of times and alternate. Jump rope in a rhythmic motion alternating legs. This is a good exercise for the legs, body coordination, and wrists.

Ankle-Strengthening Exercises

1. **Partner-Static.** Sit on table with legs hanging over the edge. Toes of the right foot should be extended downward, bottom of the foot turned away from the left side. Partner places his hand on the inside edge of the foot as close to the toes as possible, grasping the back of the ankle with the other hand for stabilization. Attempt to pull the foot inward and upward against the pressure exerted by your partner. (Tension is felt on the inside of the ankle and calf.) Hold six seconds, relax one second. Repeat three times. Repeat with the left ankle.

2. **Self-Resistant.** Without shoes, stand as straight as possible on the edge of a stair, block, or platform, toes as close to the edge as possible. Place the hands lightly on some object to help hold balance. Be sure not to support any weight with the hands. Slowly rise on the toes of the right leg as high as possible. Then lower body weight as far down as possible so that heel is below the edge of the support. Return to starting position. This movement should take approximately eighteen seconds. Do five to eight repetitions, or until leg becomes unsteady. Repeat with left leg.

Toe-Strengthening Exercises

1. **Toe Walk.** Begin in a sitting position, with knees up and feet together and flat on floor, hands resting on floor behind the hips. Press down on toes, raise arch, then release, allowing feet to move forward a few inches.

2.   For this exercise, use a large Turkish towel, and a weight which may be any object sufficiently heavy. Sit erect on a stool or a flat-topped bench with the towel spread lengthwise in front of the feet. The toes and foreparts of the feet are on the near edge of the towel; The feet are a few inches apart with the toes turned inward. Keeping the heels stationary, alternately flex the toes of each foot while gripping the towel with the toes and the outer borders of the feet and drawing the feet inward and upward (supination). In this way the towel is drawn toward the feet. Continue the exercise until enough of the towel has been drawn under the feet to make a small heap. Respread the towel and repeat the exercise several times. (*Note:* A light weight should be placed on the far end of the towel after the technique of the exercise has been mastered. The weight should be increased as the feet and toe muscles are strengthened.)

Needless to say, the above list is only a sampling of what may be done in the way of adaptive exercises for the handicapped. It should be noted, however, that overnight results cannot be expected in any program. It is imperative the children not be pushed too hard at any time during the remediation period. Severely handicapped children should be worked with individually.

This program is very good for a number of reasons. First of all, it helps to clarify the child's self-concept by orienting him in space. This program also correlates with two points of Frostig's program (Frostig, 1964): (1) Perception of position in space—it shows the same-and-different relationships of space orientations; and (2) perception of spatial relationships—it shows a correlation of fast, slow, etc. By using this program and building into it our own ideas and experiences, we, as educators, may be able to do a better job in remediation of physically handicapped people.

SKILLS

These exercises in perceptual-motor skills are designed to be used in a group situation. But if the students are too hyperactive to be in a group, they can still perform them individually.

The instructor should use a whistle. Explain to the pupils that when they hear the whistle they are to stop right where they are and be extremely quiet; then they are to follow your next command. This procedure is to encourage them to follow verbal directions as well as the whistle command. It will also help them to change actions quickly. Tell the pupils they are not to touch anyone and they are to let no one touch them. Where possible, they should be able to hold their arms out to the side at shoulder height and not touch anyone.

Position in Space

1. Walk forward—fast, then very slow.
2. Walk backward—fast, then very slow.
3. Walk sideways (right or left)—fast, then very slow.
4. Move as tall as you can—fast, then very slow.
5. Move as low as you can—fast, then very slow.
6. Skip—fast, then very slow.
7. Use combinations of the above, fast and slow.

Use the Walking Board:

1. Walk forward—have pupil gradually increase speed as accuracy develops.
2. Walk backward—have pupil gradually increase speed as accuracy develops.
3. Walk sideways—have pupil gradually increase speed as accuracy develops.
4. Use a mixture of the first three.

Allow only one pupil at a time on the Walking Board. You may want to use music to set the tempo.

The Walking Board may be either a 2 x 4 or a 4 x 4; the illustration shows the correct shape of the end supports.

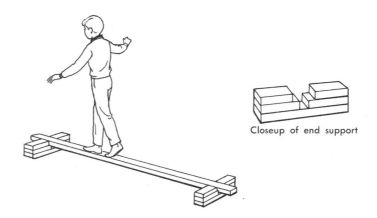

Closeup of end support

Sequence

1. **Wooden Soldier.** Pupils stand at attention and move arms quickly to various positions on command. Arms must be kept stiff like wooden soldiers.

    a.   Arms forward to shoulder height.

    b.   Arms extended overhead.

    c.   Arms sideward to shoulder height.

    d.   Arms at sides in position of attention.

The instructor could call out the positions by number. Numbers are given fast and arms are snapped into position. The instructor may request that only the left or the right arm be moved. Or he could direct that the arms move to different positions, i.e., left arm forward and right arm to the side.

2. **Tall as a Tree.** (1) *Tall as a tree,* (2) *small as a bee,* (3) *limp as a rag,* (4) *big as a bag.*

Children act out each of the commands as they are given by the instructor. The required response may be demonstrated by the instructor or left entirely up to the imagination of the pupils. When the pupils become familiar with this activity, the commands may be given quickly and in mixed order.

Vocal and Sequence

1. **Blast-off.** Pupils stand erect and, as they start counting "10, 9, 8, 7, 6, 5, 4, 3, 2, 1, *blast-off*," gradually lower their bodies

to squatting position. On *blast-off* they jump as high as they can with arms extended upward.

2. **Marching Soldiers.** The pupils stand at attention and march: *left, right, left, right.* Then graduate to the call *your left, your left, your left-right-left.* Have the pupils call commands out loud and sharply. If pupils catch on well, use *Sound-off.*

> Instructor: *Sound-off!*
> Pupils: *One, two!*
> Instructor: *Sound-off!*
> Pupils: *Three, four!*
> Instructor: *Cadence count!*
> Pupils: *One, two,* (very loud) *three, four!*

Vocal

1. **Hopping Frog.** Pupils squat on "lily pad" with hands on the floor. They hop straight up and down, then hop from one lily pad to another while croaking like a frog.

2. **Birds Learning to Fly.** Stretch one "wing" and then the other. Flap wings slowly at first and then more rapidly. Jump off the floor and flap wings as many times as possible while in the air. Other actions: birds look up at the sky, tuck wings under, hop around, drink water at a brook, fly around in a circle, peck at the ground (kneeling), or huddle in their nests being sure to chirp like birds.

3. **Puppy Run.** Bend over and place hands on the floor. Take short running steps with the hands and feet. Encourage imaginative movements and free expression. (Let pupils give their impression of a puppy in actions and sounds.)

4. **Bear Walk.** Bend over and place hands on the floor. Walk on hands and feet without bending knees or elbows. Pupils should imitate the slow, lumbering gait of a bear, using appropriate hip and shoulder action. Other bear actions may also be mimicked while using the growling bear sounds.

5. **Duck Waddle.** Do a full squat and grasp ankles with hands. Waddle forward like a duck, taking small steps and swaying the buttocks from side to side while mimicking duck sounds. Back should be straight. Shoulders should be swung forward and back as steps are taken.

6. **Mule Kick.** Stand erect. Then do a full squat and place the hands on the floor in front of the feet. Lean forward, thrust

both legs up and out quickly, then go back to squat position, making horse sounds.

7.   **Rabbit Hop.** Do a full squat. Raise arms forward. Lean body forward. When you begin to fall off balance forward, push off both feet and reach forward with both hands. When hands hit, extend the legs as in the mule kick. Then double the legs up quickly and bring them forward to the squat position again. Repeat. The pupils should learn to make no sound at all.

8.   **Indians.** Have pupils use imaginations and dance and yell like Indians in a big war-party circle.

9.   **Airplane.** Stand erect with arms extended out to sides at shoulder height. Move fast while making airplane sounds. Have pupils land and take off.

10.   **Inch Worm.** Stand erect. Place the hands on the floor in front of the feet. "Walk" the hands out as far as possible. Then walk the feet up to the hands. Keep the knees straight. Feet should be moved as close to the hands as possible. Walking steps of hands and feet should be short. Remember, inch worms do not make sounds.

11.   **Robots.** Stand erect and move arms, head, and legs stiffly like robots.

Visual-Motor

1. Different courses of action
Have the children study a pattern on the chalkboard, then carry out the activities it shows.

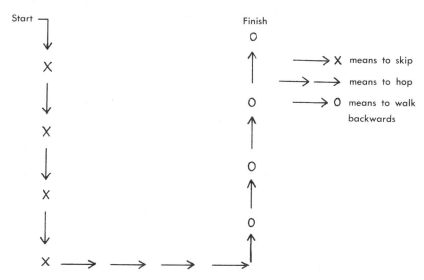

Use any combination that is needed to help any one child. Space the pupils so they will not bump into each other. Plenty of room is needed.

2. **Obstacle Course.** Use a broom handle or similar object which is approximately three feet in length. Hold one end of the handle firmly and place the other end against the wall so that the handle extends parallel to the floor and is at the level of the pupil's knees. The pupil faces the stick and attempts to step over it. Let each pupil have a try. Repeat. Then place the handle about two inches below the pupil's shoulder height. The pupil goes under it. Let each pupil have a turn. Repeat. Finally, pull the end of the broom handle away from the wall just far enough so the pupil can go between the end of it and the wall if he turns his body sidewise. Each pupil gets a turn. Repeat.

PHYSICAL FITNESS PROGRAMS

It has been demonstrated that physical, mental, and social competencies improve as a child becomes physically fit. It has also been shown that, in many cases, poorly adjusted adults could have been helped to live more socially acceptable and satisfying lives had their problems been identified earlier and a program of physical fitness been provided throughout their developmental periods.

In a study investigating the physical abilities and psychomotor functions of a group of children in a pre-vocational unit of special education in Amarillo, Texas, the results supported the hypothesis that a structured program of physical education combined with four specific techniques of psycho-educational therapy would improve the psychomotor function, physical condition, and social behavior of mildly retarded adolescents. The AAHPER Youth Fitness Tests were used as one of the measuring instruments throughout this study. This group of adolescents made almost unbelievable gains on three of the tasks in this test. (The gain was observably higher in the sit-up test, the softball throw, and the 600-yard run-walk test.) Not only did this group improve markedly in motor areas that were trained, but they also improved noticeably in spontaneity and interpersonal relationships. Thus, the total learning function was enhanced for these students (Giles, 1968).

Physical fitness is a basic objective of physical education. It is essential that all students learn to attain and appreciate a high level of physical development so that foundation skills of sports and other activities can be engaged in with confidence and pleasure. Success comes when the pupil chooses to participate in school sport programs; when the pupil, and later the adult, participates in vigorous recreational activities. Each individual should learn to enjoy taking part in vigorous exercise appropriate to his age and general ability.

The following selected principles must undergird any effective physical fitness program:

1. Programs to improve physical fitness must provide vigorous activities that will develop the physique, increase the efficiency of the cardiovascular system, and contribute to the development of physical skills.

2. Progressive resistive exercises involving increased work loads for longer periods are essential to increase the level of fitness.

3. Endurance develops in proportion to the total work done over a period of time.

4. Strength is increased through activities requiring more than 50 percent of the total strength capacity.

5. Organic efficiency is improved where rhythmical muscular activity is continued over long, unbroken periods.

6. Physical fitness is directly proportional to the levels of strength, power, and endurance achieved.

7. The school physical-education program should include a core of developmental and conditioning activities appropriate to each grade level. These activities should be carefully identified and stressed in progressive order.

8. The school health-education program provides knowledge and understanding based on scientific facts and principles in order to develop desirable health attitudes and behavior for promotion of physical fitness.

The AAHPER Youth Fitness Test (President's Council on Physical Fitness, 1967) includes seven tasks which can be administered in a gymnasium or outdoors. These tests are:

1. Pull-up (with flexed-arm hang for girls): for judging arm and shoulder girdle strength.

2. Sit-up: for judging efficiency of abdominal and hip flexor muscles.

3. Shuttle run: for judging speed and change of direction.

4. Standing broad jump: for judging explosive muscle power of leg extensors.

5. Fifty-yard dash: for judging speed.

6. Softball throw for distance: for judging skill and coordination.

7. Six-hundred-yard run-walk: for judging cardiovascular efficiency.

ALL LEVELS

SPORTS AND GAMES

1. **Ringmaster.** Players form a circle, with one player, called the Ringmaster, in the center. The Ringmaster pretends to snap a whip and calls out the name of an animal. All those in the circle imitate the animal named. This procedure continues with different animals. Finally the Ringmaster calls, *We will all join in the circus parade,* and everyone moves around the circle imitating any animal. Ringmaster then chooses another player to take his place. (*Grade 1*)

2.   **Bouncing Ball.** Children choose partners, with one becoming a ball and the other the bouncer. The one who is the bouncer pushes on the partner's head as he would in bouncing a ball. The partner does a deep-knee-bend and returns to standing position. (*Grade 1*)

3.   **Circle Ball.** Players form a circle with a leader in the center. The leader tosses the ball to each player in the circle, who then tosses it back. When the leader drops the ball, he exchanges places with a player in the circle. (*Grade 1*)

4.   **Circle Relay.** Players form circles of six to eight players. Number One in each circle is given a handkerchief. He runs to his right around the circle and gives the handkerchief to Number Two, who repeats the same procedure. The relay continues until each person has had a turn. The first circle to finish is the winner. (*Grade 2*)

5.   **Elephant Walk.** Each child stands and bends forward at the waist. He clasps his hands and lets his arms hang in imitation of an elephant's trunk. The arms are swung from side to side as the child walks with back rounded and knees slightly bent. (*Grade 2*)

6.   **Target Toss.** Players form a group of four to eight. Each group has a beanbag and a circle drawn on the floor. Each group forms a straight line twenty feet from the circle. Each child tosses the beanbag at the target and receives one point for getting it in the circle. The group with the greatest number of points at the end of the playing time wins. (*Grade 2*)

7.   **Call Ball.** Six to ten players form a circle. One player who is in the center is *It*. He tosses the ball into the air and calls a player's name. This player must catch the ball before it bounces more than once. If the player succeeds, he becomes the new *It*. If not, the one in the center remains until a player successfully catches the ball. (*Grade 3*)

8.   **Hop Tag.** Eight to ten players spread around the playing area. One player who is *It* hops around trying to tag another player who is also hopping. When another player is tagged, he becomes the new *It*. (*Grade 3*)

9.   **Three Deep.** Two circles of from ten to twenty-five players are formed with one circle inside the other. Each child in the inside circle stands directly in front of a child in the outside circle. One child is chosen to chase another around the outside of the circles. The one being chased may step in front of a child on the inside circle to avoid being tagged. The outside player

of this group then becomes the one being chased. If the runner is tagged, he turns and chases the tagger. (*Grade 3*)

10. **Post Ball.** Two or more teams participate. They form parallel lines, teammates one behind the other, about three feet apart. A leader stands facing each line, about twelve feet away. On signal, the leader tosses a ball to the first player in the line, who catches it, throws the ball back, and squats in line. The leader repeats the same procedure with each one in the line. The team finishing first and dropping the ball the least number of times wins the game. (*Grade 4*)

11. **Chain Tag.** One player is *It*. He tags another player, and the two join hands and run to tag other players. Each player who is tagged joins the chain at the end. Hands must remain joined and the players at the beginning and end of the chain are allowed to tag. (*Grade 4*)

12. **Circle Weave Relay.** Players form circles, six to eight players to each. One player from each circle starts the relay by running to the outside of the player to his right, to the inside of the next, and continues weaving in this pattern around the circle to the starting position. He tags the next player to his right, who similarly runs to his right around the circle. The relay continues until everyone in the circle has had his turn. The team to complete the relay first is the winner. (*Grade 4*)

13. **Bull in the Ring.** Ten to twelve players form a circle with hands joined. One player, the Bull, is inside this circle. The Bull tries to break through the circle or slip under the hands. If he gets out, all players chase him. The player who did the tagging becomes the new Bull. The Bull is allowed three tries to break through. If he fails, he chooses the new Bull. (*Grade 5*)

14. **Leap Frog.** Players take squatting positions four to five feet apart in a line. One player runs toward the end of the line and leaps over each player in succession by placing his hands, fingers forward, on the player's shoulders and pushing off as he jumps. When he reaches the front of the line, he squats down. The last person in the line rises and follows the same procedure until everyone has had an opportunity to leap the entire line. This could also be played in teams or in relay races. (*Grade 5*)

15. **Bat Ball.** Players divide into two teams, one at bat and one in the field. A volleyball or soccer ball is used. The first player at bat hits the ball into the field and runs to a base and home. If the player makes the complete trip without the fielder catch-

ing the fly or hitting him below the waist with the ball, one run is scored. Three outs and teams change. The team with the most runs wins. The bat and ball could be plastic. (*Grade 5*)

16. Hot Potato. Players form a circle with six to twenty players in each circle. Players all sit crosslegged and roll or punch balls across the circle. Three or four balls are kept going at once. Players try to knock the ball past other players through the circle. The player permitting the least number of balls to go through the circle wins. An extra player retrieves all the balls going out of the circle. No ball higher than the shoulders counts. Balls may not be bounced or thrown. (*Grade 6*)

17. Walking Chairs. Children form a line, standing behind each other with their hands on the waist of the one in front. All bend knees to sit on the knees of the one behind. Last person must balance himself in the sitting position; they rock forward and backward. (*Grade 6*)

18. Chinese Stand Up. Partners stand back-to-back and lock elbows with each other. They push against each other's back and with small steps walk forward and sit on the floor. To stand up, the partners keep arms locked and bend the knees with the feet close to the body. They brace their back up against each other's back, extend legs, and come to a standing position. (*Grade 6*)

19. Indian Wrestle. Partners stand facing opposite directions beside each other. The outsides of the right feet are placed together. Right hands are joined. The two players push and pull until one person's right foot is lifted from position. The person whose right foot remains in position wins. (*Grade 7*)

20. Line Dodge Ball. Players standing side-by-side form two lines twenty feet apart with a four-foot square drawn in the middle. One person stands in this box, and the other players take turns trying to hit him below the waist with the ball. The player may dodge the ball but must keep one foot in the box. When hit, the player changes places with the one who hit him. (*Grade 7*)

21. Hand Wrestle. Partners lie on their abdomens on the floor, facing each other with their right hands grasped and right elbows together. They push on each other's hand, attempting to force the opponent's hand to the floor. The one forcing the other's hand down wins. (*Grade 7*)

22. Wheelbarrow. Partners stand, one behind the other, facing the same way. The one in front places his hands on floor while the one behind lifts his legs at the knees. The first child walks forward on his hands and with his partner holding his legs in wheelbarrow fashion. This can be used in teams or in relay races. (*Grade 8*)

23. **Tug Pick-Up.** Two people hold a six-foot rope at opposite ends. A block is placed six inches behind each person. On a signal, each player tries to pick up the block behind him. Releasing the rope or permitting the other player to reach the block gives one point to the winner. One match consists of three points. (*Grade 8*)

24. **Indian Leg Wrestle.** Partners lie side-by-side on their backs, facing opposite directions. The right arms are locked together. On signal the partners raise right legs and lock knees. They attempt to throw each other over by pushing, pulling, or shoving. A match consists of two out of three victories. (*Grade 8*)

This list contains just a few of the activities or games that can be played with groups of children. There are many more that can be played individually. These games can be modified to fit your own situation by changing some of the rules and some of the equipment.

Part VI

Educational Planning

Marian T. Giles

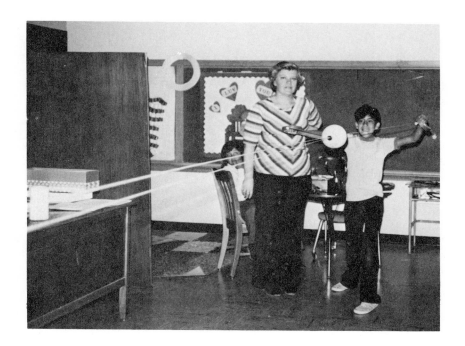

14

Guidelines for Teachers

Since the first edition of this book appeared on the bookshelves in 1969, teachers and college students in education, psychology, and speech pathology have coordinated activities from this text into programs based on particular test scores derived from the *Illinois Test of Psycholinguistic Abilities,* the *Wechsler Intelligence Tests,* the *Frostig Developmental Test of Visual Perception,* the *Wepman Auditory Discrimination Test,* and many others. This practice facilitated the work of public school supportive staffs who were assigned the tasks of testing and developing programs for hundreds of children during each year. The activities also provided empirical data for those scientifically minded diagnosticians concerned with how children learn.

Demands for diagnostic services increased, and in many schools requests were "backlogged" for as much as 6 months. Concurrently with these growing pressures, the use of teacher assessment began to pick up momentum. Intensive efforts were made to train teachers and diagnosticians to closely observe the learning behaviors of children, correlate their observations with formal test results, and to design educational plans that integrated the well-sequenced curriculum, utilized in general or special education, with the learning processes and styles of their students (Giles, 1973, 1974).

The key to this method is clearly teacher observation, informal testing, and criterion-referenced testing. The trained observer becomes the instrument (Bush & Waugh, 1976), and by this means a greater number of services can be provided. Not only does this relieve the diagnosticians of the burden of hundreds of cases, but it also gives them more time for analysis of the more critical ones. Through this process of careful observation, the teacher becomes more competent in the art of assessment, and is better skilled to interact with the diagnostician regarding the needs of the child.

To facilitate the development of the skills needed to meet this new challenge, we would like to respond to three questions often asked by teachers.

1. *What are the differences in developmental, remedial, and compensatory methods of teaching?*

Developmental: A method of exposing a student initially to a sequence of information needed for mastery of skills and abilities used in reading, spelling, math, and other subjects. This method can be used from the early childhood level to the adult level and is highly recommended when new or forgotten information is taught.

Remedial: For use when developmental techniques have been tried already. An educational method which stresses the amelioration of those skills and abilities which are measured below expected levels. It uses special techniques and materials in a highly repetitive fashion.

Compensatory: A technique which uses the students well-established abilities or strength areas as a means of mastering subject matter content or vocational skills at or above her grade or age levels. Attention is directed to developing coping skills for a successful adult life.

2. *Where should a person begin training or working with a student who has a learning problem?*

Make a genuine effort to get to know the student as soon as possible. This strategy will require visiting on a daily basis, as well as being especially observant of personality, interests, social interaction with both peers and adults, abilities, disabilities, and academic achievement levels. Check to determine what makes the student smile, relax, or become tense. Be a good listener; try to understand why and what is being said. Be aware of facial expressions which may provide clues to emotional feelings. Be a sensitive, perceptive person whose integrity and actions create trust. At the end of a period or day, fill out a behavioral checklist (Giles, 1973) on each child showing problems in learning. If the children have been observed faithfully for several weeks, much information will have been already established.

Administer pretests designed to measure a child's entering achievement levels in each area of content soon to be covered. Many learning disabled children do poorly on group tests and may respond more positively to individual assessment. Follow the principle of using testing methods by which the child will soon be taught. For example, if the majority of the child's work will require comprehension of written materials, use written tests for assessment to determine the level of achievement in that specific area.

Many formal assessment tools have been designed for teachers' use specifically.* Some of the more useful ones are designed for children who are "test shy" or highly anxious. When these tests are administered by a competent teacher the child trusts, the testing session can be intellectually stimulating and rewarding to both. In addition, if copious notes have been taken regarding the child's behavior prior to, during, and after the test is administered, the interpretations can be made with greater reliability and validity.

The observations, the notes on the checklist, and the assessment instruments may be correlated with previous test results in the child's folder. At this point, check to see if all the information has been collected. The learner is the most important facet of this program, and it is by means of this information that the child's problem is sufficiently understood to permit choice of activities for intervention. Information from the following five areas should be obtained:

a. The learner's functional problem-solving ability as obtained from intelligence tests.

b. The learning process and styles, including strength and weaknesses.

---

* Key Math, *Peabody Individual Achievement Test, Woodcock Reading Test,* Slosson, *Wide Range Achievement Test.*

    c.   Achievement data, including criterion measurement of specific behavioral objectives.

    d.   Background information: developmental, medical, educational, socioeconomic, and emotional.

    e.   Interests, and positive and negative reinforcers to be used as change agents (Stellern & Vasa, 1973).

    3.   *What teaching techniques or systems should be used?*

Efforts have been made by numerous researchers regarding effective teaching. These studies include research on teaching by the various traditional methods, language, phonics, and basal readers. All methods can be shown to be effective. Chapter One describes *constructs* for teaching approaches, which include the psycholinguistic, the Piagetian, and the structure of intellect. The reader may choose to reread this chapter, especially if the terminology therein is new. Ideas from each may afford a workable, systematic plan with which to begin training. Rather, the reader *may choose* to use the activities in this book without reference to the *constructs*. If so, the activities are indexed specifically to phonics, arithmetic, and spelling. The index is found in the appendix.

TEACHING SUGGESTIONS

Special suggestions to teachers are listed as follows. These suggestions have been found helpful in programs for learning disabled children.

1. Maintain an emotional atmosphere which is warm, supportive, and nonthreatening. Children in such an atmosphere should show increased ability to learn. With some children, physical contact, such as a friendly hand on a shoulder, will be a powerful means of communicating warmth. On the other hand, touching is not advised if the teacher finds that it makes the child uncomfortable.

Specifics:

Accentuate the positive; play up recognition for even partial success. Punitive, competitive, or authoritarian attitudes will defeat any program from the beginning. Patience, a relaxed attitude, and acceptance of the child will be of primary importance in teaching.

2. Reduce the number of distractions as much as possible, such as background noises, other children moving around, and a large number of different learning materials in sight at any given time.

Specifics:

To offset the child's distractibility, remove letters, pictures, or sentences from the blackboard before replacing them with new ones. Use preferential seating and place children where there are fewer distractions.

3. Structure the learning situation as concretely as possible.

Specifics:

Explain and define to the child specifically what is to be done or what is expected, avoiding generalizations. Say, "Write these sentences now," rather than "Do your assignment."

4. Break down the units of learning into the smallest possible steps. Determine which approach is needed for the child and choose one of the following specifics.

Specifics:

  a. Teach reading by means of individual letters and sounds instead of by the "whole word" method.
  b. Teach reading by the "whole word" method. (Usually, trial and error will determine which method is more effective.)

5. Use a variety of sensory media simultaneously.

Specifics:

Be sure the child is looking at you when you are giving directions. The child should *hear* your words and *see* your nonverbal clues and gestures. In general, visual, auditory, and tactile stimuli in each learning situation will help strengthen areas of weakness,* and at the same time allow more opportunity for understanding the directions given. By this means the child can associate what you say with something that can be seen and touched.

6. Improvise new teaching methods to fit the needs of different children.

---

* The exception to this rule is that some children cannot take stimulation through all senses at one time.

Specifics:

Look for "crutches" that will help; encourage their use. A common example is the ABC song (p. 254). Other memory tasks can also be set to music. Poems and rhymes are other examples of aids, as are rebus* pictures in reading. Experiment with a variety of methods to discover which ones are best suited for each child. This strategy is called "diagnostic teaching" and is essential in view of the wide variation of strengths and weaknesses children exhibit. It merely means trying out a variety of approaches and comparing their results.

7. Lean heavily upon drills and repetition to commit academic materials to memory. Establish routine habits of procedure for such things as putting away clothes or books. Try to establish automatic behaviors so that eventually the child will learn to react more on the basis of habit (i.e., when memory and judgment are impaired).

Specifics:

Regular reviewing and daily repetition should be an essential part of classroom procedure. Present drill material in a variety of *different* forms and situations if the child tends to perseverate. Rote repetition sometimes causes a child to perseverate.

8. "Modern math" is often not understood by children with learning disabilities. The older drill methods of teaching adding, subtracting, multiplying, and dividing may be more effective because abstract thinking used in modern math may be too difficult for them.

9. Simplify the child's tasks by giving one task at a time instead of several.

Specifics:

Give three spelling words instead of ten, or give one arithmetic problem at a time.

10. Some hyperactive children may need a shortened school day for a period of time, since a whole day is sometimes too tiring for them. If this alternative cannot be arranged, try breaking up their day with successive periods of free time and academic work. In some cases, the activities in gym classes are too physically stimulating or too demanding for children with coordination problems. If so, their programs should be modified according to their needs.

---

* Picures of objects to substitute for the names of those objects.

Specifics:

Schedule "buffer time" in between strenuous physical activities to allow the child time to quiet down when she has been over-stimulated.

11. When necessary, attempt to increase attention span to at least 15 minutes duration before attempting academic work.

Specifics:

Alternate 5-minute periods of free play with 5-minute periods of practice in attending through games such as Simon Says and Follow the Leader. Gradually, the periods of attending can be increased minute by minute and periods of free play reduced. Most children can learn within 2 weeks to attend for 15 minutes at a time if trained in this manner.

12. Employ the techniques of "error-free discrimination" so that the child's chances of making an error are so sharply reduced that success occurs at least 90 % or more of the time. When the child has a history of failure, make a special effort to avoid giving her work which is beyond her ability. Begin at a level which is low enough for success, but high enough for some element of challenge.

Specifics:

If memory is a problem, use simple multiple-choice questions instead of completion questions. Ask for information which can be answered satisfactorily.

13. Make ongoing evaluations. Structure these so that the children can see their own growth.

Specifics:

Use charts and graphs designed for each subject.

REFERENCES

Abilene Independent School District. The Abilene-Giles resource guide for evaluation and teaching. Level II (Target II). Abilene, Tex.: Author, 1976.

Bush, W. J., & Waugh. K. *Diagnosing learning disabilities* (2nd ed.). Columbus, O.: Charles E. Merrill, 1976.

Giles, M. T. A continuity model for inservice training of educators. Fort Collins, Colo.: Giles Institute for Educational Research, 1975.

Giles, M. T. *Individual learning disability classroom screening instrument-adolescent level, grades 4–12.* Evergreen, Colo.: Learning Pathways, 1973.

Stellern, J. & Vasa, S. F. A primer of diagnostic-prescriptive teaching and programming. Laramie, Wyo.: University of Wyo. Press, 1973. (Available from University of Wyoming, Laramie, Wyo. 82070).

Bibliography

Bush, W. J., & Waugh, K. W. *Diagnosing learnings disabilities*. Columbus, O.: Charles E. Merrill, 1976.

Fernald, G. M. *Remedial techniques in basic school subjects*. New York: McGraw-Hill, 1943.

Fisher, A. "The Coffee-Pot Face," *My Poetry Book*. Edited by G. Huffard. New York: Holt, Rinehart & Winston, 1956.

Frostig, M, & Horne, D. *The Frostig program for the development of visual perception*. Chicago: Follett Educational Corporation, 1964.

Garton, M. D. *Teaching the educable mentally retarded—Practical methods*. Springfield, Ill.: Charles C Thomas, 1961.

Giles, M. T. Classroom research leads to physical fitness for retarded youth. *Education and Training of the Mentally Retarded*, 1968, III (2).

Holt, J. *How children fail*. New York: Pitman, 1964.

Kephart, N. C. *The slow learner in the classroom*. Columbus, O.: Charles E. Merrill, 1960.

Kirk, S. A., & Kirk, W. *Psycholinguistic learning disabilities: Diagnosis and remediation*. Urbana: University of Illinois, 1968.

Kirk, S. A., & McCarthy, J. J. *The Illinois Test of Psycholinguistic Abilities* (Rev. ed.). Urbana: University of Illinois, 1968.

McCarthy, J. M. Learning disabilities. *Grade Teacher*, May-June, 1967, pp. 97–102.

Merrill Publishing, Charles E. *Nicky* and *Uncle Bunny*. In Merrill Reading Skilltext Series. Columbus, O.: Author, 1977.

Miller, J. G. *Using phonics first*. Amarillo, Tx.: Amarillo Public Schools, 1966.

Myers, G. C. *Creative thinking activities*. Columbus, O.: Highlights for Children, 1965.

Osgood, C. F., & Miron, M. S. *Approaches to the study of aphasia*. Urbana: University of Illinois, 1963.

Paraskevopoulos, J., & Kirk, S. A. *The development and psychometric characteristics of the revised* Illinois Test of Psycholinguistic Abilities. Urbana: Ill.: University of Illinois, 1969.

Robinson, et al. *Basic reading skills workbook*. Glenview, Ill.: Scott, Foresman and Company, 1963.

Russell, D. H. et al. *Roads to everywhere.* In Ginn Basic Readers. Boston, Mass.: Ginn and Company, 1961.

Wedemeyer, A., & Cejka, J. *Learning games for exceptional children.* Denver, Colo.: Love, 1971.

Indexes

PHONICS ACTIVITIES

Kindergarten

Addition I, 93
Addition II, 93
Alert Games, 121
Animal Names, 34
Associating What Is Heard, 70
Big and Little Box, 69
Common Sounds, 36
Completion I, 94
Completion II, 95
Do What I Say, 119
Finish My Rhyme, 94
Hearing Numbers, 37
Learning Games, 92
Letters, 152
Like Sounds, 70
Pretend Animal, 119
Rhymes, 70
Rhyming, 35
Songs and Rhymes, 118
Sound Blending, 92
Taped Sounds, 70
Teacher Listens, 93
Which Sounds Best, 94

Grade 1

Activity #4, 299
Activities for Auditory Memory,
    122
Classifying Sounds, 73
Concentration, 124
Following Verbal Directions, 38
    #2, #4, #5, #6
Grammatic Closure Activities, 96
Identifying Familiar Sounds, 39
Object Identification, 155–157
    #1–#23
Rhyming and Matching, 73
Use of Letters and Numbers, 224

Grade 2

Activity #1, 211
Categorizing and Classifying
    #3, #4, 74–75

Grade 2 (cont.)

Identifying:
    Familiar Sounds, 41
    Nonsense, 40
Language Master, 97
Other Techniques, 101
Recognizing Correct Forms of
    Words, 100
Repetition of Sounds in Environ-
    ment, 126
Rhyming Game, 278
Sequencing, 125
Training Ability to Classify, 185
Understanding Inherent Rela-
    tionship Between Words, 98

Grade 3

Activity *h*, 233
Auditory Sound Blending, 104
Automatic Closure, 101
Classifying, 76
Identifying:
    Familiar Sounds, 46
    Objects, 161

Grade 4

Activity #2
    a and *b*, 214
Automatic Closure, 106
Identifying Letter Sounds, 79
Jump Rope Songs and Chants,
    252–255
Listening, 80
Noises and Sounds, 167
Sounding Bee, 79
Sound Classification, 79
Suggested Activities
    #8, 235
Tongue Twister, 133
The Vowel Game, 78
Writing, 330

Grade 5

Alphabetizing, 137
Auditory Cues, 54

Grade 5 (cont.)

Commercial Materials, 242
Consonant Ending Sounds, 134
Facts and Opinions, 83
Hearing Syllables, 135
Listen-and-Say Puzzle, 135
Listening Activities, 55
Plurals, 109
Rhyming Words, 109
Tongue Twisters, 136
Training Games, 133
Word Analysis, 57

Grade 6

Clay Modeling, 313
Choral Reading or Speaking, 111
Funny Bunny, 315
Homonyms, 243
Memory Sequencing, 242
Prefixes and Suffixes, 244
Repetition in Sequence, 137
Sentence Completion, 112
Sorting, 196
Suffixes, 113
Tongue Twisters, 138

Grade 6 (cont.)

Use Pictures to Label, Describe
    and Categorize, 170
Word Syllables, 244

Grades 7 and 8

Activities and Exercises
    #10, 86
Activity
    #3, 244
Alphabetizing by Memory, 141
Audiovisual Aids, 89
Building Sentences, 141
Closure, 115
Identifying Familiar Sounds, 63
Initial Consonants, 141
It Happened Like This, 142
Making Comparisons in an Aural
    Message, 85
Making Inferences and Drawing
    Conclusions, 88
Pass-Along, 142
Repetition in Sequences, 139
Suggested Activities
    #2, 244
Supplying the Missing Word, 114

MATH ACTIVITIES

Number and Concept

Kindergarten

Candy Designs, 178
Chalkboard Copying, 181
Finding Identical Pictures, 179
Hearing Numbers, 37
Look and Tell, 267
Number Fun, 121
Numbers, 152
Opposites, 69
Pictures, 151
Rectangle Folding, 35
Rhythm Claps, 36

Kindergarten (cont.)

Sequencing Memory, 118
Shapes, 151
Silent Counters, 178
Speed Game, 121
Valentines, 154
Visual Closure, 204

Grade 1

Activities for Auditory Memory,
    122
Activities
    Item *h*, 210

Math (cont.)

Following Verbal Directions, 37
Visual Relationships, 182
  #3, 183
Use of Letters and Numbers, 224

Grade 2

Activity
  #24, 228
  #11, 226
Association Parts in Sequence, 187
Concepts, 161
Finding Likenesses and Differences, 160
Identifying Color, Letters, Numbers and Geometric Forms, 158
Language Master, 97
Music and Rhythm, 126
Nursery Rhymes, 127
Sequencing, 125
Visual Motor Activities
  #7, 226

Grade 3

Identifying Colors, Letters and Geometric Forms, 163
Pegboard Games, 190
Understanding and Following Verbal Directions, 43
Understanding Verbal Concepts, 42
Write About First Things, 44

Grade 4

Activity
  #3, 214
  #4, 215
  #14, 283
Classifying Pictures, 191
Different Percepts, 166
Incongruities, 193
Jump Rope Songs and Chants, 252–255
Number Activities, 167

Grade 4 (cont.)

Perception of Position in Space, 168
Quantity, 167
Repetition of Digits, 132
Rhymes, 132
Tapping Rhythm, 141
Time, 167

Grade 5

Art, 311
Bean Count, 324
Concentration Games, 136
Dial-A-Phone, 134
Fingers Out, 309
Operational Perception: A Number Game, 169
Repetition in Sequence, 133
Short-Answer Questions, 52
Teaching the Days and Months, 56
Vocal and Sequence, 351

Grade 6

Activities for Math Concepts, 172
Miscellaneous Activities, 172
  #3 and #4
Repetition in Sequence, 137
Sorting, 196
Techniques to Develop Sequencing Ability, 170
Use Pictures to Label, Describe and Categorize, 170
  #7

Grades 7 and 8

Activities and Exercises
  #4, 86
Activity
  #6, 245
Distinguishing Relevant and Irrelevant Information
  #2, 89
Games
  #4, 174

Math (cont.)

Identifying Pictures and Objects, 173
#4, 173
Repetition in Sequence, 139

Grades 7 and 8 (cont.)

Sorting, 201
Top Ten, 142
Training the Ability to Classify, 198

SPELLING ACTIVITIES*

Grade 1

Use of Letters and Numbers, 224

Grade 2

Spelling Aid, 128

Grade 3

Motor Activities, 229
Multisensory Techniques, 333
Spelling, 330
Techniques Utilizing Basic Tool
    Subjects, 328
Textured Flash Cards, 325
Writing, 330

Grade 4

Fernald Multisensory Techniques, 324
Games, 326–327
Kinesthetic Techniques, 325
Language Development Activities, 332
Sounding Bee, 79
Vowel Game, 78

Grade 5

Commercial Materials, 242
Hearing Syllables, 135
Word Analyses, 57
Words, 242

Grade 6

Common Characteristics, 84
Homonyms, 243
Memory Sequencing, 242
Prefixes and Suffixes, 244
Repetition in Sequence, 137
Typing, 242
Word Syllables, 244

Grades 7 and 8

Activity
    #3, 244
    #7, 245
C.B. Activities
    #4 and #5, 175
Sight Vocabulary, 84

SUBJECT INDEX

AAHPER Youth Fitness Test, 357
Adynamia, 251

Agrammatism, 7
Anagrams, 242
Aphasia, 7

---

* See all phonics activities, also.

Subject Index (cont.)

"A Picture-Word Book," 160
Apraxia, 250
Autokinetic Handwriting Program, 242

Basic Sight Vocabulary Cards, 242
"Billy Goat Gruff," 270
Bingo, 333
"Blondie," 171
Bowman Manipulative Books, 180

Children's Digest, 228
Civil War–1861, 201
Continental Press, 226
Cuisenaire Rods, 4, 12, 163

"Dennis the Menace," 171
Dysphasia, 251
Dolch Sentence Game, 292
Dyslexia, 7
Dysnomia, 251

Expressive language disorder, 250
Eye Gate House, Inc., 280

Filmstrips, 280
    Find Another Word
    Homonyms
    Name the Right Words
    Read and Tell
    Synonyms
First World War–1917, 201
Frostic Test of Visual Perception, 4, 365
Fruit Basket Turn Over, 225

"Hansel and Gretel," 280
Heavy, Heavy, Hangs Over Your Head, 273
"Henry," 235
Highlights for Children, 228, 230
Humpty Dumpty, 228

Illinois Test of Psycholinguistic Abilities, 4, 9, 11, 12, 17, 21, 365

"Jack and the Bean Stalk," 274, 280
Judy-See Quees, 242
Jack-In-The-Box, 300

Key Math, 4, 367

Language
    expressive, 9
    inner, 9
    receptive, 9
    development, 19
Levels
    automatic, 10
    representational, 10
Link Letters, 242
Little Golden Dictionary, 270

Magic Cards, 189
Match Game, 201
Materials for exceptional children, 183
Memory, 11
    auditory, 9
    sequential, 9, 21
    visual, 9

Name and Know Book, 268
"Nancy," 171
Neurological Impress System, 111

Paragrammatism, 7
Paraphasia, 7
Password, 201, 372
Peabody Lang. Develop. Kit, 208
Peabody Ind. Ach. Test, 367
Peanuts, 171, 235, 243
Pictionairies, 162
Physical Fitness Programs, 355–357
Process
    receptive, 9, 10
    organizing, 9, 10
    expressive, 9, 10
Put Your Finger in the Air, 300

Old Maid, 201

Remediation, 12
Revolutionary War–1776, 201
Rummy, 201

Subject Index (cont.)

Scrabble, 327
Sequencing Boards, 268
Simon Says, 371
"Simple Objects to Color," 160
Slosson Test, 367
SOI, 21, 22
Solitaire, 201
Speech-O, 327
Stanford-Binet Intelligence Test, 4
Starchips, 215
Stern (Catherine) Blocks, 4
Structure of Intellect (SOI), 21, 22

Task Analysis, 13, 14, 15
Telegraphic speech, 7

Tongue Twisters, 284
Turn the Page Books, 268

Uncle Wiggly Game, 160
Using Phonics First, 161

Wahoo, 332
Wechsler Intelligence Test, 4
Wepman Auditory Discrimination Test, 4, 365
Wide Range Achievement Test, 367
Woodcock Reading Test, 367
Word Bingo, 328
Word blindness, 7
Word deafness, 7
Wordo, 190

AUTHOR INDEX

Alon, G., 209
Atkinson, R., 10, 11, 24

Bateman, B., 28, 29
Blumstein, S., 6, 7, 24
Bouillaud, 6, 7
Bush, W. J., 1, 12, 13, 15, 23, 27, 206, 345, 304, 305, 366

Carroll, J. B., p. 5, 23
Cattell, R., 3
Cejka, J., 324
Chalfant, J., 13, 15, 23
Chomsky, N., 4
Chronister, J., 330
Clevenger, A., 111
Consilia, Sister M., 251, 263

de Hirsch, K., 250, 251, 264
Dunn, L. M., 12, 24

Eichler, 183
Ellis, J. V., 6, 24

Feldman, B., 21, 24
Fernald, G., 4, 24, 239, 245, 323, 324, 325
Fisher, A., 123
Frostig, M., 159, 184, 209, 349
Furth, H., 17, 20, 24

Galton, 3
Garton, M. D., 157
Gearhart, B. R., 29
Giles, M. T., 12, 23, 207, 291, 366, 367, 393
Goodglass, H., 6, 7, 24
Greer, J. G., 5, 25
Guilford, J. P., 4, 11, 12, 24

Hammill, D., 12, 24, 25
Head, H., 7, 24
Heckelman, R. C., 111
Hilgard, E., 9, 10, 11
Hughes, R., 215
Hunter, M., 146, 147, 148

Author Index (cont.)

Iscoe, I., 5

Jackson, J. H., 7, 24
Jansky, J. J., 250
Johnson, D., 9, 13, 24, 29, 250, 251, 264
Junkala, J., 13, 24

Karnes, M. B., 12, 24
Kass, C., 20, 25
Kephart, N. C., 160, 295, 337
Kirk, S., 5, 8, 9, 10, 11, 17, 25, 68, 266, 295
Kirk, W., 5, 9, 10, 25, 266, 295

Langford, W. S., 250
Larsen, S., 12, 24, 26
Lehtinen, L., 28, 30
Lennenberg, E., 4
Lerner, J. W., 29, 30, 250, 264
Locke, J., 3
Luria, A. R., 28, 30, 249, 250, 264

Maier, H. W., 17, 25
McCarthy, J. J., 5, 9, 10, 12, 25
McCarthy, J. M., 12, 25, 194
McGaugh, J. L., 27, 30
Meeker, M. N., 21, 25
McLeod, J., 12, 25, 28, 30
McLoughlin, J. A., 28, 30, 250, 264
Miron, M. S., 8
Miller, J., 161
Minskoff, E. H., 12, 25
Minskoff, J. G., 12, 25
Myers, G. C., 280
Myklebust, H. R., 9, 25, 27, 29, 145, 148, 146, 250, 251

Neisworth, N. T., 5, 25
Newcomer, P., 12, 25

Osgood, C. E., 4, 8, 9, 25, 26

Parker, R., 12, 26
Page, J., 137
Paraskevopoulos, J., 9, 26
Payne, S., 5
Piaget, J., 4, 16, 17, 18, 20, 21
Pick, A., 7, 26
Pribram, K., 5, 26

Quay, H., 5

Rapaport, D., 11, 26
Ringler, L. H., 28, 30
Robinson, 115

Scheffelin, M. A., 13, 15, 23
Schmidt, J., 7
Smith, J. O., 12, 24
Snyder, 183
Sowell, V., 12, 26
Stellern, J., 368
Stevens, G., 5
Strauss, A. A., 28, 30
Smith, I., 28, 30

Tarver, S., 28, 30
Thorndyke, 3
Thurstone, L. L., 3, 11, 26

Vygotsky, L. S., 4, 249, 264
Vasa, S. F., 368

Waugh, K., 13, 15, 23, 336, 367
Wachs, H., 17, 20, 24
Wallace, G., 28, 30, 250, 264
Weber, R., 157
Wedemeyer, A., 324
Weinberger, N. M., 27, 30
Whalen, R. E., 27, 30
Wiseman, D., iv, 12, 25

Young, W. E., 226

Zevely, C., 105, 251, 252, 338, 264
Zigmond, N. K., 28, 30

Materials List

Basic Reading Skills Workbook. (1963) And other materials. Scott, Foresman and Company, 1900 E. Lake Ave., Glenview, Ill. 60025.

Burns, J. V., & Wheeler, E. *Square Dances—Album D,* and others. Burns Record Company, 755 Chickadee Lane, Stratford, Conn. 06497.

Cusenaire Rods. (1958) Cusenaire Corporation of America, 12 Church St., New Rochelle, N. Y. 10805.

Dolch, E. W. *The Happy Bears.* (1956) This is a story reading pad; other materials available. Garrard Publishing, Champaign, Ill. 61820.

Eichler and Snyder. *Instructional Materials for Exceptional Children.* (1958) And other materials. Continental Press, Elizabethtown, Pa. 17022.

Films. Eye Gate House, 146-01 Archer Ave., Jamaica, N. Y. 14435.

Fitness. *AAHPER Youth Fitness Test Manual.* (1967 rev. ed.) President's Council on Physical Fitness, 1201 Sixteenth St., N.W., Washington, D. C. 20016.

Frostig, M. *The Frostig Program for the Development of Visual Perception.* (1964) Follette Educational Corporation, Chicago, Ill.

Games. Colorado Game Products, P. O. Box 475, Fort Morgan, Colo. 80701.

Heckleman's Neurological Impress System. Merced County Schools, Calif. 95340.

Judy-See Quees. The Judy Company, 310 N. Second St., Minneapolis, Minn. 55340.

Language Master and various other materials. Bell & Howell, 7100 McCormick Rd., Chicago, Ill. 60654.

Magic Cards and other materials. Ideal School Supply, 11018 S. Lavergne Ave., Oak Lawn, Ill. 60453.

Miami Linguistic Series. D. C. Heath, 125 Spring St., Lexington, Mass. 02173.

Miller, J. *Using Phonics First.* (1966) 4611 Cole, Amarillo, Tx. 79106.

Musicall Technique. Musicall, Eighth Floor, 17 W. Sixtieth St., New York 23, N. Y.

Peabody Individual Achievement Test, and *Peabody Language Development Kit.* American Guidance Associates, Publisher's Building, Circle Pines, Minn. 55014.

Periodicals:

Children's Digest and *Humpty Dumpty,* Better Reading Foundation, 52 Vanderbilt Ave., New York, N. Y. 10017.
Highlights for Children. 2300 W. Fifth Ave., Columbus, O. 43212.

Picture-Word Book, Simple Objects to Color, and other materials. Whitman Publishing, Racine, Wisc.

Reading and penmanship materials. Autokinetic, Box 2010, Amarillo, Tx. 79105.

Reading Laboratory, Kindergarten Math Program, and other materials. Science Research Associates, 259 E. Erie St., Chicago, Ill. 60611.

Tiny Tots Publishing House, 5483 W. Northwest Highway, Chicago, Ill. 60630. Various materials.

Wedemeyer and Cejka Instructional Books. Love Publishing, 6635 E. Villanove Place, Denver, Colo. 80122.

Winter Haven Lion's Publication, Box 1045, Winter Haven, Fl. 33880. Perceptual Copy Forms.